"Jake is a captivating storyteller, though each story is more like a naughty secret he couldn't keep."
—Yotam Ottolenghi

"Jake is like a son to me."
—Katie Couric

"Jake is like a son to me. A wildly embarrassing son."
—Phil Rosenthal

"Jake is any mother's dream, and by that I mean my mother is obsessed with him."
—Shoshana Bean

"Jake is the sexiest chef alive."
—benny blanco

"Jake is a shining star for the next generation of Cohens!"
—Andy Cohen

"Jake, like everything he makes, is easy and delicious."
—Ali Wong

"Jake opened my eyes to fantastic cooking and also the wonderful possibility of being gay. But, seriously, these recipes are his best yet."
—Mike Solomonov

"Jake's delicious, has a shayne punim, and makes me kvell with nachas!"
—Debra Messing

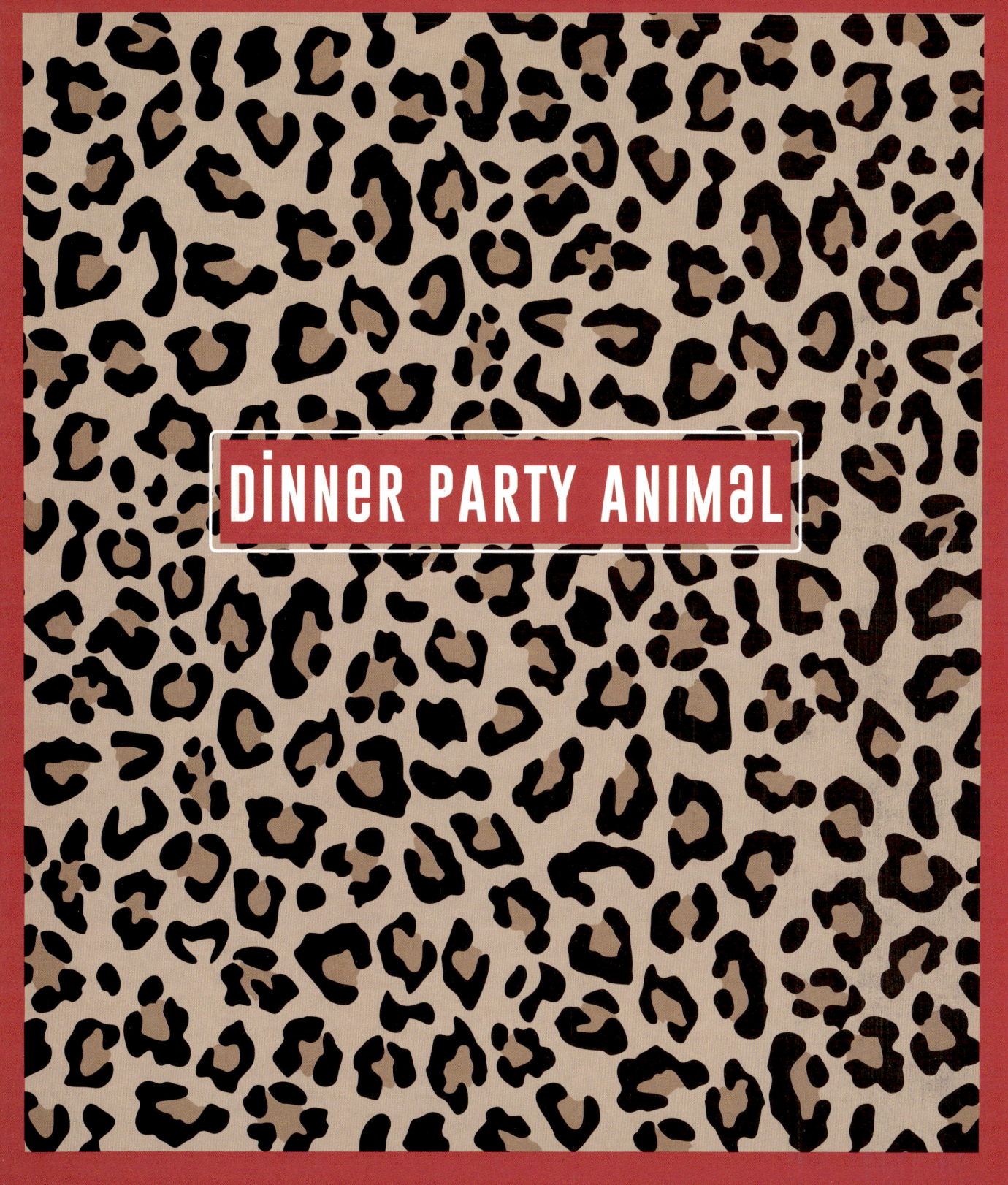

Also by Jake Cohen

Jew-ish:
Reinvented Recipes from a Modern Mensch

I Could Nosh:
Classic Jewish Recipes Revamped for Every Day

DINNER PARTY ANIMAL

RECIPES TO MAKE EVERY DAY A CELEBRATION

JAKE COHEN

Photography by Matt Taylor-Gross

HARVEST
An Imprint of WILLIAM MORROW

To my mom, the modern-day Julia Child who let me use her dining room table to host my first dinner parties

contents

Introducing a Self-Help Cookbook	1
Bagel Bonanza	17
Treat Yourself Brunch	33
Life of the Cocktail Party	47
That Was Tonight?	71
Grills Gone Wild	85
Ride or Pie	105
Veg Out	121
Mediterranean Spa Food	139
Green Machine	153
Pita Party	167
Shtetl Chic	191
Meatballs to the Wall	205
Winner Winner, Chicken Dinner	223
Steak 'n' Cake	239
Let My People Nosh	261
Gobble, Gobble	291
Just the Recipes: A Master List by Category	315
Universal Conversion Chart	317
Acknowledgments	319
Index	321

Introducing a Self-Help Cookbook

I love to party, what can I say? And while I truly mean that in every sense of the word, it's especially relevant here when it comes to a dinner party. The joy and passion I find in cooking is only partly satiated by creating delicious food. The bigger chunk of magic is getting to share all that delicious food as an ephemeral experience with others. Forgive me as I become a name-dropping monster for a minute, but I've spent the last two years throwing the wildest dinner parties with the wildest guests. Imagine Alex Edelman and Miz Cracker having a friendly philosophical debate while sharing meatballs. Imagine Doug Emhoff and Brian Derrick discussing rising antisemitism in America as they schmear bagels. Imagine the entire cast of *The Real Housewives of New York City* yelling at one another with mouths full of frittata. Imagine Benj Pasek and Shoshana Bean breaking out in song while enjoying a nice piece of salmon. Imagine Modi and Judy Gold jotting down jokes that landed well at the table in between bites of cake. Imagine Katie Couric and Jenji Kohan cross-referencing what shows they've been bingeing while passing around the carrots. Imagine Benny Blanco and Selena Gomez cozying up with a big bowl of matzo ball soup as we sing the Four Questions at Seder. The wildest part is that I don't have to because all these moments actually happened when writing this book and will forever be burned into my memory! This is all to say that gathering people at a table over a home-cooked meal is my ideal way to create meaningful memories that deepen connection.

So, I'm going to warn you now that this introduction reads kind of like a self-help book, because whether you like it or not, you just bought a self-help book. Surprise! Don't get me wrong—I'm not going to promise you woo-woo spiritual enlightenment (and that's not shade, since I'm VERY into woo-woo), but you chose this cookbook with a very specific goal in mind. You could have picked up any other cookbook that would give you delicious recipes. But you didn't. You chose a guide to throwing a dinner party. That's an intention to not just hone your cooking skills, but to do it through hospitality and building community. And that right there is not just a gift to everyone at your table, but a powerful act of self-improvement.

I need community like I need air. But it doesn't come as easily as breathing. My learning curve began in high school when I hosted my first dinner party for some friends, armed with printouts of Ina Garten's recipes for ratatouille and Parmesan polenta. While the recipes were solid, my execution was not. The ratatouille was perfumed with the stale dried herbs from my pantry that had expired many years prior. The polenta was cooked way too far in advance, congealing into gloopy slop on the plate. But none of that mattered. It was the first time this group of teenagers had a home-cooked meal made by one of their peers. We got to cosplay as adults, talking about life, and first loves, and the intense feeling of being on the cusp of adulthood. To my surprise, after I cooked for people, it seemed that they liked me more, so *I* liked me more. That holds true to this day, and I can trace my love of cooking, recipe creation, and hosting back to that first gathering—nothing is quite as soul-filling as inviting people over and feeding them a meal that you cooked yourself, with love.

But let me back up a moment.

I'd always struggled with feelings of not being worthy of friends or love. The confident Jake you see on social or in these pages today is not the Jake I was in high school! I was a shy boy struggling with my weight and sexuality at the same time, all while juggling to figure out how to build the community I so desperately craved. That dinner party was the first time my doubting inner voice was silenced. By building my own table, I felt as if I finally found where I belonged. So, I doubled down and began spending all my free time watching Food Network and experimenting in the kitchen. A dull humming in the back of my mind slowly grew to a symphony singing in my ears that the only option was to go to culinary school. I have always been one to fantasize, with the added delusion that no matter what the fantasy was, I needed to make it a reality. Naturally, I only applied to one college and that was the Culinary Institute of America, kicking off the road that led me here today, living out my dream one recipe at a time.

And while this is a story with a happy ending, it didn't end there. My craving for community never waned. Recipe development and cooking was my calling, but I was truly my happiest and most confident when I was entertaining—and Shabbat became my gateway to practice the art of doing just that. This ancient Jewish ritual involves taking Friday night to Saturday night as a day of rest, unplugging from the world and channeling all your energy toward those you love, including yourself. At a time when everyone is facedown in their phones, experiencing an epidemic of loneliness and placing all worth in the validation of either strangers or acquaintances online, Shabbat is the antidote. I've always said extending hospitality to others is the fastest way to turn strangers into friends and friends into family. And while my journey to discovering the value of hospitality was rooted in Shabbat, it didn't end there—and it may look different for you. Through hosting Shabbat dinners I discovered firsthand the magic of a dinner party. But dinner parties shouldn't be limited to Shabbat, and they don't have to feel daunting.

If you want to build a community and feel the joy of authentic personal connection, then throwing a dinner party is for you! Before you start writing your grocery list (which I've done for you, by the way—more on that later), I want you to start with this affirmation: *The intention of welcoming people into my home, where I get to be my most authentic self, and nourishing them is a powerful expression of both hospitality and self-care.* The how is definitely important (and trust me, I will guide you through every step), but it is not as crucial as the very act of entertaining itself. In other words, you don't have to turn into Martha Stewart overnight, but you very well may end up following in her footsteps. All you have to do is ignore the thoughts that pop into your head that your table is too small to host or you're too tired to entertain, or you don't even know how to cook a full meal. To put it simply, get over yourself and just do it.

And this is where I come in! My mission has always been to inspire your confidence in the kitchen through recipes that make you feel like you can cook anything. Because you can. The greatest joy I get from my work is the constant stream of messages I get from all of you expressing gratitude for the first cake recipe that made you feel like a successful baker, or the weeknight pasta that your kids now request constantly, or the holiday brisket that has now become your family's choice for celebrating every year. It's why I do what I do. And now it's time to step it up. Making one recipe is good, but I'm writing this book to give you all the other recipes that go well with that perfect dish. I'm writing this book to teach you how to manage your time, so everything is hot and ready at the same time. I'm writing this book to help you minimize any stress, so you can actually enjoy your guests, the whole reason you're throwing a party!

Introducing a Self-Help Cookbook

LET'S PARTY

As a seasoned dinner party pro,

I've spent the last two years hosting the wildest gatherings and perfecting over one hundred recipes, broken into sixteen menus, to satisfy an array of party possibilities for every desired vibe. They range from simple menus that make it easy to entertain when you don't have the luxury of extra time (like That Was Tonight?) to more involved celebrations, including holiday menus for Thanksgiving and Passover. Each menu is designed to be enjoyed in one sitting, if desired—the appetizers complement the sides, which complement the mains, and the dessert is designed as a natural finish to the meal you've just enjoyed. Everyone will enjoy, and—I assure you—no one will leave hungry!

This book is for everyone, no matter your experience or comfort in the kitchen, and you can start wherever you see fit! Each menu comes with a grocery list with everything you will need to cook the entire menu, as well as a prep list to give you guidance on what you can prep ahead to make sure everything goes smoothly the day or night of. (You're welcome: I'm giving you your Thanksgiving grocery list and timeline on lock.) I've broken down the grocery lists based on category, so you can cross-reference your pantry and spice drawer before heading to the store. The prep lists are broken down by how far in advance you can knock out each task. Look at the list and make it work with your schedule to ensure everything gets done, but on your time!

Each menu will tell you how many it feeds, and know that portions are generous with the intention that all your hard work should be rewarded with leftovers. Each recipe has an individual breakdown of how far it can be prepped or even finished in advance, with notes

on reheating and even guidance on how long leftovers will last.

I can confidently say that this book is my pride and joy, distilling years of hosting into a streamlined guide just for us! I say *us*, because we're in this together. You'll see I use *we* often in the recipe headnotes because I want you to feel like I'm right in the kitchen with you. All the extra details in this book are to help remind you that I believe in you, and you've got this. We've got this! I promise you, all this time will be well worth it. There's nothing more beautiful than bringing friends and family together around the table—it's time to start cooking and gathering for our souls.

The Food

Hospitality without breaking bread is hardly hospitality. For me it's about abundance. It's about putting the time and energy into preparing a delicious feast to experience this care tangibly with your senses. I want to see the mountain of pasta. I want to smell the aromas of freshly baked bread. I want to feel the juices of ripe tomatoes dripping down my chin. I want to hear the crunch of crackers and nuts from a cheeseboard cut through all the chatter and laughter. I want to taste the meal cooked with so much love that I smile until it hurts.

When you make the decision to invite people into your home for a meal, that is a special occasion. It should be treated as such. Go the extra mile with sourcing ingredients. Make sure you serve portions that go even beyond everyone feeling satiated. Take the time to prepare each recipe with the attention it deserves. We're rethinking the way we approach hosting, shifting any feelings of stress or burden into the affirmations of joy and privilege. It's not easy, but the best things in life never are. That's why

I developed every menu with the tips and tricks I've picked up from years of easy entertaining to help you feed a passion for hospitality. I'm still going to challenge you. I find that the easiest way to make your community feel special is to make project recipes for them. This doesn't mean they're necessarily difficult; rather, they're dishes that shift away from the normal culinary lexicon to emphasize that this gathering is a celebration, no matter the occasion.

You don't have to do this alone. Both in the figurative sense because I'm here to talk you through the entire way, but also literally. This book is a guide to being the consummate dinner party host who cooks everything, soup to nuts. If that's you, we've got this and you're going to crush it. But know that if you want to tackle these menus with your significant other, friends, or family, by all means divide and conquer. Part of this journey is discovering how you can best show up to your own table, whether having accomplished everything by yourself or with support—both are equally miraculous. It can also mean outsourcing some of the components or dishes as you seem fit. Maybe store-bought focaccia is fine for pasta night or a cake from your favorite bakery is how you want to end Steak 'n' Cake dinner. All options are valid, and you are the master of your own domain (as in, your kitchen). I will call out often which recipes I say you can skip, options for ingredient swaps, and ways you can customize menus, but you are in the driver's seat. I'm creating the structure for how I throw a dinner party with everything you need to know to re-create it. But I am always giving you permission to make it your own. Take these guides and adjust them to work for your life. It's the only way you can build a positive relationship with hospitality. Good food is the best pairing with good company. It's your job to look inside and figure out how you can provide both to those you love while being able to enjoy it all yourself.

The Booze

One thing I'm not doing is

suggesting wine pairings with every menu. It's not that I don't support wine at the shared table, but I don't like to prescribe anything but the recipes—my suggestion is to serve what you enjoy. This is also a really nice thing for guests to bring if they don't want to show up empty-handed, but you have the meal covered. I'll always tell my guests to *just bring themselves*, but when they insist, I ask them to bring a bottle of something they love to drink. That could be wine, liquor, soda, or flavored seltzer, and it makes the night so much better. Instead of pushing what I think should be sipped with dinner, they're enjoying a glass of their favorite beverage. This also passes on sommelier duties to your guests, who now get to wax poetic about their favorite Sauvignon Blanc they bought three cases of on vacation in New Zealand or the craft gin they're gaslighting you into believing won't give you a hangover. That doesn't mean you shouldn't have a backup. I have a bar cart filled with everything from Manischewitz and orange wine to gluten-free vodka and every color of tequila. It becomes almost a take-a-bottle-leave-a-bottle situation, creating the baseline that everyone has options and can trade up whenever they want. For cocktails, I'm stocked up with tonic, soda, lemons, limes, and some nice ice from those fancy silicone trays. Let your thirstiest guest step in as bartender, shaking up whatever libations the crowd wants. Oh, and always have some nostalgic sodas. No matter what vintage wine is on the table, an offer of Fresca or Dr. Brown's Black Cherry is always met with the most excitement. All gatherings and groups are different, so read the room and plan accordingly. No matter what you're serving, just be sure to toast the occasion.

The Table

You can go as wild as you want, but for me the best decor for a table is overflowing platters of gorgeous food. Past that, live your truth. If you love flowers, pick up a bouquet or set out some bud vases that fit with the season. Personally, I love a dried flower arrangement that won't just die on me and can be reused. Throw in some candles for ambiance and you've got a tablescape to be proud of. Don't overthink it! I'm not trying to discourage you if you want to make hand-painted place cards or peacock-shaped folded napkins. The internet is a wonderful, scary place where you can teach yourself almost anything! I just don't want you to think that is what you need to host. The barrier for entry is cooking a meal and inviting your loved ones. Everything else is just the icing.

Don't have enough plates? Use disposable. Don't have a big enough table? Use it as a buffet and let your guests settle all around your home. You get to set the rules, so make them work in your favor. You'll notice there are no soup recipes in this book other than a matzo ball for Passover, which is wild because soup is my life force. That was a conscious decision because between dinner and dessert plates, I do not have the dishwasher space to add bowls to the mix. Preserving my peace of mind is always priority and it must be yours, too. If the cooking is already stressing you out, don't let the table be the straw that breaks the camel's back. As you become a seasoned entertaining pro, challenge yourself to set the scene. But let that be part of the journey and don't set out to reach your destination night one. You live and you host and you learn, adapting your rituals for how they can best fit into your life and space. Now take a deep breath and let's say together: Everything looks gorgeous and I'm proud of this table in whatever form it takes!

The Music

As for music to set the tone, here, too, I'm not going to dictate a set playlist. Trust me, you don't want that from me! First off, I prep in silence. It might seem weird and counterintuitive to finding the joy in cooking, but I treat the process like a meditation. The sounds of chopping and repetitive movements of stirring or whisking keep me grounded in the present and full of gratitude for the meal ahead. But more importantly, music is so personal and, much like wine, people would always rather stick to what they like. My Spotify Wrapped for the last few years will show you that my most-listened-to album has typically been *Slut Pop* by Kim Petras, only dethroned this past year by Charli XCX's *Brat*. I could be wrong, but something tells me hyperpop isn't the vibe for your roast chicken dinner. Find a chill playlist to set the mood and just make sure the volume doesn't compete with the chatter of your guests. Maybe a little lofi moment is all you need, or you can curate something a little more specific to your musical preferences. Just don't let it add any stress—there's always a guest who's willing to step in and play DJ.

The Invitations

This should probably come first, before all the other components, because we're looking to share good food, drinks, and music with those we love. Extending hospitality is vulnerable. It's just as intimate to extend the invitation to someone as it is for them to accept it. I'll first tell you that I'm big on absolutes, so if you're inviting someone, tell them *you'd love to have them* not *if you're around and want to come*. You want your guests to feel wanted because that's the reason you're throwing a dinner party. Now, this doesn't mean you need to send a Paperless Post for every occasion. It just means there should be some formality. Maybe you have a set date that works for your schedule, or maybe you have the group that you want to host and need to discuss when everyone is available. Once you know that, communication is key. Everyone should get a message, whether by text, email, DM, or carrier pigeon, with the date, time, address, and asking for any dietary restrictions. When they ask, "What can I bring?" you can hit them with an emphatic *nothing!*, or you can choose to delegate. Nothing crazy, but it's totally acceptable to ask them to bring a bottle of something they love to drink or a dessert. While you know my response, sometimes I'll request guests bring their favorite cheese to add to a cheeseboard or their favorite flavor of ice cream to serve with dessert. This adds to the spread, makes your guests feel like they've contributed, and gives you an opportunity to get to know their likes a little better.

In terms of timing, don't go crazy and plan twelve weeks out, unless that's how you and your friends operate. But also try not to have anything planned with too short of notice either. A last-minute invitation always makes me feel like an afterthought or that I was on the B-list for invitations. And while that very well may be true, I would never want to make someone feel that way. The night before, I always send a follow-up message expressing how excited I am to see them just in case they forgot to put it in their calendar. Now here's what I want to stress the most: People will sometimes disappoint you. They'll cancel last minute, sometimes with valid reasons and sometimes with excuses just to get out of it. Or, and I truly hope this never happens to you, they just won't show up at all without a word of notice. It sucks, I know. But in those moments, you have to focus your energy and gratitude on those who pulled up a chair at your table. Don't let someone ruin your night—they don't deserve the headspace or attention. Sorry to break it to you, but we only have space for joy!

The Kitchen

Okay, time to get granular. While you don't need a ton of specialty equipment, a fully stocked kitchen is important. I made a list of all the pots, pans, and tools used throughout the book to have on hand. That doesn't mean you need all of these for every menu—this is just how I keep my kitchen stocked. For the kitchen itself, you don't need a ton of counter space or burners, and I try to keep the oven temperature consistent in recipes within the same menu. I've tested these menus in kitchens of all shapes and sizes to keep ease in mind! Oh, and please don't forget YOU NEED TO OWN A KITCHEN SCALE AND A DIGITAL THERMOMETER! These two gadgets are the fastest way to improve your cooking and baking game. I'm a strong believer that all flour for baking should be measured with a scale (135g per cup, preferably King Arthur brand) to ensure consistency and accuracy. For our thermometer, cooking meat or baking cakes by internal temperatures over minutes takes out the guesswork for a perfect result every time. Please invest in both before tackling any menu in this book! Finally, you'll see KS&P on almost every ingredient list, which just means kosher salt and pepper. I use Diamond Crystal kosher salt, which is an important distinction for the baking recipes. Pepper is always freshly and coarsely ground black peppercorns. It comes up in almost every recipe, so I thought I'd save a little ink.

Main List

- Half sheet pans (have at least 2)
- Wire rack for half sheet pan (1 is enough)
- 8-quart pot or Dutch oven
- 5-quart pot or Dutch oven
- Large high-sided skillet
- 12-inch skillet
- 10-inch skillet
- 12-inch cast-iron pan
- 2-quart saucepan
- 9 by 13-inch baking pan (have at least 2)
- 7 by 11-inch (2-quart) baking pan
- 9 by 5-inch loaf pan (have at least 2)
- 9-inch pie plate
- 9-inch round cake pan (have at least 2)
- 9-inch square baking pan
- Heatproof glass or metal bowls (have a few different sizes)
- Blender
- Food processor
- Mini food processor
- Digital scale
- Digital thermometer
- Dry measuring cups/spoons
- Liquid measuring cups (have at least a 1-cup and 4-cup)
- Knives (have at least a chef's, paring, and serrated)
- Wooden spoon
- Silicone or rubber spatula
- Pastry brush
- 2-tablespoon-sized scoop
- Pepper mill
- Butcher's twine
- Cheesecloth (optional, you can use a kitchen towel)
- Cavatelli/gnocchi board (optional, you can use a fork)
- Parchment paper
- Plastic wrap
- Foil
- Sealable containers (for prep and leftovers!)
- Sealable plastic bags
- Box grater
- Mortar and pestle
- Stand mixer
- Electric hand mixer
- Immersion blender
- Bench scraper
- Potato masher

The Conversation

While I have no doubt that you are perfectly capable of leading a conversation, or at least know how to pick good middlers for your table, I'm going to give you just a little bit of guidance.

What's the best compliment you've ever received and why did it resonate?
—JAKE COHEN

What's a dream job for many that would be your worst nightmare and why?
—BENJ PASEK

When you die, if you could come back as Bette Midler or Barbra Streisand, who are you choosing and why?
—BENNY BLANCO

If they created a new $1,000 bill, whose face would you put on it and why?
—BRIAN DERRICK

What's a line of dialogue out of the craziest night of your life? Context encouraged.
—TAFFY BRODESSER-AKNER

What's the last news story that made you smile?
—KATIE COURIC

When did you first know you were special?
—JENJI KOHAN

What are you reading? Not to say I judge people who don't read but . . . okay, I judge people who don't read.
—ISAAC MIZRAHI

I think a great dinner party question that really brings on the fun is "What do you think of the situation in the Middle East?"
—JUDY GOLD

What's the biggest change you've seen in yourself over the last ten years?
—ALEX EDELMAN

Would you tell me a story from your day?
—MIZ CRACKER

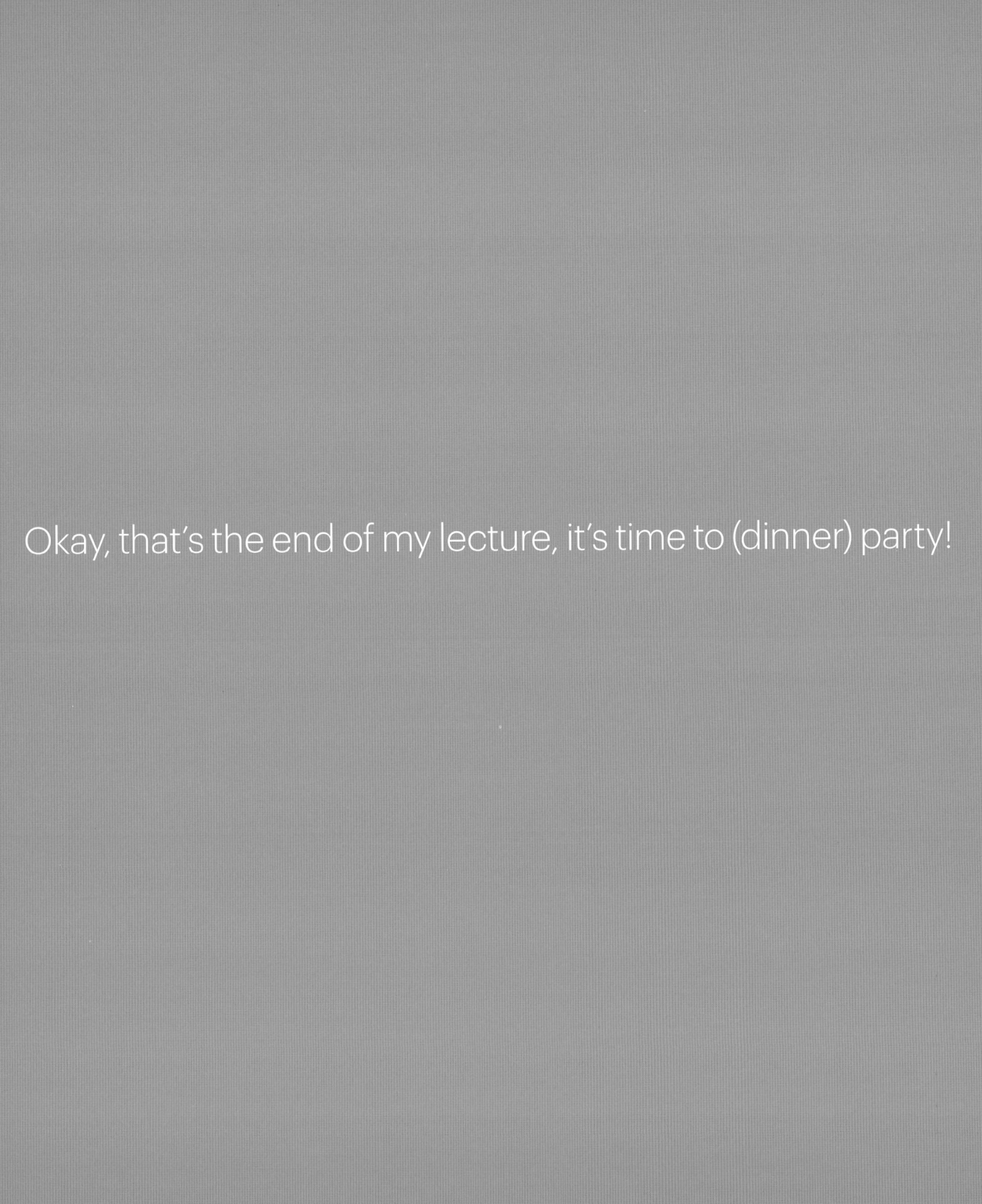

Hot and fresh NYC-style bagels with the works.

BAGEL BONƏNZƏ

MENU

Bagels
Dirty Martini–Cured Salmon
Wasabi-Lime Tuna Salad
Whipped Schmear
Bagel Toppings Salad

GROCERY LIST

PANTRY
7 c (945g) bread flour
1 c (200g) granulated sugar
¾ c mayonnaise
½ c barley malt syrup
½ c pitted Castelvetrano olives
⅓ c seltzer
3 tbsp olive oil
2 tbsp dry gin
1 tbsp prepared wasabi paste
2 tsp honey
1 tsp (3g) active dry yeast
½ tsp baking soda
3 (6-oz) cans water-packed tuna
1 jar capers (3 tbsp drained)

SPICES, SEASONINGS, AND FLAVORINGS
2 tsp dried juniper berries
Everything bagel seasoning (½ c per 4 bagels)
Sesame seeds or poppy seeds (½ c per 4 bagels)
Flaky sea salt (2 tsp per 4 bagels)
KS&P (at least 2 c kosher salt and 1 jar whole black peppercorns to be safe)

SEAFOOD
1 (2-lb) salmon fillet, skin-on

PRODUCE
3 heirloom tomatoes
2 medium red onions
2 lemons
1 lime
1 English cucumber
1 bunch celery
1 small bunch dill

REFRIGERATED
4 (8-oz) blocks cream cheese

PREP LIST

3 Days in Advance
- Make the Dirty Martini–Cured Salmon

Up to 2 Days Ahead
- Make the Whipped Schmear

Up to 1 Day Ahead
- Make the dough for the Bagels (if proofing in the refrigerator overnight)
- Make the Wasabi-Lime Tuna Salad
- Make the dressing for the Bagel Toppings Salad

2 Hours Before Guests Arrive
- Shape, boil, and bake the Bagels

1 Hour Before Guests Arrive
- Assemble the Bagel Toppings Salad
- Slice the Dirty Martini–Cured Salmon

Right Before Guests Arrive
- Dress the Bagel Toppings Salad
- Reheat the Bagels, if needed (about 5 minutes)

Game Time Pep Talk
The Dirty Martini–Cured Salmon, Whipped Schmear, Wasabi-Lime Tuna Salad, and Bagel Toppings Salad should be ready and on the table. Once your bagels are warm, time to slice them and serve the whole spread. You've got this!

Sho♥

I swore I'd never make bagels, yet here we are. You can blame PopUp Bagels, one of my favorite shops in NYC. Their whole shtick is pumping out a constant stream of bagels from their ovens, screaming HOT BAGELS as they pull out every tray, so everyone gets the pleasure of tearing into a warm, still-steaming bagel. It's one of life's greatest pleasures that I wanted to bring into my own kitchen, since a bagel brunch is my ideal daytime entertaining experience. Now here's where you'll probably roll your eyes, but homemade bagels are easier than you think! I've now thrown dozens of bagel bonanzas that have tested every possible combination of overnight proofing in the fridge, freezing and thawing dough, doubling the recipe (it doubles beautifully!), reheating leftovers, and more to give you the most streamlined recipe for hot, golden bagels that are crispy and chewy on the outside and fluffy on the inside. Yes, we're hand-rolling our bagels before boiling, covering in seeds, and baking, but I promise, as long as you use a kitchen scale, the hardest part of the recipe is just getting your hands on the barley malt syrup (you can easily order it online, but it's sometimes available in the alternative sweetener section of the grocery store by the maple syrup and molasses). You don't *have* to scream HOT BAGELS when you serve them, but it's highly encouraged!

Makes 1 dozen bagels | Prep Time: 45 minutes, plus overnight and 1 hour proofing time | Cook Time: 25 minutes

Dough
2½ cups (567g) water, heated to 115°F
3 tablespoons (63g) barley malt syrup
1 teaspoon (3g) active dry yeast

7 cups (945g) bread flour, plus more for dusting
2 tablespoons (18g) kosher salt
1 tablespoon olive oil, for greasing

Boiling and Baking
3 tablespoons (63g) barley malt syrup
½ teaspoon baking soda
Everything bagel seasoning (½ cup per 4 bagels)

Sesame seeds or poppy seeds (½ cup per 4 bagels)
Flaky sea salt (2 teaspoons per 4 bagels)

1. Make the dough: In the bowl of a stand mixer fitted with the whisk attachment, mix the warm water and barley malt syrup to dissolve, then sprinkle the yeast over the top. Let stand until foamy, 5 to 10 minutes. Switch to the dough hook. Add the flour and salt to the mixture in the bowl and, beginning on low speed and gradually increasing to medium, knead until a smooth, elastic dough forms, 3 to 4 minutes. Transfer to a lightly floured work surface and, with floured hands, continue to knead by hand, dusting with flour as needed, until a very smooth ball forms, another 3 to 5 minutes. Toward the end of the kneading time, if the dough is streaky or tearing, cover with a kitchen towel or plastic wrap and let

(cont.)

rest for 1 minute so the gluten can relax before continuing to knead. (Alternatively, if you make this dough entirely by hand, it will require about 10 minutes of kneading on a clean work surface after incorporating the flour.) Grease a large bowl with the olive oil and add the dough, tossing gently to coat. Cover tightly with plastic wrap and refrigerate overnight. (Alternatively, you can let the dough double in size on the counter in a warm place for 1½ to 2 hours.)

2. The next morning, at least 2 hours before serving, transfer the dough to a clean work surface and divide into 12 equal pieces (about 130g per piece). Cup your hand and fingers around each piece of dough and roll on the work surface into a tight ball. Cover the dough balls with a warm, damp towel and let rest for 15 minutes.

3. Working with one dough ball at a time, use both hands to roll the ball into a 10-inch rope, then wrap the rope around your four fingers (all but the thumb) overlapping the ropes by 1 inch on the bottom side of your fingers. (Keep a small bowl of water nearby to dab the ends of the rope with your fingers, if needed, to help them adhere.) Roll the dough back and forth on the surface, using light pressure from your upper palm to seal the overlapped ends of the rope. Place the shaped bagel back under the damp towel and repeat until all the bagels are shaped. Once all are shaped and covered, let sit on the counter for 45 minutes, or until puffy.

4. Meanwhile, prepare to boil and bake the bagels: Preheat the oven to 450°F. Set an oven rack in the center of the oven. Line a sheet pan with a wire rack. Line another sheet pan with parchment paper. Bring a large pot filled halfway with water to a boil. Remove from the heat and carefully whisk in the barley malt syrup and baking soda, which will bubble up vigorously. Return to the heat and to a boil. Place the everything bagel seasoning and sesame seeds each in separate shallow bowls or plates.

5. Working in 3 batches, use wet hands to transfer 4 bagels to the pot and boil, flipping once with a metal spider or slotted spoon, for 1 minute per side. Transfer to the wire rack–lined sheet pan to drain.

6. Working quickly while the bagels are still wet, dip both sides of each bagel in the everything bagel seasoning to fully coat, then transfer to the parchment-lined sheet pan. Once the water returns to a boil, repeat step 5, dipping the second batch in the sesame or poppy seeds and sprinkling the flaky salt over the third batch, transferring both to the parchment-lined sheet pan (you'll have 3 rows of 4 bagels).

7. Bake until golden brown, about 20 minutes. Transfer to a wire rack to cool slightly, then slice and serve warm.

Make Ahead You can make the bagels to completion and freeze (see Leftovers below for reheating instructions), or you can freeze the shaped bagels before you let them go through their second rise. Place the shaped bagels on a parchment-lined sheet pan and wrap with plastic wrap, then freeze for up to 3 months. (Once frozen, the bagels can be transferred to a sealable plastic bag to store in the freezer.) The night before you want to bake them, transfer the tray to the refrigerator to thaw overnight. (If the bagels were stored in a bag, arrange on a parchment-lined sheet pan and cover with plastic wrap before thawing in the refrigerator.) The next morning, let them sit on the counter while you start to prepare to boil and bake them (step 4), then continue with the recipe.

Leftovers 2 days at room temperature for the first 48 hours after baking. 1 month in the freezer for any longer. To reheat, microwave for 30 seconds for room-temperature bagels and 1 minute for frozen bagels, then transfer to a 400°F oven to bake for 5 to 7 minutes, until crisp.

Bagel Bonanza

Dirty Martini–Cured Salmon

What is a bagel bonanza without a platter of lox? And while I'm all about crowning my schmeared bagel with Nova, I don't have the time or equipment to be cold-smoking salmon. (Though if that's a journey you want to take, I wish you well!) Instead, we're going to let some salmon chill out in the fridge and soak in a martini. Well, I guess not exactly, but we will dry brine the salmon in a juniper and lemon–infused salt and sugar mixture with some chopped olives and gin for the same effect. After three days, we're left with a firmer, flavor-packed piece of salmon ready to slice and sandwich. While I think this recipe is relatively low lift as long as you have a sharp knife, it is the one part of this menu I give you permission to skip and source your favorite appetizing variety.

Serves 6 to 8 | Prep Time: 30 minutes, plus 3 days curing

⅔ cup kosher salt
⅔ cup (133g) granulated sugar
2 teaspoons dried juniper berries
2 teaspoons finely grated lemon zest

1 (2-pound) salmon fillet, skin-on
½ cup pitted Castelvetrano olives, finely chopped
2 tablespoons dry gin

1. In a mini food processor, combine the salt, sugar, juniper berries, and lemon zest. Pulse until the juniper berries are finely crushed.

2. Lay a sheet of parchment on a sheet pan and place the salmon fillet on top, skin-side down. Sprinkle the salt mixture over all sides of the salmon, lifting the fillet to coat the entire surface. Scatter the olives over the top, then drizzle with the gin. Fold the parchment to enclose the salmon, then wrap tightly with plastic wrap. Place another sheet pan on top of the salmon and weigh it down with a cast-iron pan. Place in the refrigerator for 3 days.

3. After 3 days, remove the salmon from the package. Use a damp paper towel to wipe away the curing mixture and transfer the salmon to a cutting board with the tail end pointing to the right. Using a very sharp knife (ideally a long, thin slicing knife) and beginning a few inches from the tail end, slice thin strips at a 45-degree angle toward the tail. (The first few will be ugly, but you'll get the hang of it!) Arrange the cured salmon on a platter, then cover and refrigerate until ready to serve.

Make Ahead That's the whole point of the recipe! Make sure to start this recipe 3 days before serving.

Leftovers 5 days in the refrigerator or 1 month in the freezer.

Wasabi-Lime Tuna Salad

Of all of the recipes in this entire book, this tuna salad was the dish I received the most texts asking for the recipe after serving it to friends and family. And, of course, it's one of the easiest dishes in this book! We're just adding a little sweet and spicy pop to a simple tuna salad with wasabi paste and sugar. That means the first step in this recipe is ordering in a nice sushi takeout dinner to source our wasabi (you can find tubes of it in most grocery stores, but my way is more fun). However the wasabi is procured, the most important part of this recipe is that we use a stand mixer to make it, which allows everything to emulsify with the tuna and never gets watery. A double batch is encouraged, since there can never be too much tuna!

Makes about 1 quart | Prep Time: 15 minutes

3 (6-ounce) cans water-packed tuna, drained
¾ cup mayonnaise
¾ cup minced red onion
¾ cup minced celery
¼ cup minced celery leaves

1 tablespoon prepared wasabi paste
1 tablespoon granulated sugar
1 lime, zested and juiced
KS&P

In the bowl of a stand mixer fitted with the paddle attachment, combine the tuna, mayonnaise, red onion, celery, celery leaves, wasabi, sugar, lime zest and juice, and a heavy pinch each of salt and pepper. Mix on low speed until well combined and the tuna is finely shredded. Taste and adjust the seasoning with salt and pepper, then serve.

Make Ahead Tuna salad can be made up to 1 day in advance, stored in an airtight container in the refrigerator.

Leftovers 4 days in the refrigerator.

whipped schmear

Feel free to make any of the ten flavored schmears in my last book, *I Could Nosh*, for this bagel brunch. Or keep it simple and delicious with my secret recipe for a basic, fluffy whipped cream cheese. The goal is a schmear that can be made in advance and served straight from the fridge, while still being able to spread seamlessly. The secret is SELTZER! By whipping room-temperature cream cheese with seltzer in the mixer, you incorporate as much air as possible for the perfect texture. It's the same trick used by every NYC bagel shop so they can keep their display case of cream cheeses cold while still cranking through the morning breakfast rush orders. We've got enough going on with this menu, so we're keeping our schmear plain, but feel free to split this recipe and stir sliced scallions into half for a little variety.

Makes 1 quart | Prep Time: 10 minutes

4 (8-ounce) blocks cream cheese, at room temperature
⅓ cup seltzer
KS

In the bowl of a stand mixer fitted with the whisk attachment, combine the cream cheese, seltzer, and a heavy pinch of salt. Mix on low speed to incorporate, then increase the speed to medium and whip until light and fluffy, scraping the sides as needed. Transfer to an airtight container and refrigerate until ready to serve.

Make Ahead Whipped schmear can be made up to 2 days in advance, stored in an airtight container in the refrigerator.

Leftovers 5 days in the refrigerator.

Bagel Toppings Salad

It's honestly crazy that we've just been putting plain ol' tomatoes and red onion on our bagels without seasoning them first. If we're going to put in the work to make bagels from scratch and cure our own salmon, we have to give our veg the same level of love! So, we're consolidating all our fresh bagel accoutrements into a summery salad by shingling slices of heirloom tomatoes, red onion, and cucumber and covering them with a lemon-caper dressing, fresh dill, and flaky salt. It's a fast and easy way to help our toppings reach new heights.

Serves 6 to 8 | Prep Time: 15 minutes

Dressing
3 tablespoons drained capers, roughly chopped
2 tablespoons olive oil
2 tablespoons freshly squeezed lemon juice
2 teaspoons honey
KS&P

Salad
3 heirloom tomatoes, thinly sliced
1 medium red onion, thinly sliced into rings
1 English cucumber, thinly sliced on the bias
¼ cup roughly chopped fresh dill
Flaky sea salt, for garnish

1. Make the dressing: In a small bowl, whisk together the capers, olive oil, lemon juice, honey, and a heavy pinch each of salt and pepper. Set aside.

2. Make the salad: Arrange the tomato, red onion, and cucumber slices on a platter, alternating between each.

3. Right before serving, spoon the dressing over the salad. Sprinkle the dill and a heavy pinch of flaky salt on top, then serve.

Make Ahead Dressing can be made (step 1) up to 1 day in advance, stored in an airtight container in the refrigerator. Salad can be assembled up to 1 hour before serving, only dressing it right before serving.

Leftovers 2 days in the refrigerator.

A decadent **diner spread,** but just a bit fancier.

TREAT YOURSELF BRUNCH

MENU

Blueberry Corn Muffins
Challah French Toast Sticks
Herby Cottage Cheese Frittata
Maple-Candied Bacon
Saffron Hash Browns

GROCERY LIST

PANTRY
1¼ c (169g) all-purpose flour
2 c (400g) granulated sugar
1 c (140g) yellow cornmeal
1 c olive oil
⅓ c maple syrup, plus extra for the French Toast Sticks
¼ c (48g) potato starch (or cornstarch)
1 tbsp turbinado sugar
2 tsp baking powder
1 tsp baking soda
Nonstick cooking spray
Confectioners' sugar

SPICES, SEASONINGS, AND FLAVORINGS
2 tbsp ground cinnamon
1 tsp almond extract (or vanilla extract)
½ tsp smoked paprika
¼ tsp saffron threads
Pinch of cayenne pepper
KS&P (at least 2 c kosher salt and 1 jar whole black peppercorns to be safe)

BREAD
1 (20-oz) loaf challah

MEAT
1 lb bacon

PRODUCE
3 lb (5 medium) russet potatoes
2 c fresh blueberries
4 medium scallions
1 medium onion
1 lemon
1 bunch (2 c) fresh parsley
1 bunch (2 c) fresh dill

REFRIGERATED
8 oz (2 sticks) unsalted butter
4 c whole milk
1 c cottage cheese (any fat %)
½ c plain Greek yogurt (any fat %)
22 large eggs

PREP LIST

Up to 2 Days Ahead
- Bake the challah bread pudding for the French Toast Sticks

Up to 1 Day Ahead
- Bake the Blueberry Corn Muffins
- Make the Herby Cottage Cheese Frittata

1 Hour Before Guests Arrive
- Slice and sear the French Toast Sticks
- Make the Maple-Candied Bacon
- Make the Saffron Hash Browns
- Keep the oven at 425°F

Right Before Guests Arrive
- Reheat the French Toast Sticks (5 to 10 minutes)
- Reheat the Maple-Candied Bacon (about 5 minutes)
- Reheat the Saffron Hash Browns (8 to 10 minutes)
- Reheat the Herby Cottage Cheese Frittata (optional, 8 to 10 minutes)

Game Time Pep Talk
The muffins should already be out on the table. Everything else should be reheating in the oven, ready to plate up and serve. If space in your oven is an issue, heat the French Toast Sticks and Frittata first, then the Maple-Candied Bacon and Saffron Hash Browns right before serving. This is one of the easiest menus for game time. You've got this!

Jenna, Brynn & Erin

BLUEBERRY CORN MUFFINS

We get the best of both worlds, because we deserve it! Don't get me wrong, I love a little corn muffin moment, but that requires the full basket service with butter and jam for schmearing. Here we can get that same vibe wrapped up in one breakfast treat by marrying a just-sweet-enough cornmeal batter with yogurt and blueberries for a rich tender crumb bursting with pockets of jammy fruit. It's a moist morning affirmation that we can indeed have it all!

Makes 12 muffins | Prep Time: 15 minutes | Cook Time: 25 minutes

Nonstick cooking spray
1 cup (200g) granulated sugar
2 teaspoons finely grated lemon zest
4 ounces (1 stick) unsalted butter, melted
½ cup olive oil
½ cup plain Greek yogurt (any fat %)
1 teaspoon almond extract (or vanilla extract)
2 large eggs

1¼ cups (169g) all-purpose flour
1 cup (140g) yellow cornmeal
2 teaspoons baking powder
1 teaspoon baking soda
1 teaspoon kosher salt
2 cups fresh blueberries
1 tablespoon turbinado sugar, for garnish

1. Preheat the oven to 350°F. Grease a 12-cup standard muffin tin with nonstick cooking spray.

2. In a large bowl, combine the granulated sugar with the lemon zest and rub with your fingers until well combined. Whisk in the melted butter and olive oil, followed by the yogurt, almond extract, and eggs until smooth. Add the flour, cornmeal, baking powder, baking soda, and salt in a pile on top. Using a rubber spatula, gently stir together the dry ingredients piled above the wet ingredients a few times before folding together until incorporated. Fold the blueberries into the batter. Divide the batter among the muffin tins. Sprinkle the turbinado sugar over the muffins.

3. Bake for 20 to 25 minutes, until golden brown and the muffins have reached an internal temperature of 190°F. Let cool for 5 minutes in the pan, then transfer to a platter and serve warm.

Make Ahead Muffins can be baked up to 1 day in advance, stored in an airtight container at room temperature.

Leftovers 5 days at room temperature.

challah French toast sticks

French toast for a crowd can be a challenge. You've got to make sure your bread is well soaked (but not falling apart), you're often working two pans at once for quick batch cooking (while getting everything else on the table), and you want it all to stay warm (without letting it dry out in the oven). But don't worry, I gotchu. We start by making a quick challah bread pudding the night before brunch, so the next morning we just slice it into batons to fry up in a little butter until warmed through and golden. There's plenty of surface area for crispy edges, but most importantly, the center is pure custardy bliss. It even heats up beautifully in the oven, so all frying can be done before guests arrive. Flavor aside, it can function as a delicious Jenga tower, ready to be covered in syrup and toppled over.

Serves 6 to 8 | Prep Time: 30 minutes, plus soaking and cooling time | Cook Time: 1 hour

1 (20-ounce) loaf challah, cut into 1-inch pieces
1 cup (200g) granulated sugar
2 teaspoons ground cinnamon
1 teaspoon kosher salt
6 large eggs

4 cups whole milk
4 tablespoons (2 ounces) unsalted butter, for frying
Confectioners' sugar, for garnish
Maple syrup, for serving

1. Preheat the oven to 350°F. Line a 9 by 13-inch baking dish with parchment paper, leaving overhang on at least 2 sides.

2. Spread the challah on a sheet pan in an even layer. Bake for 15 minutes, or until lightly golden and crisp, then let cool on the pan.

3. In a large bowl, whisk the granulated sugar, cinnamon, salt, and eggs until smooth, then slowly whisk in the milk until fully incorporated.

4. Transfer the toasted challah to the prepared baking dish. Pour the milk mixture over the bread and let sit on the counter to soak for 45 minutes, using your hands to lightly press the bread in an even layer to soak up the milk.

5. Bake for 35 to 40 minutes, until set but with a little jiggle. Let cool completely in the pan.

6. Use an offset spatula to ensure none of the edges are sticking to the pan, then carefully transfer the French toast block to a cutting board arranged horizontally. Trim the outer ¼ inch of the block, which makes for a great chef's snack, then slice the block in half lengthwise and slice crosswise every 1½ inches to make batons.

7. In a large skillet, heat 2 tablespoons butter over medium-high heat. Add half of the French toast sticks and cook, turning as needed, until golden brown, 4 to 5 minutes. Transfer to a platter and repeat with the remaining butter and French toast sticks.

8. Once all the French toast sticks are on the platter, garnish with confectioners' sugar and serve with maple syrup.

Make Ahead French toast sticks can be made up until slicing and pan-searing (through step 5) up to 2 days in advance, covered in plastic wrap, and kept in the refrigerator. They can be pan-seared (step 7) up to 1 hour before serving, held on a parchment-lined sheet pan to reheat in the oven.

Leftovers 5 days in the refrigerator.

Herby Cottage Cheese Frittata

It's time to drop the cottage cheese slander. And no matter how much I wish it was, big cottage isn't paying me to say that. There's no better way to sneak in creamy protein to your breakfast, whether oatmeal, toast, or especially eggs. For this frittata, a scoop of cottage cheese adds the same rich fluffiness as a splash of cream, while keeping things light to leave plenty of room for French Toast Sticks. Tons of fresh herbs brighten it all up to give very vague vibes of a Persian kuku sabzi, which intentionally pairs perfectly with the Saffron Hash Browns. Let this recipe be your gateway into the cottage cheese craze, but if you're a determined hater (booooo, do better), you can swap in a cup of crumbled feta and I won't be mad . . . just disappointed!

Serves 6 to 8 | Prep Time: 15 minutes | Cook Time: 20 minutes

- 12 large eggs
- 1 cup cottage cheese (any fat %)
- 1 teaspoon kosher salt
- ½ teaspoon freshly ground black pepper
- 4 medium scallions, thinly sliced
- 1 bunch (2 cups) fresh parsley, leaves and tender stems finely chopped
- 1 bunch (2 cups) fresh dill, fronds and tender stems finely chopped
- 2 tablespoons olive oil

1. Preheat the oven to 425°F.
2. In a large bowl, whisk the eggs until smooth, then whisk in the cottage cheese, salt, pepper, scallions, parsley, and dill.
3. In a 10-inch ovenproof cast-iron or nonstick skillet, heat the olive oil over medium-high heat. Add the egg mixture and cook for 1 minute, stirring often. Smooth the eggs in an even layer with a spatula, then transfer to the oven. Bake for 16 to 18 minutes, until just set. Transfer to a platter, then slice and serve.

Make Ahead Frittata can be made up to 1 day before serving, stored, unsliced, on a platter covered in plastic wrap in the refrigerator. If only baking, about 1 hour before serving, let the frittata cool in the pan for easy reheating. Frittata can be served at room temperature or reheated in the oven before slicing and serving.

Leftovers 5 days in the refrigerator.

Maple-Candied Bacon

Obviously, bacon is a staple ingredient for treating yourself and needs a seat at our brunch table. Whether piled on a bagel with egg and cheese, sandwiched between lettuce and tomato on sourdough, or sprinkled over a wedge salad, it's pretty perfect as is. But we can always strive for improvement. For this recipe, we're shellacking our bacon with a spiced maple syrup as it bakes. The syrup caramelizes around each strip, achieving the ideal crispy-yet-still-slightly-chewy texture with a dark golden hue. It's a sweet, salty, and smoky side that couldn't be easier to throw together yet garners absurd amounts of praise. Now, that's perfection.

Serves 6 to 8 | Prep Time: 10 minutes | Cook Time: 15 minutes

1 pound bacon
⅓ cup maple syrup
½ teaspoon ground cinnamon
½ teaspoon smoked paprika
Pinch of cayenne pepper

1. Preheat the oven to 425°F. Line 2 sheet pans with foil.

2. Arrange the bacon on the prepared sheet pans spaced ¼ inch apart. Bake for 10 minutes.

3. Meanwhile, in a small bowl, stir together the maple syrup, cinnamon, smoked paprika, and cayenne to combine.

4. After 10 minutes, flip the bacon and brush each strip with the maple mixture. Bake for another 5 to 6 minutes, until golden and crisp. Transfer to a platter and serve.

Make Ahead Bacon can be cooked up to 1 hour before serving, consolidated to a clean, parchment-lined sheet pan for reheating.

Leftovers 5 days in the refrigerator.

Saffron Hash Browns

Ever since I snuck some saffron into my latke recipe in *Jew-ish*, it has been one of my favorite ingredients to throw on a blank potato canvas. Is it expensive? Yes. Is it worth it? Absolutely. Luckily, a little goes a long way if you use a mortar and pestle to grind the threads first, infusing the most color and flavor. (I bought a cheap little set online reserved just for saffron!) Naturally, my saffron-stained-spud obsession resulted in this giant golden hash brown. Past the fancy stuff, we're just grating potatoes to fry up until extra crispy on the outside thanks to some added potato starch, while the center stays tender and creamy. I mean, it's a giant saffron latke, how could it not be amazing?

Serves 6 to 8 | Prep Time: 15 minutes | Cook Time: 10 minutes

- 2 large eggs
- ¼ teaspoon saffron threads, finely ground with a mortar and pestle
- 3 pounds (5 medium) russet potatoes, peeled
- 1 medium onion, peeled
- ¼ cup (48g) potato starch (or cornstarch)
- 2 teaspoons kosher salt
- ¼ cup olive oil

1. In a large bowl, whisk together the eggs and saffron until smooth, then set aside.
2. Using a box grater or a food processor fitted with the shredding disc, coarsely grate the potatoes and onion. Transfer to a medium bowl lined with cheesecloth or a thin dish towel and wring the cloth to squeeze out any liquid into the bowl. Set the bowl of liquid aside to sit for 5 minutes. Put the squeezed potatoes and onion into the bowl with the eggs, then add the potato starch and salt and mix until well incorporated.
3. Pour off and discard the reserved liquid from the medium bowl, revealing a thin layer of white potato starch stuck to the bottom. Stir the potato starch into the potato mixture.
4. In a 12-inch cast-iron or nonstick skillet, heat the olive oil over medium-high heat until shimmering. Add the potato mixture and spread in an even layer across the pan. Cook until golden brown around the sides and bottom, 4 to 5 minutes.
5. Place a low-rimmed plate or platter, slightly larger than the pan, over the hash browns. Remove from the heat and, using a kitchen towel or oven mitts, invert them together away from you quickly, with confidence. Carefully shimmy the flipped hash browns back into the pan, using a rubber spatula to tuck in the edges. Return to the heat and cook until the bottom is golden brown, 4 to 5 minutes more.
6. Transfer to a cutting board and cut into squares or wedges, then transfer to a platter and serve.

Make Ahead Hash browns can be made up to 1 hour before serving, transferred to a wire rack–lined sheet pan, ready to be reheated in the oven until crisp.

Leftovers 5 days in the refrigerator.

Skip dinner, let's just do **noshes** galore and get everyone full and drunk!

Life of the Cocktail Party

MENU

Cucumber-Basil Shrub
Honey-Ginger Syrup
Rose Grenadine

Party Animal Mix
Marinated Party Mix
Au Poivre Dip

Minty Pea & White Bean Dip
Maple-Candied Nuts
Cacio e Pepe Cheese Twists

Cheeseburger
Arayes Sliders
Raspberry Goat Cheese Bars

GROCERY LIST

PANTRY

1 lb mixed olives
8 oz peppadew peppers
3 c Corn Chex
3 c mini pretzels
3 c (about 11 oz) mixed raw nuts, such as walnuts, cashews, pecans, and/or almonds
3 c (600g) granulated sugar
2 c (270g) all-purpose flour
1½ c honey

1 c M&M's (optional)
1 c white wine vinegar
1 c olive oil
1 c mayonnaise
1 c raspberry jam
½ c maple syrup
5 tbsp ketchup
¼ c neutral oil, such as vegetable, avocado, or sunflower
¼ c Worcestershire sauce

¼ c minced pickles (dill or bread and butter)
¼ c cognac, brandy, dry sherry, or bourbon
¼ c Dijon mustard
2 tbsp light brown sugar
2 tbsp red wine vinegar
1 tsp hot sauce
1 tsp baking powder
1 (15-oz) can cannellini beans

1 (14-oz) can artichoke hearts
1 (9¼-oz) bag Fritos
1 (8½-oz) bag Cheetos
1 (7-oz) bag bagel or pita chips
1 (5-oz) bag barbecue potato chips
1 bag ruffled potato chips, for the Au Poivre Dip
3 to 4 boxes assorted crackers, for a cheese board

SPICES, SEASONINGS, AND FLAVORINGS

1 tbsp rose water
2 tsp dried lavender flowers (optional)

2 tsp sesame seeds
2 tsp smoked paprika
1½ tsp garlic powder

1 tsp fennel seeds
1 tsp coriander seeds
½ tsp crushed red pepper

KS&P (at least 2 c kosher salt and 1 jar whole black peppercorns to be safe)

BREAD

6 pitas

MEAT

3 lb ground beef (preferably 80% lean)

PRODUCE

12 oz (1 medium) English cucumber
3 c pomegranate juice
1 c fresh basil leaves
4 lemons

4 medium shallots
1 orange
1 medium yellow onion
1 bunch mint (½ c leaves)

1 bunch chives (½ c minced)
1 small bunch rosemary (2 tbsp leaves)
1 small bunch thyme (1 tsp leaves)

1 head garlic (3 cloves)
1 (4-in) knob ginger
About 2 pounds assorted crudités, for the Minty Pea & White Bean Dip

REFRIGERATED

12 oz (3 sticks) plus 2 tbsp unsalted butter
8 oz sharp cheddar cheese

4 oz goat cheese
1 c finely grated Pecorino Romano cheese

2 large eggs
1 (16-oz) container full-fat sour cream

4 to 5 cheeses (each about 8 oz), for a cheese board

FROZEN

2 sheets puff pastry (from one 17.3-oz package)

1 (10-oz) bag frozen peas

PREP LIST

Up to 1 Week Ahead
- Make the Cucumber-Basil Shrub
- Make the Honey-Ginger Syrup
- Make the Rose Grenadine
- Make the Party Animal Mix
- Make the Marinated Party Mix
- Make the Maple-Candied Nuts

Up to 2 Days Ahead
- Make the Au Poivre Dip
- Make the Minty Pea & White Bean Dip
- Make the burger sauce for the Cheeseburger Arayes

Up to 1 Day Ahead
- Make the Cacio e Pepe Cheese Twists
- Make the Raspberry Goat Cheese Bars
- Chill any wines or beverages

Day Of
- Prep any crudités for dips and cheeses for a cheese board
- Slice the Raspberry Goat Cheese Bars
- Assemble the Cheeseburger Arayes

1 Hour Before Guests Arrive
- Assemble a cheese board
- Build your table, transferring all dishes to bowls or platters
- Build your bar
- Sear the Cheeseburger Arayes

Right Before Guests Arrive
- Bake the Cheeseburger Arayes

Game Time Pep Talk
This one is pretty easy since your cheese board, Party Animal Mix, Maple-Candied Nuts, Au Poivre Dip, Minty Pea & White Bean Dip, Cacio e Pepe Cheese Twists, and Raspberry Goat Cheese Bars should be out on the table alongside any crudités, crackers, and/or chips. You should have a bar set up with the Cucumber-Basil Shrub, Honey-Ginger Syrup, and Rose Grenadine alongside an array of spirits, mixers like seltzer, tonic, and ginger beer, and ice. The only thing you should have to deal with is pulling the Cheeseburger Arayes out of the oven to serve with their dipping sauce. If you decided to make them in advance, flash them in the 450°F oven to reheat (about 5 minutes if recently baked or 10 minutes if fully cooled). You've got this!

Navot

cucumber-basil shrub

Welcome to the magical world of shrubs, the mixer of my dreams! Also known as "drinking vinegar," shrubs take any combo of fruit, vegetables, and/or herbs and macerate them with sugar into a syrup before mixing them with vinegar, preserving all that flavor with the perfect balance of sweetness and acidity. While my go-to is to simply pour a little over ice and top with seltzer, they're also perfect for spiking with the spirit of your choice. For this shrub, cucumber and basil add both a stunning green hue and refreshing vegetal flavor that tastes like you're either recharging at the spa or getting drunk there. Either way, call it self-care.

Makes 2 cups | Prep Time: 10 minutes, plus 24 hours chilling

12 ounces (1 medium) English cucumber, thinly sliced
1 cup fresh basil leaves, roughly chopped
1 cup (200g) granulated sugar
Pinch of kosher salt
1 cup white wine vinegar

1. In a medium bowl, combine the cucumber, basil, sugar, and salt. Toss with a wooden spoon to combine and lightly mash the cucumber. Transfer to an airtight container and refrigerate for 24 hours, shaking the container once or twice.
2. After 24 hours, shake vigorously to ensure all the sugar is dissolved. Strain into a clean container, then stir in the vinegar to combine. Seal and store in the refrigerator.

Make Ahead Shrub can be made up to 1 week in advance, stored in the refrigerator.

Leftovers 1 month in the refrigerator.

Honey-Ginger Syrup

You can always make a simple syrup with sugar, but when you swap in honey you've discovered a way to infuse both richness and floral sweetness to any drink. Here, the simple yet classic combo of honey, ginger, and lemon zest adds cozy vibes for a syrup that's just as potent in adding zing to a cocktail as it is to rounding out any tea party, whether hot or iced.

Makes 2 cups | Prep Time: 5 minutes, plus cooling and overnight chilling | Cook Time: 5 minutes

1 cup honey
1 cup water
Pinch of kosher salt

1 (4-inch) knob ginger, thinly sliced
1 lemon, zested with a peeler

In a small saucepan, combine the honey, water, salt, ginger, and lemon zest. Bring to a simmer over medium-high heat and cook for 2 minutes, then cool completely. Transfer to an airtight container and refrigerate overnight. The next day, strain into a clean airtight container, discarding any solids. Seal and store in the refrigerator.

Make Ahead Syrup can be made up to 1 week in advance, stored in the refrigerator.

Leftovers 1 month in the refrigerator.

Rose Grenadine

Embrace your inner child and treat yourself to a grown-up Shirley Temple. Instead of the fluorescent red grenadine that reminds me of every bar mitzvah I've ever attended, this homemade version cooks down pomegranate juice with sugar and lemon until you have a tart, ruby-colored syrup that we're going to perfume with just a little rose water for a hint of ethereal sweetness. Spike some in your ginger ale or Sprite, or if you're anything like me, in a giant ice-filled cup of Fresca. Then, the only question is whether you want to make it dirty or keep it clean.

Makes 2 cups | Prep Time: 5 minutes, plus cooling time and overnight chilling | Cook Time: 20 minutes

3 cups pomegranate juice
1 cup (200g) granulated sugar
2 tablespoons freshly squeezed lemon juice

Pinch of kosher salt
1 tablespoon rose water

In a medium saucepan, combine the pomegranate juice, sugar, lemon juice, salt, and rose water. Bring to simmer over medium-high heat and cook, reducing the heat to maintain a simmer, until the mixture has reduced to 2 cups, about 20 minutes. Let cool completely, then stir in the rose water. Transfer to an airtight container and refrigerate overnight before using.

Make Ahead Grenadine can be made up to 1 week in advance, stored in the refrigerator.

Leftovers 2 weeks in the refrigerator.

Party Animal Mix

I'm the person who's always picking out the things I love in a party mix, leaving behind a pile of rejects to be pushed onto someone else. But now, it's my party, and I'll mix what I want to. This is truly my dream party snack mix, taking my favorite chips and tossing them in a spiced butter mixture before baking low and slow into a crunchy combo that is so saturated in flavor, salt, sugar, and fat that you're probably releasing dopamine just by reading this recipe. We've got our corn chips, Cheetos, bagel chips, barbecue potato chips (must be BBQ!), Corn Chex (the superior Chex), and mini pretzels. Once the mixture is cooled, the power move is tossing in M&M's for the sweet and salty combo that sounds so wrong but tastes so right. Never have I made a recipe so intentionally for the munchies, and yet it's ideal snacking for a cocktail party. Ready to party?

Serves 12 to 15 | Prep Time: 15 minutes, plus cooling time | Cook Time: 1 hour

- 1 (9¼-ounce) bag Fritos
- 1 (8½-ounce) bag Cheetos
- 1 (7-ounce) bag bagel or pita chips
- 1 (5-ounce) bag barbecue potato chips
- 3 cups Corn Chex
- 3 cups mini pretzels
- 4 ounces (1 stick) unsalted butter
- ¼ cup Worcestershire sauce
- 2 tablespoons light brown sugar
- 1 teaspoon smoked paprika
- 1 teaspoon garlic powder
- 1 teaspoon kosher salt
- ½ teaspoon freshly ground black pepper
- 1 cup M&M's (optional)

1. Preheat the oven to 250°F.
2. Divide the Fritos, Cheetos, bagel chips, potato chips, Chex, and pretzels between 2 sheet pans.
3. In a medium saucepan, melt the butter over medium heat. Add the Worcestershire sauce, brown sugar, paprika, garlic powder, salt, and pepper and cook for 2 minutes. Drizzle the butter mixture over both trays, dividing it equally. Using a spoon or your hands, toss until everything is well coated.
4. Bake for about 1 hour, stirring each tray every 20 minutes, until dry and golden. Let cool completely, then stir in the M&M's (if using) and transfer to sealable bags.

Make Ahead Party mix can be made up to 1 week in advance, stored in sealable plastic bags or airtight containers at room temperature.

Leftovers 2 weeks at room temperature.

Marinated Party Mix

This marinated party mix is the negroni to the Party Animal Mix's Four Loko. Instead of various bags of chips, we're venturing into the olive bar and making my dream blend of briny snacks I want to enjoy alongside a cheese board. Since we can't forget it's a party, we're going to zhuzh this combo of olives, peppadew peppers, and artichoke hearts with a little olive oil marinade infused with rosemary, fennel seeds, and orange zest. Unlike my Party Animal Mix, here everything is negotiable! Itching for some gherkins? Go for it! Want to switch up the spices and aromatics? By all means! Think of this as more of a technique to explore, so you never leave out a sad, bone-dry bowl of Castelvetrano olives again!

Serves 12 to 15 | Prep Time: 10 minutes, plus cooling time and overnight chilling | Cook Time: 5 minutes

1 pound mixed olives, drained
8 ounces peppadew peppers, drained
1 (14-ounce) can artichoke hearts, drained and halved
¾ cup olive oil
2 tablespoons rosemary leaves
1 teaspoon fennel seeds
1 teaspoon coriander seeds
½ teaspoon crushed red pepper
6 (2-inch) strips orange zest, zested with a peeler
1 garlic clove, minced
2 tablespoons red wine vinegar

In a large heatproof bowl, combine the olives, peppers, and artichoke hearts. In a small saucepan, combine the olive oil, rosemary, fennel seeds, coriander seeds, crushed red pepper, orange zest, and garlic. Bring to a simmer over medium heat and cook for 1 minute, then pour over the olive mixture. Add the vinegar and toss to combine. Transfer to an airtight container and refrigerate overnight before serving.

Make Ahead Marinated party mix can be made up to 1 week in advance, stored in the refrigerator.

Leftovers 1 week in the refrigerator.

AU POIVRE DIP

You can always catch me at the bowl of onion dip at any party, alternating between potato chips and celery stalks since I'm all about that balance. As a result, I feel an intense responsibility to only share a dip recipe that will make your guests find a higher power within the swirls of sour cream, or at least grab their attention away from whatever cute boy they're flirting with to compliment the chef. After perfecting the steak au poivre recipe for my Steak 'n' Cake menu, the classic French sauce was front of mind when I was figuring out how I could switch things up. So I cooked down shallots with tons of black pepper before deglazing with cognac for an intense mélange of sweetness and rich onion flavor to stir into a tub of sour cream. It's everything you love about onion dip, but just a little fancier and ready in a fraction of the time. Everybody wins, especially your taste buds.

Makes 2½ cups | Prep Time: 15 minutes, plus cooling time | Cook Time: 10 minutes

2 tablespoons unsalted butter
4 medium shallots, minced
2 teaspoons coarsely ground black pepper
1 teaspoon thyme leaves, minced
KS

¼ cup cognac, brandy, dry sherry, or bourbon
1 (16-ounce) container full-fat sour cream
½ cup minced fresh chives
Ruffled potato chips, for serving

1. In a medium saucepan, melt the butter over medium heat. Add the shallots, black pepper, thyme, and 2 heavy pinches of salt. Cook, stirring often, until jammy and just beginning to caramelize, 6 to 8 minutes. Pour in the cognac and cook, stirring continuously, until completely reduced, 3 to 4 minutes. Transfer to a medium bowl and let cool completely.

2. To the cooled shallot mixture, stir in the sour cream and chives until well combined. Taste and adjust the seasoning with salt, then serve with potato chips.

Make Ahead Dip can be made up to 2 days in advance, stored in the refrigerator.

Leftovers 5 days in the refrigerator.

Minty Pea & White Bean Dip

Every party needs a dish that gives you the opportunity to obnoxiously say, "And would you ever guess it's vegan?!" Just kidding, I want to make sure there's something for everyone, whether they're vegan or lactose intolerant (let's be real, aren't we all?) or just trying to not eat their weight in gouda, and this recipe checks all the boxes. My typical rule is if I do one dairy-based dip, I always want it balanced with a plant-based one. Instead of the predictable hummus, I've been obsessed with throwing a bag of thawed, frozen peas and a whole can of white beans in the food processor with mint and garlic to puree into a creamy, verdant spread that thickens up in the fridge since we're all about that prep-ahead life. Frame it with a bouquet of crudités and you're ready to go skinny dipping.

Makes about 3 cups | Prep Time: 10 minutes, plus 4 hours chilling time

1 (15-ounce) can cannellini beans, drained
1 (10-ounce) bag frozen peas, thawed
½ cup fresh mint leaves
2 tablespoons olive oil
2 garlic cloves, thinly sliced
1 lemon, zested and juiced
KS&P
Assorted crudités, for serving

In a food processor, combine the beans, peas, mint, olive oil, garlic, lemon zest and juice, and a heavy pinch each of salt and pepper. Process until mainly smooth, then taste and adjust the seasoning with salt and pepper.

Make Ahead Dip can be made up to 2 days in advance, stored in the refrigerator.

Leftovers 5 days in the refrigerator.

Maple-Candied Nuts

While NYC offers some rather pungent odors, I find no greater joy than the momentary whiff of a Nuts 4 Nuts cart, temporarily replacing the aroma of hot garbage with toasty caramelized nuts. And you, too, can bring that olfactory joy to your home (without the hot garbage hopefully) with this easy app that never fails to have my friends texting me for the recipe. It's as simple as cooking toasted nuts with maple syrup, sesame seeds, and spices until all the water in the syrup evaporates, coating the nuts in sandy, sweet crystals of maple sugar. Once cooled, there's no stickiness, which is an important consideration so your guests won't be inclined to lick their fingers or pick at their teeth. (Not that I'm judging.) And any combo of raw nuts will do, so you can take this as an opportunity to finally clean out your pantry for a snack that everyone will go nuts for.

Makes 3 cups | Prep Time: 10 minutes, plus cooling time | Cook Time: 10 minutes

- 3 cups (about 11 ounces) mixed raw nuts, such as walnuts, cashews, pecans, and/or almonds
- ½ cup maple syrup
- 2 teaspoons sesame seeds
- 1 teaspoon kosher salt
- 1 teaspoon smoked paprika
- ½ teaspoon garlic powder
- ½ teaspoon freshly ground black pepper

1. Line a sheet pan with parchment paper.

2. In a medium saucepan, heat the nuts over medium heat. Cook, stirring often, until fragrant but not toasted, 2 to 3 minutes. Stir in the maple syrup, sesame seeds, and salt. Cook until the syrup is vigorously bubbling and has almost completely evaporated, 4 to 5 minutes. Stir in the salt, smoked paprika, garlic powder, and pepper. Continue to cook until the maple syrup crystallizes around each nut so it has a sandy appearance, about 2 minutes more. Transfer the candied nuts to the prepared pan and spread in an even layer, then let cool completely.

3. Once cooled, break up any clusters with your hands, then serve.

Make Ahead Nuts can be made up to 1 week in advance, stored in an airtight container at room temperature.

Leftovers 2 weeks at room temperature.

cacio e pepe cheese twists

My journey to learn how to host and entertain was a long one that wasn't always filled with me doing all the cooking. While I'm giving you everything you need to take the reins from soup to maple-candied nuts, that wasn't my reality when I was a twenty-four-year-old just starting to host gatherings at my mother's apartment. Instead of baking challah or appetizers or dessert, I gladly outsourced, serving a dairy haul from Murray's Cheese to start and all the bread and sweets from Breads Bakery. And while we can spend all day praising their chocolate babka, right now we need to focus on the magic of their cheese straws, using up strips of laminated dough, coated with cheese, and baked until flaky and crisp. Like I tell you in my introduction, you should never feel like you have to do it all to have it all. So if you feel like taking on the challenge, you only need four ingredients and thirty-five minutes to make my version, perfumed with chunks of pepper for a universally adored cacio e pepe moment. But if one more recipe feels like you might lose your mind, then by all means, and in my best Ina Garten voice, *store-bought is fine*!

Makes 24 twists | Prep Time: 15 minutes | Cook Time: 20 minutes

2 sheets store-bought puff pastry (from one 17.3-ounce package), thawed
1 large egg, beaten
1 cup finely grated Pecorino Romano cheese
4 teaspoons coarsely ground black pepper

1. Preheat the oven to 375°F. Line 2 sheet pans with parchment paper.

2. On a cutting board, unfold 1 sheet of puff pastry with the creases running vertically. Brush the sheet liberally with egg. Sprinkle ¼ cup of the cheese and 1 teaspoon of the pepper evenly over the egg wash, pressing the cheese gently to stick. Flip the puff pastry over and repeat brushing with egg and sprinkling on another ¼ cup cheese and 1 teaspoon pepper.

3. Using a knife, pizza wheel, or pastry cutter, cut the sheet into 12 even strips. Twist both ends of each strip in opposite directions a few times. Place each twist on the prepared pan, spacing them ½ inch apart.

4. Repeat steps 2 and 3 with the remaining sheet of puff pastry, egg, cheese, and pepper and place on the second prepared sheet pan.

5. Bake for about 20 minutes, rotating the trays halfway through, until golden and crisp. Let cool slightly on the pan, then serve.

Make Ahead Twists can be made up to 1 day in advance, stored in an airtight container at room temperature.

Leftovers 3 days at room temperature.

Life of the Cocktail Party

cheeseburger arayes sliders

The whole point of this cocktail party is to feed as many people as you can fit in your home while still being able to mingle and nosh and even turn up, if you're into something like that. Every other recipe in this menu is prepped in advance and plated before your guests arrive, so you truly can be the host with the most. I just wanted one hot, substantial bite to round it all out since we're not serving a formal dinner. And since I've already done a million variations on pigs in a blanket, I felt like it was time to venture away from hot dogs and into the world of sliders. But instead of a classic slider, I took inspiration from a recipe mashup I had made with my culinary bestie Ben Gingi, where we took Middle Eastern arayes (spiced meat–stuffed pitas that are grilled until crispy and golden) in an Italian American direction by stuffing them with a meatball mixture and dipping them in marinara once cooked. It couldn't be further from tradition, yet it made so much sense in my mouth. With the same taste of blasphemy, I decided to make a cheeseburger version, stuffing pitas with beef and chunks of cheddar. (Cyberbully me all you want, this recipe changed my life.) You get a crispy crust of beef and cheddar matched with gooey cheese pockets throughout and the perfect ratio of burger to bread. And that's before you've even dipped it in my burger sauce. Now, let me put my host hat back on, since it's also such an iconic recipe for easy entertaining. You can not only have the arayes pre-assembled, but you can even pre-sear them so you just have to pop a sheet pan in the oven when the party is bumping. All that hype aside, I still want you to consider this to be the extra-credit recipe for this menu, so feel free to skip it even if I know you'll regret it. (Did you expect no guilt? I am still my mother's son!)

Makes 24 cheeseburger arayes sliders | Prep Time: 30 minutes | Cook Time: 20 minutes

Burger Sauce
1 cup mayonnaise
¼ cup ketchup
¼ cup minced pickles (dill or bread and butter)
3 tablespoons Dijon mustard
1 teaspoon hot sauce
KS&P

Arayes
3 pounds ground beef (preferably 80% lean)
8 ounces sharp cheddar cheese, finely chopped
1 medium yellow onion, minced
1 tablespoon kosher salt
1 tablespoon ketchup
1 tablespoon Dijon mustard
6 pitas, halved
¼ cup neutral oil, such as vegetable, avocado, or sunflower

1. Make the burger sauce: In a medium bowl, stir together the mayonnaise, ketchup, pickles, mustard, and hot sauce until well combined. Taste and adjust the seasoning with salt and pepper.

2. Make the arayes: Preheat the oven to 450°F. Line a sheet pan with a wire rack.

3. In a large bowl, mix together the beef, cheddar, onion, salt, ketchup, and mustard until well combined. Stuff the beef mixture into the pita pocket halves, dividing evenly for 12 arayes.

4. In a large nonstick or cast-iron skillet, heat the oil over medium-high heat. Working in 2 batches, place half of the arayes meat-side down and cook until golden, 3 to 4 minutes. Transfer the arayes to the prepared sheet pan, placing them on their sides (pita-side down). Repeat with the remaining arayes. Using a pastry brush, brush the pitas with some of the oil from the pan.

5. Bake for 5 minutes, then flip the arayes to the other side and bake for another 5 minutes. Transfer to a cutting board and cut each arayes in half, then arrange on a platter and serve with the burger sauce.

Make Ahead Burger sauce (step 1) can be made up to 2 days in advance, stored in an airtight container in the refrigerator. Arayes can be stuffed (step 3) a few hours in advance of cooking. They can be just seared and ready to bake in the oven (step 4) up to 30 minutes before your guests arrive, finishing in the oven (step 5) when everyone has arrived. Alternatively, the arayes can be fully cooked (steps 4 and 5) and held on the wire rack–lined tray up to 1 hour before your guests arrive, reheating in the oven before slicing and serving.

Leftovers 5 days in the refrigerator.

Life of the Cocktail Party

Raspberry Goat Cheese Bars

At any cocktail party, I like to make one easy dessert to sweeten the spread, while also understanding that people will end up bringing desserts even if you told them to just bring themselves. Since we are going for simple, I gravitate toward anything in bar form that can be pre-baked and pre-sliced. For these bars, I revisited the dough from my great-grandmother's apple cake recipe, which is the gift that keeps on giving! You'll find the full recipe for Nanny's Apple Cake in *I Could Nosh*, but the dough is so unbelievably versatile that it also makes an appearance in the Plum Crumb Bars in *Jew-ish*, as well as here. It works as both a crust and a crumble, simultaneously creating a chewy bottom and crispy top, which perfectly describes my ideal dessert/man. This time around, I flavored the dough with lemon zest and lavender for a summery brightness to pair with the effortless, yet unexpected, filling of raspberry jam and tangy goat cheese. It's a flawless final bite to wrap up this menu and evening. Well, I guess depending on what you have planned for the afters.

Makes 24 bars | Prep Time: 20 minutes, plus cooling time | Cook Time: 60 minutes

- 1 cup (200g) granulated sugar
- 2 teaspoons finely grated lemon zest
- 2 teaspoons dried lavender flowers (optional)
- 2 cups (270g) all-purpose flour
- 1 teaspoon baking powder
- 1 teaspoon kosher salt
- 8 ounces (2 sticks) unsalted butter, cold and cubed
- 1 large egg, lightly beaten
- 1 cup raspberry jam
- 4 ounces goat cheese

1. Preheat the oven to 350°F. Set an oven rack in the center of the oven. Line a 9-inch square baking pan with parchment paper.

2. In a food processor, combine the sugar, lemon zest, and lavender, if using. Process for 1 minute, or until well incorporated. Add the flour, baking powder, and salt and pulse to combine. Add the butter and pulse until it forms pea-sized crumbles. Add the egg and pulse until the dough just comes together.

3. Press two-thirds of the dough into the prepared pan in an even layer. Spread the raspberry jam evenly over the dough, then crumble the goat cheese evenly over the jam. Pinch off small pieces of the remaining one-third dough and scatter them over the top.

4. Bake on the center rack for 55 to 60 minutes, until golden. Let cool completely, then transfer to a cutting board, cut into bars, and serve. (I find 4 rows and 6 columns make for the best size for a cocktail party.)

Make Ahead Bars can be made up to 1 day in advance, stored in an airtight container in the refrigerator.

Leftovers 5 days in the refrigerator.

MENU

Sun-Dried Tomato & Yogurt Dip

Creamy Pistachio Salad

Spicy Sausage Gnocchi Bake with Pesto Ricotta

Peanut Butter Hot Fudge Sundaes

GROCERY LIST

PANTRY
- 2 lb shelf-stable, packaged gnocchi
- 8 tbsp olive oil
- 1½ c (300g) granulated sugar
- ½ tsp baking soda
- ¾ c honey-roasted peanuts or roasted, salted peanuts
- ¾ c dark chocolate chips
- ½ c smooth peanut butter
- ½ c shelled, roasted, and salted pistachios
- ½ c dry red wine
- ¼ c white wine vinegar
- 1 tbsp honey
- 1 tsp Dijon mustard
- 1 (24-oz) jar marinara sauce
- 1 (10-oz) jar sun-dried tomatoes, in oil
- Crackers

SPICES, SEASONINGS, AND FLAVORINGS
- 1 tsp vanilla extract
- ½ tsp crushed red pepper
- Flaky sea salt
- KS&P (at least 2 c kosher salt and 1 jar whole black peppercorns to be safe)

MEAT
- 12 oz spicy Italian sausage

PRODUCE
- 3 heads of romaine lettuce
- 1 bunch red radishes
- 1 head garlic (6 cloves)
- Assorted crudités

REFRIGERATED
- 8 oz shredded mozzarella cheese
- 1 c heavy cream
- 1 c plain Greek yogurt (any fat %)
- 1 c ricotta cheese (any fat %)
- ½ c prepared pesto
- 2 tbsp unsalted butter
- 1 small chunk Parmesan cheese (for about ½ c grated)
- 1 large egg

FROZEN
- 1 quart vanilla ice cream

PREP LIST

Up to 2 Days Ahead
(if you remembered it was tonight)
- Make the Sun-Dried Tomato & Yogurt Dip
- Make the dressing for the Creamy Pistachio Salad
- Make the peanut brittle for the Peanut Butter Hot Fudge Sundaes
- Make the hot fudge for the Peanut Butter Hot Fudge Sundaes

1 Hour Before Guests Arrive
- Prep the vegetables for the Creamy Pistachio Salad
- Assemble the Gnocchi Bake
- Assemble any crudités or crackers for serving with the Sun-Dried Tomato & Yogurt Dip

Right Before Guests Arrive
- Assemble the Creamy Pistachio Salad
- Bake the Gnocchi Bake

Game Time Pep Talk
The Sun-Dried Tomato & Yogurt Dip should be in a bowl already on the table alongside any crudités or crackers for serving. The Creamy Pistachio Salad can be tossed and on the table. The Gnocchi Bake should be in the oven and what you're waiting on. For the Peanut Butter Hot Fudge Sundaes, the fudge should be in a saucepan on the stove, ready to be whisked over medium heat to reheat for 2 to 3 minutes, until glossy. The brittle should be ready and broken up. The ice cream should be in the freezer, but pull it out about 10 minutes before scooping and assembling. You've got this!

Idan & Jason
My challah Prince!

sun-dried tomato & yogurt dip

It all started with a desire to find out: Will it mayo? By that I mean, could I blend an entire jar of sun-dried tomatoes in their oil with an egg yolk to emulsify into mayo? Not only was it possible, but the crimson mayo that formed became one of the best sandwich spreads I've ever had. I was a wild man with an immersion blender who couldn't stop there. As I explored all the variations of my new discovery, I naturally tried adding some non-fat Greek yogurt to the mix since I'm just as big on dip culture as I am on sandwich schmears. The result was a velvety spread with all that rich, intense tomato flavor and sweetness, balanced by the tangy yogurt and a little punch from garlic. It's become my secret weapon for both personal snacking and entertaining, wowing everyone who swoops in with a carrot stick or cracker.

Makes about 2 cups | Prep Time: 5 minutes

1 (10-ounce) jar sun-dried tomatoes, in oil
1 cup plain Greek yogurt (any fat %)
2 garlic cloves, finely grated

1 large egg yolk
KS&P
Crudités and/or crackers, for serving

In a quart container or medium bowl, combine the sun-dried tomatoes, yogurt, garlic, egg yolk, and 2 heavy pinches each of salt and pepper. Using an immersion blender, blend until smooth and emulsified. Taste and adjust the seasoning with salt and pepper. Serve with crudités and/or crackers.

Make Ahead Dip can be made up to 2 days in advance, stored in an airtight container in the refrigerator.

Leftovers 4 days in the refrigerator.

Creamy Pistachio Salad

There's only one restaurant in the world I gatekeep, and it's this little Italian spot in New York's Hudson Valley that makes the best fresh pasta and chicken Parm in the world. They have no social media accounts and you still have to call to make reservations. The chef, who is the only one cooking every night, always picks up the phone and ends every call with a "Ciao, babe." It's just a perfect spot and always packed with the local community, so we're going to keep it that way! Every meal for me there starts with a big salad with their pistachio dressing, inspiring this recipe so I can share a taste of my favorite hidden gem. We pop everything into a quart container and hit it with an immersion blender (though a food processor will do the trick, too) to form an emulsified yet chunky dressing that's best described as a pistachio-flavored Caesar. Since we're throwing this menu together quickly, we're just using romaine and radishes, though feel free to get creative with the mix-ins. I will say this secret restaurant always includes a combo of grapes and olives in their salad that seems so wrong but tastes so right.

Serves 4 to 6 | Prep Time: 15 minutes

Dressing
½ cup shelled, roasted, and salted pistachios
6 tablespoons olive oil
6 tablespoons water
¼ cup white wine vinegar
¼ cup freshly grated Parmesan cheese
1 tablespoon honey
1 teaspoon Dijon mustard
KS&P

Salad
3 heads of romaine, leaves roughly torn
1 bunch red radishes, trimmed and thinly sliced
KS
Freshly grated Parmesan cheese, for garnish

1. Make the dressing: In a quart container or medium bowl, combine the pistachios, olive oil, water, vinegar, Parmesan, honey, mustard, and a heavy pinch each of salt and pepper. Using an immersion blender, blend until a chunky but emulsified dressing forms. Taste and adjust the seasoning with salt and pepper.

2. Assemble the salad: In a large bowl, toss the romaine and radishes with the dressing. Taste and adjust the seasoning with salt. Top with freshly grated Parmesan and serve.

Make Ahead Dressing (step 1) can be made up to 2 days in advance, stored in an airtight container in the refrigerator.

Leftovers 1 day in the refrigerator.

spicy sausage gnocchi bake with pesto ricotta

Over the last few years, I've become a big proponent of sheet pan store-bought gnocchi dinners, since you can throw the gnocchi right into the oven without boiling. From there, I had the crazy adjacent idea of making a baked ziti but swapping the ziti with gnocchi so you could make it in one pan without the added time of cooking the pasta. Now, here's where things get crazy . . . go ahead and buy store-bought marinara and pesto while you're at it and don't feel guilty for one second. We're infusing the sauce with spicy Italian sausage, garlic, and red wine to quickly make it taste like we let it simmer all day. When the bubbly, cheesy pan hits the table, nobody will ever guess how easy it was to throw together, and why should they? Take the compliments and the credit—you deserve it!

Serves 4 to 6 | Prep Time: 10 minutes | Cook Time: 40 minutes

Pesto Ricotta
1 cup ricotta cheese (any fat %)
½ cup pesto, store-bought or homemade
KS&P

Gnocchi Bake
2 tablespoons olive oil
12 ounces spicy Italian sausage, casing removed
½ teaspoon crushed red pepper
4 garlic cloves, thinly sliced
½ cup dry red wine
1 (24-ounce) jar marinara sauce, or 3 cups homemade
KS&P
2 pounds shelf-stable packaged gnocchi
8 ounces shredded mozzarella cheese

1. Make the pesto ricotta: In a medium bowl, stir the ricotta, pesto, and a heavy pinch each of salt and pepper until well combined.

2. Make the gnocchi bake: Preheat the oven to 400°F.

3. In a large cast-iron pan or ovenproof skillet, heat the olive oil over medium-high heat. Add the sausage and cook, using a wooden spoon to break it up into crumbles, until lightly golden, 4 to 5 minutes. Stir in the crushed red pepper and garlic and cook for 1 minute. Pour in the wine and cook for 1 minute, using the wooden spoon to scrape up any browned bits on the bottom of the pan. Stir in the sauce, then taste and adjust the seasoning with salt and pepper. Add the gnocchi and toss to coat in the sauce, then dollop on the pesto ricotta and top with the shredded mozzarella.

4. Bake for 25 to 30 minutes, until golden brown and bubbling, then serve.

Make Ahead Gnocchi bake can be assembled and ready to bake (through step 3) up to an hour before baking and serving.

Leftovers 4 days in the refrigerator.

Peanut Butter Hot Fudge Sundaes

As a society, we don't have enough ice cream socials. Maybe it's just because I impulsively bought a set of twelve banana split dishes off Amazon over the pandemic, but I try to have a sundae moment whenever I can with those I love. When it's done right, you can satisfy everyone's inner child and sweet tooth at the same time. It doesn't hurt that it also takes a fraction of the time to prepare compared to most other desserts. For this sundae, we're going to cover vanilla ice cream with a rich, glossy peanut butter hot fudge, caramelized shards of peanut brittle, and a pinch of flaky salt for a dreamy combo of both hot and cold, crunchy and smooth, chocolate and vanilla, and sweet and salty. (Who said we can't have it all?) What makes this such a go-to recipe for me is that it works just as well as a last-minute resort as it does for a pre-planned spectacle. The brittle can be made right before your guests arrive and will be cooled and ready to shatter by dessert time, but it also can be made days in advance. Same deal with the hot fudge, which can be drizzled freshly whisked, or you can be like me and always keep a pint in your freezer, because you never know when the mood will strike!

Serves 4 to 6 | Prep Time: 15 minutes, plus cooling time | Cook Time: 15 minutes

Peanut Brittle
1 cup (200g) granulated sugar
3 tablespoons water
2 tablespoons unsalted butter
1 teaspoon kosher salt
½ teaspoon baking soda
¾ cup honey-roasted peanuts or roasted, salted peanuts

Hot Fudge
1 cup heavy cream
½ cup (100g) granulated sugar
1 teaspoon vanilla extract
½ teaspoon kosher salt
¾ cup dark chocolate chips
½ cup smooth peanut butter

Sundaes
1 quart vanilla ice cream
Flaky sea salt, for garnish

1. Make the peanut brittle: Line a sheet pan with parchment paper. In a medium saucepan, heat the sugar and water over medium-high heat. Cook, shaking and swirling the pan often (but do not stir), until dark amber in color, 8 to 10 minutes. Working quickly, remove from the heat and, using a silicone spatula, stir in the butter, salt, and baking soda, followed by the peanuts. Pour onto the prepared sheet pan, using the spatula to spread into an even layer. Let cool completely.

2. Using the handle of a wooden spoon or knife, smash the brittle to break it into small pieces.

3. Make the hot fudge: In a medium saucepan, combine the heavy cream, sugar, vanilla, and salt. Bring to a simmer over medium-high heat and cook, whisking continuously, until the sugar has dissolved, about 1 minute. Remove from the heat and add the chocolate chips and peanut butter. Whisk until a smooth hot fudge forms. If serving shortly, cover and set aside.

4. Assemble your sundaes: Warm the hot fudge over medium-low heat, whisking to ensure it's glossy and emulsified. Scoop the ice cream into small bowls. Spoon a few tablespoons of hot fudge over the ice cream, then top each with a handful of peanut brittle and a pinch of flaky salt. Serve immediately.

Make Ahead Peanut brittle (steps 1 and 2) can be made up to 2 days in advance, stored in an airtight container at room temperature. Hot fudge (step 3) can be made up to 2 days in advance, stored in an airtight container in the refrigerator, or 1 month in advance, stored in an airtight container in the freezer. Reheat the hot fudge in a saucepan over medium heat, whisking to re-emulsify.

Leftovers Brittle for up to 1 week at room temperature. Hot fudge for 5 days in the refrigerator or 1 month in the freezer.

That Was Tonight?

A summer **soirée** that's prepped ahead so you just need to grill and chill.

grills gone wild

MENU

Heirloom Tomato Toasts with Goat Cheese Schmear

Honey Mustard Potato Salad with Cornichons & Dill

Green Bean & Grilled Corn Salad with Honey-Lime Vinaigrette

Scallion Chimichurri

Honey-Balsamic Grilled Chicken & Summer Veg

Burgers Provençal

Apple Pie Calzone

GROCERY LIST

PANTRY
- 3½ c (473g) all-purpose flour
- 2½ c olive oil
- 1¼ c (250g) granulated sugar
- 1 c neutral oil, such as vegetable, avocado, or sunflower
- ¼ c red wine vinegar
- ¾ c honey
- ½ c mayonnaise
- ¼ c balsamic vinegar
- ¼ c Dijon mustard
- ¼ c vodka
- 3 tbsp cornstarch
- 2 tbsp whole grain Dijon mustard
- 1 tsp hot sauce
- 1 tsp Worcestershire sauce (optional)
- 1 jar cornichons (enough for ½ c sliced, plus 2 tablespoons minced)

SPICES, SEASONINGS, AND FLAVORINGS
- 2 tbsp herbes de Provence
- 2 tbsp ground cinnamon
- 1 tsp ground ginger
- 1 tsp freshly grated nutmeg
- Flaky sea salt
- KS&P (at least 2 c kosher salt and 1 jar whole black peppercorns to be safe)

BREAD
- 8 brioche or potato buns
- 1 large loaf sourdough bread

MEAT
- 3 lb ground beef (preferably 80% lean)
- 3 lb boneless, skinless chicken breasts

PRODUCE
- 4 lb baby potatoes
- 3 lb green beans
- 3 lb (8 to 9 medium) Honeycrisp apples
- 6 heirloom tomatoes
- 6 ears corn
- 6 medium (1 bunch) scallions
- 4 medium zucchini
- 4 lemons
- 3 medium red onions
- 3 medium bell peppers (preferably a mix of colors)
- 2 limes
- 2 heads garlic (10 cloves)
- 1 medium eggplant
- 1 Fresno or jalapeño chile
- 1 bunch basil (¾ c minced, plus more for garnish)
- 1 bunch dill (½ c minced)
- 1 bunch oregano (3 tbsp minced)
- 1 bunch chives (2 tbsp minced)
- 1 head butter lettuce

REFRIGERATED
- 9 oz (2¼ sticks) unsalted butter, cold and cubed
- 4 oz goat cheese
- 2 (8-oz) packages cream cheese
- 1 large egg

PREP LIST

Up to 2 Days Ahead
- Roast the potatoes for the Honey Mustard Potato Salad
- Blanch the green beans for the Green Bean & Grilled Corn Salad
- Make the sauce for the Burgers Provençal

Up to 1 Day Ahead
- Make the schmear for the Heirloom Tomato Toasts
- Make the dressing for the Honey Mustard Potato Salad
- Make the dressing for the Green Bean & Grilled Corn Salad
- Make the Scallion Chimichurri
- Marinate the chicken and vegetables for the Honey-Balsamic Grilled Chicken & Summer Veg
- Shape the patties for the Burgers Provençal
- Make the dough for the Apple Pie Calzone
- Make the filling for the Apple Pie Calzone

Day Of
- Slice the potatoes and assemble the Honey Mustard Potato Salad
- Grill the corn for the Green Bean & Grilled Corn Salad
- Assemble and bake the Apple Pie Calzone

1 Hour Before Guests Arrive
- Slice the tomatoes for the Heirloom Tomato Toasts
- Assemble the Green Bean & Grilled Corn Salad
- Prep the buns and lettuce for the Burgers Provençal

Right Before Guests Arrive
- Grill the bread for the Heirloom Tomato Toasts
- Grill the Honey-Balsamic Grilled Chicken & Summer Veg (hold in a 200°F oven)

Right Before Serving
- Assemble the Heirloom Tomato Toasts
- Grill the Burgers Provençal

Game Time Pep Talk
This is definitely a menu that requires a little extra attention at game time. The Green Bean & Grilled Corn Salad, Honey Mustard Potato Salad, and Scallion Chimichurri should all be ready and on the table. The Grilled Chicken & Summer Veg should be already grilled and held warm in the oven, ready to be plated. The Heirloom Tomato Toasts should be assembled shortly before serving so they don't get soggy but can be done before grilling the Burgers Provençal. All of the accoutrements for the burgers should be on the table so when the burgers are ready, it's time to serve everything. The Apple Pie Calzone should be ready to slice and serve, with the option to always flash in the oven for 5 to 10 minutes to warm through. You've got this!

Rachel♡

Heirloom Tomato Toasts with Goat Cheese Schmear

All summer gatherings should start with juicy, peak-season heirloom tomatoes! I run to the farmer's market to stock up on every color and start to work my way through them at every meal, whether on a morning bagel, lunch-time sandwich, or evening salad. But my all-time favorite way to serve them is on grilled sourdough with some cream cheese. Imagine watching the sun set somewhere in the country while you listen to the crunch of the toast break through sounds of birds chirping. You recount your shopping stories, reminding everyone that the bread was baked just a few minutes away and the tomatoes were picked just down the road. Tomato juice is dripping down your chin, but you're in a bathing suit, so you don't mind a little mess. Now, I unfortunately can't provide the country home or pool, but I can talk you through the tartines that pair so well with this fantasy! We can leave the bread to the local bakers and the tomatoes to the local farmers, but we get to control how we dress them up. Here, we're swirling our cream cheese with goat cheese, fresh basil, and lemon zest for a bright and tangy schmear to hold up our heirlooms. It's the toast with the most, packing the best parts of summer into every bite.

Serves 8 to 10 | Prep Time: 20 minutes | Cook Time: 5 minutes

Goat Cheese Schmear

- 2 (8-ounce) packages cream cheese, at room temperature
- 4 ounces goat cheese, at room temperature
- ¼ cup minced fresh basil leaves
- 1 teaspoon finely grated lemon zest
- 1 garlic clove, finely grated
- KS&P

Tomato Toasts

- 1 large loaf sourdough bread, sliced 1 inch thick
- Olive oil, for grilling and drizzling
- 6 heirloom tomatoes, sliced ¼ inch thick
- Flaky sea salt, for garnish
- Torn fresh basil leaves, for garnish

1. Make the goat cheese schmear: In a large bowl, combine the cream cheese, goat cheese, basil, lemon zest, garlic, and 2 heavy pinches each of salt and pepper. Using a spatula (or electric hand mixer), stir until well combined. Taste and adjust the seasoning with salt and pepper, then store in an airtight container in the refrigerator until 1 hour before serving.

2. Make the tomato toasts: Start a charcoal fire or heat a gas grill to medium-high. Drizzle both sides of each slice of bread with olive oil. Place the bread on the grill and cook, flipping once, until lightly golden and crisp, about 1 minute per side. Transfer to a cutting board.

3. Spread the schmear over each piece of grilled bread, then shingle the tomato slices on top. Drizzle each toast with olive oil, then garnish with flaky salt and basil. Slice each toast in half, then transfer to a platter and serve.

Make Ahead Schmear (step 1) can be made up to 1 day in advance. Tomatoes can be sliced up to 1 hour before serving. Toasts (steps 2 and 3) should be grilled and assembled only shortly before serving.

Leftovers Doesn't hold well!

Honey Mustard Potato Salad with Cornichons & Dill

There's a time and a place for a luscious, mayo-heavy potato salad, but not today. Mayo haters rejoice! Instead, we're tossing roasted baby potatoes with a bright honey-mustard dressing to balance our starchy spuds, rounding it all out with cornichons for crunchy tang and dill for freshness. We roast our potatoes whole and then halve them, creating large chunks that break apart ever so slightly when tossed with our dressing for extra creaminess. And like all potato salads, this recipe only gets better with time, making it an ideal side to make ahead so our potatoes can soak up all that flavor.

Serves 8 to 10 | Prep Time: 15 minutes, plus cooling time | Cook Time: 30 minutes

Roasted Potatoes
- 4 pounds baby potatoes
- 2 tablespoons olive oil
- KS&P

Dressing
- ¼ cup freshly squeezed lemon juice
- 3 tablespoons Dijon mustard
- 3 tablespoons honey
- 2 garlic cloves, finely grated
- KS&P
- ½ cup neutral oil, such as vegetable, avocado, or sunflower
- ½ cup sliced cornichons
- ½ cup minced fresh dill

1. Roast the potatoes: Preheat the oven to 450°F.

2. On a sheet pan, toss the potatoes with the olive oil and 2 heavy pinches each of salt and pepper to coat. Roast for 30 minutes, or until golden and tender. Let cool completely on the pan.

3. Meanwhile, make the dressing: In a large bowl, whisk the lemon juice, mustard, honey, garlic, and 2 heavy pinches each of salt and pepper until smooth. Slowly whisk in the neutral oil until emulsified, then stir in the cornichons and dill.

4. Slice the cooled potatoes in half, then add them to the bowl with the dressing and toss to coat. Taste and adjust the seasoning with salt and pepper. Let the salad sit at room temperature for at least 1 hour before serving.

Make Ahead Roast the potatoes (steps 1 and 2) up to 2 days in advance, letting them cool completely before storing them in an airtight container in the refrigerator, unsliced. Dressing (step 3) can be made up to 1 day in advance, though for any longer than a few hours, keep the dill on the side to preserve color and flavor. Potato salad can be dressed (step 4) a few hours in advance, in the refrigerator if longer than 1 hour.

Leftovers 5 days in the refrigerator.

Green Bean & Grilled Corn Salad with Honey-Lime Vinaigrette

While I'm not above gnawing at a corn cob like a typewriter, my move is always grilling corn and cutting off the charred, sweet kernels to throw into one of my sides. Here, we're tossing them with blanched green beans and a honey-lime vinaigrette to create a refreshing salad bursting with sweetness and acidity. And you can always pivot this recipe depending on your vibe. For a crunchier option, swap the tender green beans with chopped cucumbers, tomatoes, and/or snap peas. In peak corn season, you can even skip the grill and slice off the kernels raw since they're at their sweetest. Everything can be prepped in advance, so however you toss it together, it's going to be the salad of the summer.

Serves 8 to 10 | Prep Time: 30 minutes, plus cooling time | Cook Time: 15 minutes

Green Beans
KS
3 pounds green beans, trimmed

Dressing
½ cup olive oil
½ cup minced fresh basil
¼ cup honey

2 limes, zested and juiced
½ medium red onion, thinly sliced
KS&P

Grilled Corn
6 ears corn, husked
2 tablespoons olive oil

KS&P

1. Blanch the green beans: Bring a large pot of salted water to a boil. Fill a large bowl with ice and water.
2. Cook the green beans until bright green and tender, 3 to 4 minutes. Use a large metal spider or tongs to transfer to the ice bath for a few minutes until chilled, then drain.
3. Make the dressing: In a medium jar or pint container, combine the olive oil, basil, honey, lime juice and zest, red onion, and 2 heavy pinches each of salt and pepper. Seal closed and shake vigorously, then set aside.
4. Grill the corn: Start a charcoal fire or heat a gas grill to medium-high. Brush the corn with the olive oil and season with a heavy pinch each of salt and pepper. Grill, turning occasionally, until lightly charred, 8 to 10 minutes. Transfer to a sheet pan or platter to cool, then slice the kernels off each cob.
5. In a large bowl, toss the green beans and corn kernels with the dressing to coat. Taste and adjust the season with salt and pepper, then serve.

Make Ahead Green beans can be blanched and drained (steps 1 and 2) up to 2 days in advance, stored in an airtight container in the refrigerator. Dressing (step 3) can be made up to 1 day in advance, though for any longer than a few hours, keep the basil on the side to preserve color and flavor. Corn (step 4) can be grilled a few hours in advance. Salad can be dressed (step 5) up to 1 hour in advance.

Leftovers 5 days in the refrigerator.

Grills Gone Wild

scallion chimichurri

This is the spicy, tangy, herby condiment to dress up anything and everything. We're just making a simple chimichurri but swapping the parsley with scallions for some extra bite. It's meant to go over our Honey-Balsamic Grilled Chicken & Summer Veg (recipe follows), but honestly, why stop there? Leave out a bowl and let your guests go wild, since it would be great spooned over every dish (I'd probably avoid the apple pie, but you do you). And while it's a quick recipe that doesn't require any cooking, if you're looking for extra credit, I'll sometimes lightly grill the scallions before slicing for a hint of char and sweetness.

Makes about 1½ cups | Prep Time: 10 minutes, plus 1 hour marinating time

- ½ cup olive oil
- ¼ cup red wine vinegar
- 3 tablespoons minced fresh oregano leaves
- 6 medium (1 bunch) scallions, trimmed and thinly sliced
- 3 garlic cloves, minced
- 1 Fresno or jalapeño chile, stemmed, seeded, if desired, and minced
- KS&P

In a medium bowl, stir together the olive oil, vinegar, oregano, scallions, garlic, chile, and 2 heavy pinches each of salt and pepper to combine. Let marinate for 1 hour, then taste and adjust the seasoning with salt and pepper.

Make Ahead Chimichurri can be made up to 1 day in advance, stored in an airtight container in the refrigerator.

Leftovers 4 days in the refrigerator.

Honey-Balsamic Grilled Chicken & Summer Veg

To this day, my mother's secret to grilling just about anything is marinating it first with a bottle of Wish-Bone Italian Dressing. And, honestly, tea. Salad dressing makes the best marinade, since the acidity tenderizes meat, the sugar helps veggies caramelize, and everything ends up seasoned perfectly. But you know, I can give my mom her flowers for the cooking tip while still not settling for the bottled stuff. Instead, we're whisking up a quick honey-balsamic vinaigrette to toss our chicken and veggies with before hitting the grill. Feel free to play around with the dressing, swapping vinegars or sweeteners, adding herbs, or raiding your pantry to spice things up. Or just use a bottle of your favorite store-bought dressing, I'm not your mother, and you know mine would give you her blessing.

Serves 8 to 10 | Prep Time: 20 minutes, plus marinating time | Cook Time: 20 minutes

½ cup olive oil
¼ cup balsamic vinegar
¼ cup honey
1 tablespoon kosher salt
1 tablespoon Dijon mustard
1 teaspoon hot sauce
2 garlic cloves, finely grated

3 pounds boneless, skinless chicken breasts, halved lengthwise into cutlets
4 medium zucchini, halved lengthwise
3 medium bell peppers (preferably a mix of colors), stemmed, cored, and quartered
2 red onions, quartered
1 medium eggplant, cut into 1-inch slices
Neutral oil, such as vegetable, avocado, or sunflower, for grilling

1. In a medium bowl, whisk together the olive oil, vinegar, honey, salt, mustard, hot sauce, and garlic until smooth.

2. Place the chicken in a large bowl. Place the zucchini, bell peppers, red onions, and eggplant in another large bowl. Pour half of the marinade on each, tossing to coat, then cover both with plastic wrap and refrigerate to marinate for at least 1 hour, but preferably overnight.

3. When ready to grill, start a charcoal fire or heat a gas grill to high. Dip a rolled-up paper towel in neutral oil and, using tongs, brush the grates of the grill to grease. Grill the vegetables first, turning as needed with tongs, until charred and tender, 8 to 10 minutes. Transfer to a platter and tent with foil. Grill the chicken, flipping once, until it's lightly charred and reaches an internal temperature of 165°F, about 4 minutes per side. Transfer the chicken to the platter with the vegetables, then serve.

Make Ahead Before you start grilling, preheat the oven to 200°F. Transfer the freshly grilled chicken and vegetables to a sheet pan and hold in the oven to keep warm for about 15 minutes, while you grill the burgers (following recipe) and finish the spread.

Leftovers 5 days in the refrigerator.

Burgers Provençal

This recipe began in the lavender fields of Provence at a dear family friend's home enjoying the majestic French countryside. Days were spent frolicking through the local markets followed by quick meals I'd throw together to enjoy poolside. These burgers were one of the first things I made, embracing summer grilling season with some light tweaking to adjust to the scenery. Ground beef is seasoned with herbes de Provence and garlic, perfuming the burgers with rosemary and lavender when grilled. Served simply on brioche buns with a Dijon and cornichon-swirled mayo and torn lettuce, these burgers are simple yet sophisticated, and dare I say romantic! So get ready to fall in love . . . with this recipe, at least.

Makes 8 burgers | Prep Time: 25 minutes | Cook Time: 10 minutes

Sauce
½ cup mayonnaise
2 tablespoons whole grain Dijon mustard
2 tablespoons minced cornichons
2 tablespoons minced fresh chives
1 teaspoon Worcestershire sauce (optional)
KS&P

Burgers
3 pounds ground beef (preferably 80% lean)
2 tablespoons herbes de Provence
2 garlic cloves, finely grated
Neutral oil, such as vegetable, avocado, or sunflower, for grilling
KS&P

Assembly
8 brioche or potato buns, halved, toasted or untoasted
Torn butter lettuce

1. Make the sauce: In a medium bowl, stir the mayonnaise, mustard, cornichons, chives, Worcestershire sauce, if using, and a heavy pinch each of salt and pepper to combine.

2. Make the burgers: In a large bowl, mix the beef with the herbes de Provence and garlic until well incorporated, then form into 8 burger patties about 1 inch thick, and make a very light indentation with your thumb in the center of each.

3. Start a charcoal fire or heat a gas grill to high. Dip a rolled-up paper towel in oil and, using tongs, brush the grates of the grill to grease. Season both sides of each patty with a heavy pinch each of salt and black pepper. Place the patties on the grill and cook undisturbed until golden, 3 to 4 minutes, then flip with a metal spatula and continue to cook for another 3 to 4 minutes for medium-rare. Transfer to a platter and let rest for 5 minutes.

4. Assemble the burgers: Serve on the buns with the sauce and lettuce.

Make Ahead Sauce (step 1) can be made up to 2 days in advance, stored in an airtight container in the refrigerator. Burger patties (step 2) can be formed up to 1 day in advance, held in the refrigerator layered between parchment paper on a sheet pan and tightly covered with plastic wrap.

Leftovers 4 days in the refrigerator.

Grills Gone Wild

Apple Pie Calzone

Summer is all about wrapping the season's best fruit in a flaky buttery crust to be crowned with a giant scoop of vanilla ice cream, right? I've been very much in my galette era for the past few years, providing the most surface area for a crispy, golden crust, while also being a bit less fussy to throw together compared to a standard pie. The one thing I was missing was the joy of a precooked fruit filling, pulling out all those juices and thickening them with cornstarch into a jammy, sweet gel suspending chunks of tender fruit. I'm a big believer that we can and should have it all, so this recipe was born. We're rolling out our pie dough as if we're making a galette, but then adding a precooked apple filling (though peaches or cherries would be stunning here, too) on half of the dough so we can fold over the other half to seal it into our pie calzone. Is it an actual calzone? No! But you immediately get the concept, and "jumbo hand-pie" doesn't have the same ring to it, you know? Maybe just call it the best dessert you'll bake all summer.

Serves 8 to 10 | Prep Time: 30 minutes, plus chilling and cooling time | Cook Time: 55 minutes

Dough
- ½ cup ice-cold water
- ¼ cup vodka
- 3 cups (405g) all-purpose flour
- 1 tablespoon granulated sugar
- 1 teaspoon kosher salt
- 8 ounces (2 sticks) unsalted butter, cold and cubed

Filling
- 2 tablespoons unsalted butter
- 3 pounds (8 to 9 medium) Honeycrisp apples, peeled and cut into ½-inch pieces
- 1 cup (200g) granulated sugar
- 2 tablespoons freshly squeezed lemon juice
- 2 teaspoons ground cinnamon
- 1 teaspoon ground ginger
- 1 teaspoon freshly grated nutmeg
- 1 teaspoon kosher salt
- 3 tablespoons cornstarch
- 3 tablespoons water

Calzone
- All-purpose flour, for dusting
- 1 large egg, beaten
- 2 tablespoons granulated sugar

1. **Make the dough:** Combine the water and vodka in the same measuring cup. In a large bowl, stir together the flour, sugar, and salt to combine. Add the butter and, using your fingers, pinch it into the flour until you have pea-sized crumbles. Pour in the vodka mixture, then knead with your hands until a solid ball of dough forms. Press into a disk and wrap in plastic wrap. Chill for at least 1 hour.

(cont.)

2. Meanwhile, make the filling: In a large pot, melt the butter over medium-high heat. Add the apples, sugar, lemon juice, cinnamon, ginger, nutmeg, and salt. Cook until the apples are just tender, 8 to 10 minutes. In a small bowl, stir together the cornstarch and water to combine, then stir into the apples. Cook until thickened, 1 to 2 minutes. Transfer to a large heatproof bowl and let cool completely.

3. Assemble the calzone: Preheat the oven to 375°F. Line a sheet pan with parchment paper.

4. Dust a clean work surface with flour. Roll the dough into a 16-inch circle, dusting with more flour as needed. Brush off any excess flour, then transfer to the prepared pan, letting half of the dough overhang on one of the long sides of the pan. Spread the filling evenly on the half of the dough on the pan, leaving a 1-inch border clean. Fold the overhanging dough over the filling to enclose it, pressing the edges to seal. Tuck the outer edges of the calzone underneath itself for a clean half-circle, then use your fingers or a fork to crimp the crust as if you were baking a pie. Brush the calzone with the beaten egg and sprinkle with the granulated sugar, then use a paring knife to make 3 (2-inch) parallel slits at the top.

5. Bake for 45 to 50 minutes, until golden brown. Let cool completely, then slice and serve.

Make Ahead Dough (step 1) can be made up to 1 month in advance, stored in a sealable plastic bag in the freezer and thawed in the refrigerator overnight before assembling, or 1 day in advance, covered tightly in plastic wrap and stored in the refrigerator. Filling (step 2) can be made up to 1 day in advance, stored in an airtight container in the refrigerator. Calzone can be assembled and baked (steps 3, 4, and 5) any time the day it's being served.

Leftovers 3 days at room temperature.

RIDE OR PIE

MENU

Caramelized Onion, Date & Brie Hand Pies

Veg-Heavy Shepherd's Pie

Chicken & Biscuits Pot Pie

Banana Cream Pie with Biscoff Crust

GROCERY LIST

PANTRY

8 oz (32) Biscoff cookies
3 c (405g) all-purpose flour
3 c chicken stock
1 c (8 medium) Medjool dates, pitted

½ c (100g) plus 2 tablespoons granulated sugar
½ c (56g) plus 2 tablespoons cornstarch
½ c plus 1 tablespoon olive oil

¼ c (30g) confectioners' sugar
2 tbsp balsamic vinegar
1 tbsp Worcestershire sauce
1 tbsp baking powder

1 (15-oz) can cannellini beans, drained
1 (15-oz) can diced tomatoes, preferably fire-roasted
1 (6-oz) can tomato paste

SPICES, SEASONINGS, AND FLAVORINGS

1 tbsp vanilla bean paste or extract

1 tsp almond extract (or vanilla extract)

½ tsp ground cinnamon

KS&P (at least 2 c kosher salt and 1 jar whole black peppercorns to be safe)

MEAT

1½ lb (6 medium) boneless, skinless chicken thighs
1 lb lean ground lamb

PRODUCE

2½ lb (4 medium) russet potatoes
1 lb sliced cremini mushrooms
4 thyme sprigs
3 medium red bell peppers

3 medium carrots
3 celery stalks
3 medium yellow onions
2 medium sweet onions
2 bay leaves

2 ripe bananas
1 head garlic (9 cloves)
1 lemon
1 bunch green kale
1 bunch chives (¼ c minced)

1 small bunch sage
1 small bunch thyme
1 small bunch parsley
1 small bunch dill

REFRIGERATED

12 oz (3 sticks) unsalted butter

12 oz Brie cheese
2 c whole milk

2 c heavy cream
1 c buttermilk

4 tbsp (2 oz) unsalted butter
7 large eggs

FROZEN

4 sheets store-bought puff pastry (from two 17.3-oz packages)

PREP LIST

Up to 5 Days Ahead
- Make the filling for the Caramelized Onion, Date & Brie Hand Pies

Up to 2 Days Ahead
- Make the Banana Cream Pie (minus the whipped cream topping)

Up to 1 Day Ahead
- Assemble the Caramelized Onion, Date & Brie Hand Pies
- Prep and assemble Veg-Heavy Shepherd's Pie
- Make the crust for the Chicken & Biscuits Pot Pie
- Make the filling for the Chicken & Biscuits Pot Pie

Day Of
- Finish the Banana Cream Pie with the whipped cream topping

1 Hour Before Guests Arrive
- Bake the Caramelized Onion, Date & Brie Hand Pies
- Bake the Veg-Heavy Shepherd's Pie
- Assemble and bake the Chicken & Biscuits Pot Pie

Right Before Guests Arrive
- Keep your oven at 400°F to flash the pies as needed to reheat.

Game Time Pep Talk

Depending on the vibe, you can serve Caramelized Onion, Date & Brie Hand Pies as an appetizer or part of the full spread, either way flashing them in the oven until hot and crisp (about 5 minutes if recently baked or 10 minutes if fully cooled). Same deal for the Veg-Heavy Shepherd's Pie and the Chicken & Biscuits Pot Pie, since you should be either waiting for both to finish if baking fresh or, if prepared in advance, reheating them (about 15 minutes if recently baked or 25 to 30 minutes if fully cooled). The Banana Cream Pie should be finished and in the refrigerator ready to slice. You've got this!

Taffela :)

Caramelized Onion, Date & Brie Hand Pies

You know, I just never really understood a baked Brie. I'm not saying that topping a wheel of Brie cheese with some yummy accoutrement and wrapping it with puff pastry won't taste good. But how do you *actually* eat it? It's not like you cut everyone a wedge to eat with a fork and knife while they *ooh* and *ahh* and ask you what kind of jam you schmeared on top. I feel like I always see it served with toast or crackers on the side to scoop up the oozing cheese with shards of the once crispy, now soggy puff pastry. And after you've torn it apart, is there a world in which you can enjoy the leftovers? I'm sorry, it just doesn't feel like a fully formed thought, which is why I decided to solve this problem that very well may not exist. After careful consideration, I have found the solution is a hand pie! By sandwiching cubes of Brie with a sweet and savory combo of balsamic-glazed onions and dates between rectangles of puff pastry, you get the ideal portion of gooey cheese in a crispy, golden personal pocket. It can be easily picked up and enjoyed, without the need for any additional carbs. I made sure you'll end up with a dozen, because not only will you be going for seconds, but the leftover hand pies crisp up beautifully in the toaster oven. Imaginary problem solved!

Makes 12 hand pies | Prep Time: 30 minutes, plus cooling time | Cook Time: 40 minutes

Onion & Date Filling
- ¼ cup water
- 4 tablespoons (2 ounces) unsalted butter
- 2 tablespoons balsamic vinegar
- 2 medium sweet onions, thinly sliced
- 2 thyme sprigs
- KS&P
- 1 cup (8 medium) Medjool dates, pitted and finely chopped

Hand Pies
- All-purpose flour, for dusting
- 4 sheets store-bought puff pastry (from two 17.3-ounce packages), thawed
- 12 ounces Brie cheese, cubed
- 2 large egg whites, beaten (save the yolks for Veg-Heavy Shepherd's Pie, page 111)

1. Make the onion and date filling: In a large skillet, combine the water, butter, vinegar, onions, thyme, and 2 heavy pinches each of salt and pepper over medium-high heat. Cover and cook for about 10 minutes, shaking the pan occasionally, until the onions have softened. Uncover and reduce the heat to medium. Cook, stirring often, until caramelized, 15 to 20 minutes more. Transfer to a heatproof bowl and stir in the chopped dates, then let cool completely, discarding the thyme sprigs.

(cont.)

2. Prepare the hand pies: Preheat the oven to 400°F. Line 2 sheet pans with parchment paper.

3. Lightly dust a clean work surface with flour. Unfold 1 sheet of puff pastry with the creases running vertically. Using a knife, pastry cutter, or pizza wheel, cut along the creases to form 3 equal columns, then once crosswise along the center, forming 6 equal rectangles. Repeat with the remaining 3 sheets of puff pastry for a total of 24 rectangles.

4. Lay 6 rectangles of puff pastry out on each prepared sheet pan, spacing each rectangle 2 inches apart. Spread 2 tablespoons of the onion filling over the puff pastry, keeping the outer 1-inch border clear. Divide the cubes of Brie over the onion filling, then brush the outer border of each with the beaten egg white. Top each with 1 of the remaining 12 rectangles of puff pastry, crimping the edges with a fork to seal each hand pie. Brush liberally with the remaining beaten egg white. Using a paring knife, cut a 1-inch diagonal slit on the top of each hand pie.

5. Bake, rotating halfway through, for 15 to 20 minutes, until golden and crisp. Let cool slightly, then serve warm.

Make Ahead Filling (step 1) can be made up to 5 days in advance, stored in an airtight container in the refrigerator. Hand pies can be assembled (steps 3 and 4) up to 1 day in advance without egg wash, stored covered in the refrigerator. Hand pies can be baked (step 5) up to 1 hour before serving, reheating in the oven as needed.

Leftovers 5 days in the refrigerator.

veg-heavy shepherd's pie

If there's one thing about me, I'm going to take a hearty comfort classic and throw in a ton of veggies. It's partly because I try to be mindful of how much meat I'm eating, partly because I like to bulk things up so I can keep up with my appetite, and partly because if I round out a dish, then I don't feel like I need to make any sides (especially here, since any side would have to be a pie). I gave shepherd's pie the veg-heavy treatment and can confirm it checks all the aforementioned boxes, plus it yields fantastic leftovers. The base is equal parts ground lamb and mushrooms, cooked down in a rich tomato sauce with peppers and onions, though you can always pivot into a cottage pie moment by swapping in ground beef or go fully veg with double mushrooms or crumbled tofu. On top, garlicky potatoes are cooked and mashed in chicken stock so you get all the creaminess without any dairy. And it's just as easy to whip up both layers and throw it in the oven as it is to have the pie assembled the day before and ready to bake before your guests show up. Since you went heavy on the veg, you can go heavy on the portions.

Serves 8 to 10 | Prep Time: 30 minutes | Cook Time: 1 hour

Meat Sauce

- 2 tablespoons olive oil
- 1 pound sliced cremini mushrooms
- 3 medium red bell peppers, stemmed, cored, and finely chopped
- 3 garlic cloves, thinly sliced
- 2 medium yellow onions, finely chopped
- 2 bay leaves
- 2 thyme sprigs
- KS&P
- 1 pound lean ground lamb
- 1 (6-ounce) can tomato paste
- 1 (15-ounce) can diced tomatoes, preferably fire-roasted
- 1 tablespoon Worcestershire sauce

Mashed Potatoes

- ¼ cup olive oil
- 6 garlic cloves, minced
- 2½ pounds (4 medium) russet potatoes, peeled and cut into 1-inch pieces
- 2 cups chicken stock
- KS&P
- 2 large egg yolks (save the whites for Caramelized Onion, Date & Brie Hand Pies, page 109)
- ¼ cup minced fresh chives

(cont.)

1. Preheat the oven to 400°F.

2. Make the meat sauce: In a large pot or Dutch oven, heat the olive oil over medium-high heat. Add the mushrooms, peppers, garlic, onions, bay leaves, thyme, and 2 heavy pinches each of salt and pepper. Cook, stirring often, until all the liquid from the mushrooms and vegetables has completely evaporated and they begin to caramelize, 15 to 20 minutes.

3. Add the lamb with another 2 pinches each of salt and pepper. Cook, using a spoon to break up the lamb into small crumbles, until no longer pink, 3 to 4 minutes. Stir in the tomato paste, followed by the diced tomatoes and Worcestershire sauce. Reduce the heat to medium and cook, stirring often, until the liquid has reduced and the tomato has lightly caramelized, 6 to 8 minutes. Remove from the heat, then taste and adjust the seasoning with salt and pepper. Transfer to a 9 by 13-inch baking dish in an even layer, discarding the bay leaves and thyme stems. Set aside.

4. Make the mashed potatoes: In a medium pot, heat the olive oil and garlic over medium heat. Cook until the edges of the garlic begin to turn golden, then add the potatoes, chicken stock, and 2 heavy pinches each of salt and pepper. Bring to a simmer. Cover and cook until the potatoes are very tender, 12 to 15 minutes. Remove from the heat and mash with a potato masher until smooth and thickened. Taste and adjust the seasoning with salt and pepper. Stir in the egg yolks, followed by the chives until well incorporated. Spread the mashed potatoes over the meat sauce in an even layer. Drag a fork over the top to make a streaked design.

5. Bake for 25 to 30 minutes, until golden. Let cool slightly, then serve.

Make Ahead Shepherd's pie can be assembled and ready to bake (through step 4) up to 1 day in advance, covered and stored in the refrigerator. It can be baked (step 5) up to 1 hour before guests arrive, reheating in the oven as needed. If baking from pre-assembled and chilled, bake for 35 to 40 minutes.

Leftovers 5 days in the refrigerator.

chicken & biscuits pot pie

I find no greater order at any diner or deli than the random, yet magical, combo of matzo ball soup and chicken pot pie. It came to define my comfort-food ideal, distilling everything warm and cozy into one dynamic duo. Since I've been conditioned to enjoy the two together, in this recipe I opted for a chicken filling that gives major Jewish penicillin vibes. I'm talking juicy chunks of chicken, tender veggies, and tons of herbs, plus the surprise addition of white beans for body and kale for freshness. For the crust, I feel strongly that a double pie crust is too much work with too much potential for disaster, while a sheet of puff pastry isn't enough work, resulting in a lackluster, and often soggy, pot pie. My Goldilocks crust is a buttermilk biscuit dough, rolled into a thin layer to drape over our filling, creating flaky, golden layers on top, while underneath gently soaking up the filling for a dumpling-like texture. This pot pie is the ultimate marriage of classic comfort with a contemporary twist. Just don't forget to make it with love.

Serves 8 to 10 | Prep Time: 40 minutes, plus 1 hour chilling time | Cook Time: 1 hour

Biscuit Crust
- 2½ cups (338g) all-purpose flour, plus more for dusting
- 1 tablespoon baking powder
- 1 teaspoon kosher salt
- 1 teaspoon minced fresh sage
- 1 teaspoon minced fresh thyme leaves
- 8 ounces (2 sticks) unsalted butter, cold and cubed
- 1 cup buttermilk

Filling
- 3 tablespoons olive oil
- 3 medium carrots, diced
- 3 celery stalks, diced
- 3 garlic cloves, thinly sliced
- 1 medium yellow onion, diced
- KS&P
- 1½ pounds (6 medium) boneless, skinless chicken thighs, cut into ¾-inch pieces
- 1 (15-ounce) can cannellini beans, drained
- 3 cups chicken stock
- 1 tablespoon minced fresh sage
- 1 teaspoon minced fresh thyme leaves
- 1 bunch green kale, stemmed and roughly chopped
- 6 tablespoons cornstarch
- 6 tablespoons water
- ½ cup minced fresh parsley leaves and tender stems
- ½ cup minced fresh dill
- 2 teaspoons lemon zest

Baking
- 1 large egg yolk, lightly beaten

(cont.)

1. Make the biscuit crust: In a large bowl, whisk together the flour, baking powder, salt, sage, and thyme to combine. Add the butter and, using your fingers, pinch the butter into the flour mixture until pea-sized crumbles form. Using your hand, knead in the buttermilk until a shaggy dough forms. Transfer to a clean work surface. Using a bench scraper, cut the dough in half, then stack the two halves and press down with your hands to flatten into a disk. Repeat this cut-and-press process, dusting with flour as needed to prevent sticking, for a total of 8 times. Cover in plastic wrap and refrigerate the dough for 1 hour.

2. Meanwhile, prepare the filling: In a medium pot or Dutch oven, heat the olive oil over medium-high heat. Add the carrots, celery, garlic, onion, and 2 heavy pinches each of salt and pepper. Cook until softened and beginning to brown, 6 to 7 minutes. Stir in the chicken, beans, stock, sage, thyme, and another heavy pinch each of salt and pepper, then bring to a simmer. Cover and cook, reducing the heat to maintain a simmer and stirring occasionally, until the chicken is cooked through, about 10 minutes. Stir in the kale and cook until just wilted, 1 to 2 minutes.

3. In a small bowl, whisk together the cornstarch and water until smooth. Stir into the simmering chicken mixture and cook until thickened, about 2 minutes. Remove from the heat and stir in the parsley, dill, and lemon zest. Taste and adjust the seasoning with salt and pepper.

4. Transfer the filling to a 9 by 13-inch baking dish or 12-inch cast-iron skillet. Cover and set aside.

5. Bake the pot pie: Preheat the oven to 400°F.

6. On a lightly dusted work surface, roll out the crust, dusting with more flour as needed, to be just larger than the size of your baking dish or cast-iron skillet. Drape the dough over the dish and trim any overhang greater than ½ inch of dough. Using your fingers, crimp the dough to the edge of the baking dish. Brush the crust with the egg yolk. Cut a series of 4 slits in the crust either on the bias parallel to one another (for a 9 by 13-inch baking dish) or arranged like the hands of a clock (for a round 12-inch cast-iron skillet).

7. Bake until golden brown and bubbling, 40 to 45 minutes. Let cool slightly, then serve.

Make Ahead Biscuit crust (step 1) can be made up to 1 day in advance, stored in the refrigerator. Filling can be made up to 1 day in advance, stored in an airtight container in the refrigerator. Pie can be assembled (step 6) up to 1 hour in advance of baking and serving.

Leftovers 5 days in the refrigerator.

Banana Cream Pie with Biscoff Crust

Let's be real, who doesn't love a cream pie? A banana cream pie, especially. It was one of the first things I ever baked by myself. Well, baked is a little bit of a stretch. I used a store-bought graham cracker crust and filled it with instant vanilla pudding, bananas (that I sliced myself!), and a spray can of whipped cream. And yet, as a teenager just starting to explore the kitchen, it helped reinforce a growing feeling that this was the path I was meant to be on. Much has changed since then, though for the sake of page count, I'm going to focus on my BCP technique. We've graduated from both store-bought and graham crackers, opting to bake a crust of crushed Biscoff cookies with melted butter, adding rich notes of caramel and warm spices. Our filling layers slices of ripe banana with a homemade vanilla custard that comes together in minutes (practically instant!) and uses the fancy vanilla bean paste, because you're worth it. Once you let the pie set up in the fridge, it's topped with fresh whipped cream perfumed with almond extract, my secret for bringing out the nuttiness in the crust while pairing so stunningly with the top notes of banana and vanilla. Put all those components together and you've managed to turn an unassuming pie into a lick-the-plate-then-have-two-more-slices experience. And while I'll always be grateful for that first attempt and the journey it helped kick off, it's just as easy to extend some gratitude for this pie replacing that garbage one.

Serves 8 to 10 | Prep Time: 35 minutes, plus cooling time and overnight chilling | Cook Time: 25 minutes

Crust
8 ounces (32) Biscoff cookies
6 tablespoons unsalted butter, melted
2 tablespoons granulated sugar
½ teaspoon kosher salt

Custard Filling
½ cup (100g) granulated sugar
¼ cup (28g) cornstarch
1 teaspoon kosher salt
4 large egg yolks
2 cups whole milk
½ cup heavy cream
1 tablespoon vanilla bean paste (or vanilla extract)
2 tablespoons unsalted butter
2 ripe bananas, peeled and thinly sliced

Topping
1½ cups heavy cream
¼ cup (30g) confectioners' sugar
1 teaspoon almond extract (or vanilla extract)
½ teaspoon kosher salt
Ground cinnamon, for garnish

(cont.)

1. Make the crust: Preheat the oven to 350°F.

2. In a food processor, pulse the cookies into fine crumbs. Add the butter, sugar, and salt and pulse until well incorporated. Transfer to a pie dish and, using your hands or a measuring cup, press the crust evenly across the bottom of the pan and up the sides.

3. Bake for 20 minutes, or until lightly golden. Set aside to cool.

4. Meanwhile, make the custard filling: In a medium bowl, whisk together the sugar, cornstarch, salt, and egg yolks until thick and pale yellow in color, about 2 minutes. In a medium saucepan, combine the milk, cream, and vanilla and bring to a simmer over medium heat. Slowly whisk the simmering milk mixture into the egg yolk mixture, then return to the saucepan. Whisk over medium heat until thickened, about 1 minute, then remove from the heat and whisk in the butter. Transfer to a heatproof bowl.

5. To assemble the pie, layer 1 sliced banana over the crust, then spread half of the custard over it evenly. Repeat with the remaining sliced banana and custard. Place plastic wrap or parchment directly over the custard and let cool completely, then refrigerate overnight.

6. An hour before serving, make the topping: In a medium bowl, combine the heavy cream, confectioners' sugar, almond extract, and salt. Using a whisk or electric hand mixer, whip until soft peaks form. Remove and discard the plastic or parchment covering the custard and spread the whipped cream evenly over the pie. Garnish with a pinch of cinnamon, then hold in the refrigerator uncovered until ready to slice and serve.

Make Ahead Banana cream pie can be made up until topping (through step 5) up to 2 days in advance.

Leftovers 5 days in the refrigerator.

veg out

MENU

Sumac-Smashed Cucumber Salad
Harissa Carrot Salad
Kale & Pomegranate Salad
Lemony Turmeric Rice
Tofu Curry with Roasted Cauliflower, Sweet Potatoes & Chickpeas
Chocolate-Covered Halva-Stuffed Dates

GROCERY LIST

PANTRY

- 12 oz (2 c) dark chocolate chips
- 8 oz halva
- 3 c long-grain basmati rice
- 1⅓ c olive oil
- ½ c toasted sunflower seeds
- ¼ c date syrup (or packed brown sugar)
- 2 tbsp pomegranate molasses
- 1 tbsp coconut oil
- 24 Medjool dates
- 1 (28-oz) can diced tomatoes, preferably fire-roasted
- 1 (28-oz) can tomato puree
- 1 (15-oz) can coconut milk
- 1 (15-oz) can chickpeas

SPICES, SEASONINGS, AND FLAVORINGS

- 3 tbsp Madras curry powder
- 3 tbsp harissa paste
- 2 tsp ground cumin
- 2 tsp ground turmeric
- 2 tsp ground sumac
- Flaky sea salt
- KS&P (at least 2 c kosher salt and 1 jar whole black peppercorns to be safe)

PRODUCE

- 3 lb medium carrots
- 5 lemons
- 3 medium red onions
- 3 English cucumbers
- 3 bunches lacinato kale
- 1 orange
- 1 pomegranate (¾ c arils)
- 1 medium cauliflower (about 1½ lb)
- 1 medium sweet potato (about 12 oz)
- 1 jalapeño (optional)
- 1 bunch scallions
- 1 bunch cilantro
- 1 bunch mint
- 1 head garlic (6 cloves)

REFRIGERATED

- 1 (14-oz) block extra-firm tofu

PREP LIST

Up to 2 Days Ahead
- Roast the carrots for the Harissa Carrot Salad
- Make the dressing for the Kale & Pomegranate Salad
- Make the Tofu Curry (see note in recipe for all make-ahead options)
- Make the Chocolate-Covered Halva-Stuffed Dates

Up to 1 Day Ahead
- Make the dressing for the Sumac-Smashed Cucumber Salad
- Make the dressing for the Harissa Carrot Salad
- Prep the kale for the Kale & Pomegranate Salad

Day Of
- Prep the vegetables for the Sumac-Smashed Cucumber Salad

1 Hour Before Guests Arrive
- Assemble the Harissa Carrot Salad
- Assemble the Kale & Pomegranate Salad
- Reheat the Tofu Curry

Right Before Guests Arrive
- Cook the Lemony Turmeric Rice

Right Before Serving
- Assemble the Sumac-Smashed Cucumber Salad
- Finish the Lemony Turmeric Rice

Game Time Pep Talk
This one is easy. The Harissa Carrot Salad, Sumac-Smashed Cucumber Salad, and Kale & Pomegranate Salad should all be ready and already on the table. The Tofu Curry should be warm on the stovetop. All you should have to do is finish the Lemony Turmeric Rice before serving everything. The Chocolate-Covered Halva-Stuffed Dates should be all done and in the refrigerator, ready to pull out when it's time for dessert. You've got this!

Modi & Leo ♥

sumac-smashed cucumber salad

Think of this recipe as a Middle Eastern take on a Chinese smashed cucumber salad. It's become my go-to side dish whenever I want something crunchy and citrusy to pair with almost any menu, since we love versatility. The technique of smashing our cucumbers allows us to get so much more surface area to catch a simple lemon dressing, speckled with tart sumac and just a bit of date syrup for sweetness. It's a smashing success, every time!

Serves 6 to 8 | Prep Time: 20 minutes

Dressing
¼ cup olive oil
¼ cup freshly squeezed lemon juice
1 tablespoon date syrup (or brown sugar)
2 teaspoons ground sumac
1 garlic clove, finely grated
KS&P

Salad
1 medium red onion, thinly sliced
3 English cucumbers
¼ cup torn fresh mint leaves
KS&P

1. Make the dressing: In a small jar or sealable container, combine the olive oil, lemon juice, date syrup, sumac, garlic, and 2 heavy pinches each of salt and pepper. Seal the container and shake to combine.

2. Make the salad: In a large bowl, toss the red onion with the dressing to coat. Let sit for 10 minutes.

3. Meanwhile, use the side of your knife and the palm of your hand to smash down each cucumber (alternatively, use a mallet or the bottom of small saucepan to smash). Use your hands to roughly tear the cucumber or use your knife to cut rough chunks.

4. Transfer the smashed cucumber and mint to the bowl with the onion and toss well to combine. Taste and adjust the seasoning with salt and pepper, then serve.

Make Ahead Dressing can be made up to 1 day in advance. Cucumbers can be smashed a few hours before serving, stored in an airtight container in the refrigerator until dressing.

Leftovers 3 days in the refrigerator.

Harissa Carrot Salad

I mentioned in my first book, *Jew-ish*, that one of my mother's frequented side dishes was baby carrots steamed in the microwave. While you'll have to reference the Citrusy Cumin-Roasted Carrots recipe in that book to learn more about the tearful family fight they caused, today we're keeping things positive and focusing on the love for steamed carrots that she instilled in me. This sweet and spicy carrot salad is the self-actualized version of those sad baby carrots. We're roasting full-sized carrots to toss with a spicy dressing of orange juice, herbs, and harissa, a spicy North African red chile paste. Hopefully there will be no tears at your table, but I can confidently say if there are, it won't be because of this recipe.

Serves 6 to 8 | Prep Time: 20 minutes, plus cooling time | Cook Time: 40 minutes

Roasted Carrots
3 pounds medium carrots, tops removed
2 tablespoons olive oil
KS&P

Dressing
¼ cup freshly squeezed orange juice
¼ cup minced fresh cilantro
¼ cup minced fresh mint leaves
3 tablespoons harissa paste
2 tablespoons olive oil
1 tablespoon date syrup (or brown sugar)
KS&P

1. Roast the carrots: Preheat the oven to 400°F.
2. Place a sheet of foil on a sheet pan. Add the carrots, olive oil, and 2 heavy pinches each of salt and pepper, then toss to coat. Place another sheet of foil on top and pinch the edges to seal into a pouch.
3. Roast for 30 to 40 minutes, until tender. Remove from the oven and let cool completely in the pouch.
4. Meanwhile, make the dressing: In a large bowl, whisk together the orange juice, cilantro, mint, harissa, olive oil, date syrup, and 2 heavy pinches each of salt and pepper.
5. Transfer the cooled carrots to a cutting board and slice into ¼-inch coins. In a large bowl, toss the carrots with the harissa dressing to coat. Taste and adjust the seasoning with salt and pepper, then serve.

Make Ahead Carrots can be roasted (through step 3) up to 2 days in advance, stored in an airtight container in the refrigerator. Dressing (step 4) can be made up to 1 day in advance, stored in an airtight container in the refrigerator. Salad can be fully assembled up to 1 hour before serving.

Leftovers 5 days in the refrigerator.

kale & pomegranate salad

This salad is all about TEXTURE. We're thinly slicing kale (no massaging necessary!) to toss with a lemony dressing that gets a sweet and tart pop from pomegranate molasses, a dark, thick syrup of reduced pomegranate juice and my favorite Middle Eastern pantry staple. Finished with pomegranate arils and toasted sunflower seeds for crunch, this side salad has everything we could want from our greens, ready in twenty minutes flat.

Serves 6 to 8 | Prep Time: 20 minutes

Dressing
⅓ cup olive oil
¼ cup freshly squeezed lemon juice
2 tablespoons pomegranate molasses

1 garlic clove, finely grated
KS&P

Salad
3 bunches lacinato kale, stemmed and thinly sliced
¾ cup pomegranate arils

½ cup toasted sunflower seeds
KS&P

1. Make the dressing: In a small jar or sealable container, combine the olive oil, lemon juice, pomegranate molasses, garlic, and 2 heavy pinches each of salt and pepper. Seal the container and shake to combine. Refrigerate until ready to dress.

2. Assemble the salad: In a large bowl, toss the sliced kale, pomegranate seeds, and sunflower seeds with the dressing to coat. Taste and adjust the seasoning with salt and pepper, then serve.

Make Ahead Dressing (step 1) can be made up to 2 days in advance, stored in an airtight container in the refrigerator. Kale can be prepped up to 1 day in advance, stored in an airtight container in the refrigerator. Salad (step 2) can be fully assembled up to 1 hour before serving.

Leftovers 5 days in the refrigerator.

LEMONY TURMERIC RICE

We're making a simple yet perfect pot of rice, stained yellow with turmeric and brightened with the juice and zest of a lemon. It's nothing crazy, just a fluffy and flavorful side to soak up this menu's curry. And while I'm never opposed to serving plain rice, this slight adjustment to add some color and acidity couldn't be any simpler and makes you seem like you did a lot more than prepare a pilaf. As always, take the credit and compliments—you deserve them!

Serves 6 to 8 | Prep Time: 5 minutes | Cook Time: 25 minutes

3 tablespoons olive oil
2 teaspoons ground turmeric
3 cups long-grain basmati rice, rinsed

4½ cups water
2 teaspoons kosher salt
1 medium lemon

1. In a medium pot, heat the olive oil over medium heat. Add the turmeric, followed by the rice, and cook, stirring continuously, for 1 minute, or until fragrant. Stir in the water and salt, then bring to a simmer. Cover, reduce the heat to medium-low, and cook until the liquid is absorbed and the rice is cooked, about 15 minutes. Remove from the heat and let sit for 5 minutes.

2. Take off the lid, then zest and juice the lemon over the rice. Use a fork to fluff the rice, then serve.

Make Ahead Cook the rice through step 1 just before your guests arrive and keep warm. Complete step 2 right before serving.

Leftovers 3 days in the refrigerator.

Tofu Curry with Roasted Cauliflower, Sweet Potatoes & Chickpeas

Our story/recipe begins in the Fire Island Pines, one of the many communities on the thirty-two-mile barrier island off the southern coast of Long Island, New York. This predominantly gay enclave features no cars, one small grocery store that makes a mean chicken salad, and few dining options other than cooking at home or eating a tub of the aforementioned chicken salad. That means summer rentals in the Pines involve detailed planning with your housemates to break up cooking duty. And while most nights there are designated groups tackling dinner, I always cook our Friday night Shabbat meal solo since I'm both a control freak and want to get my shift out of the way before the partying begins. But one weekend, it seemed as if every single housemate had a different dietary restriction, be it kosher or gluten-free or lactose-intolerant or vegetarian. I threw together this tofu curry to make sure everyone would be fed and happy, and it ended up becoming one of my favorite entertaining recipes both on and off the island. We're taking one sheet pan to roast chickpeas, cauliflower, and sweet potatoes and one pot to braise tofu in a spiced tomato and coconut sauce. Stir the two together and we've got a plant-based curry ready to be spooned over rice and devoured. And while it's great fresh, I can say from experience it tastes even better in the early hours of the morning after a night of dancing.

Serves 6 to 8 | Prep Time: 30 minutes | Cook Time: 35 minutes

Tofu
1 (14-ounce) block extra-firm tofu, drained

Roasted Veg
1 (15-ounce) can chickpeas, drained and rinsed
1 medium cauliflower (about 1½ pounds), cut into 1-inch florets
1 medium sweet potato (about 12 ounces), cut into ¾-inch pieces
3 tablespoons olive oil
1 tablespoon Madras curry powder
1 teaspoon ground cumin
KS&P

Curry
2 tablespoons olive oil
2 medium red onions, diced
4 garlic cloves, thinly sliced
1 jalapeño, stemmed, seeded, and minced (optional)
KS&P
2 tablespoons Madras curry powder
1 teaspoon ground cumin
1 (28-ounce) can diced tomatoes, preferably fire-roasted
1 (28-ounce) can tomato puree
1 (15-ounce) can coconut milk
2 tablespoons date syrup (or brown sugar)
Sliced scallions, for garnish

(cont.)

1. Prep the tofu: Line a quarter sheet pan or plate with paper towels. Place the tofu on top, then place more paper towels and another quarter sheet pan or plate over the tofu. Place the cans of tomatoes on the top pan to weigh down and press excess liquid out of the tofu for at least 20 minutes. (This is the perfect step to do before you prep all the vegetables for this recipe.) Once pressed, cut the tofu into 1-inch pieces.

2. Make the roasted veg: Preheat the oven to 400°F. On a sheet pan, toss the chickpeas, cauliflower, and sweet potatoes with the olive oil, curry powder, cumin, and 2 heavy pinches each of salt and pepper to coat. Roast, tossing halfway through, for 25 to 30 minutes, until the vegetables are tender and lightly golden. Taste and adjust the seasoning with salt and pepper.

3. Meanwhile, make the curry: In a large pot or Dutch oven, heat the olive oil over medium-high heat. Add the onions, garlic, and jalapeño, if using, with 2 heavy pinches each of salt and pepper. Cook until softened and beginning to caramelize, 4 to 5 minutes. Stir in the curry powder and cumin and cook for 1 minute, or until fragrant. Stir in the diced tomatoes, tomato puree, coconut milk, and date syrup, followed by the tofu and 2 heavy pinches each of salt and pepper. Bring to a simmer, then cover and cook, reducing the heat to maintain a simmer, for 20 minutes. Taste and adjust the seasoning with salt and pepper.

4. Gently stir the roasted veg into the curry and simmer for 5 minutes to combine. Garnish with sliced scallions, then serve.

Make Ahead You have many options! Tofu can be pressed up to 2 days in advance and stored in an airtight container in the refrigerator. Roasted veg can be made up to 2 days in advance and stored in an airtight container in the refrigerator. Curry can be made to completion up to 2 days in advance and stored in an airtight container in the refrigerator.

Leftovers 5 days in the refrigerator.

chocolate-covered halva-stuffed dates

Describe your perfect date. Well, it's this recipe. We're stuffing Medjool dates, the fudgiest of all the dates, with halva, a Middle Eastern sesame candy, and covering the whole thing in dark chocolate. Once they set in the fridge, we have fun-sized candy bars for adults, which comes in handy since it's hard to stop at one. Feel free to go rogue with your filling, as I'm no stranger to swapping the halva here with peanut butter. Any way you stuff it, it's going to be a date to remember.

Makes 24 dates | Prep Time: 20 minutes, plus chilling time | Cook Time: 5 minutes

24 Medjool dates
8 ounces halva, crumbled
12 ounces (2 cups) dark chocolate chips
1 tablespoon coconut oil
Flaky sea salt, for garnish

1. Using a paring knife, make a small slit lengthwise in each date, then open to remove and discard the pit. Stuff each date with a heaping teaspoon of halva crumbles, then lightly pinch each closed. Place on a parchment-lined sheet pan.
2. Set a medium metal or heatproof glass bowl over a small pot of simmering water, making sure the bottom of the bowl doesn't touch the water. Put the chocolate chips and coconut oil in the bowl and heat, stirring occasionally, until completely melted and combined, then remove from the heat.
3. Using 2 forks and working one at a time, dip the stuffed dates in the chocolate, letting any excess drip off before transferring back to the parchment-lined sheet pan. Once all the dates are covered in chocolate, sprinkle a pinch of flaky salt on top of each.
4. Place the sheet pan in the refrigerator until the chocolate is set, about 30 minutes. Transfer the dates to an airtight container and refrigerate until ready to serve.

Make Ahead Chocolate-covered halva-stuffed dates can be made up to 2 days in advance, stored in an airtight container in the refrigerator.

Leftovers 1 week in the refrigerator.

When you want to eat like you're on **a romantic vacation** somewhere in the Greek isles.

mediterranean spa food

MENU

Socca with Artichoke & Arugula Salad

Roasted Tomato & Halloumi Salad

Spanakorizo (Greek Spinach and Feta Rice)

Steamed Whitefish with Caramelized Fennel & Green Olive Salad

Saffron Panna Cotta

GROCERY LIST

PANTRY

1¾ c olive oil
1½ c long-grain white rice
1¼ c white wine
1 c chickpea flour
1 c pitted Castelvetrano olives
3 tbsp balsamic vinegar
2 tbsp white wine vinegar
1 c honey
1 (15-oz) can artichokes hearts, drained
1 (¼-oz) package gelatin

SPICES, SEASONINGS, AND FLAVORINGS

2 tsp dried oregano
1 tsp rose water (optional)
¼ tsp saffron threads
Pinch of crushed red pepper
KS&P (at least 2 c kosher salt and 1 jar whole black peppercorns to be safe)

SEAFOOD

2 lb whitefish fillets, such as halibut, cod, or haddock

PRODUCE

2 lb (8 medium) plum tomatoes
2 lb (2 pints) cherry tomatoes
1 lb strawberries
3 c arugula
2 medium fennel bulbs
1 medium yellow onion
1 medium red onion
1 lemon
1 head garlic (5 cloves)
1 bunch parsley (1 c minced)
1 bunch dill (½ c minced)
1 small bunch rosemary (2 tsp minced)

REFRIGERATED

1 lb halloumi cheese
8 oz feta cheese
3 c plain Greek yogurt (any fat %)
½ c whole milk

FROZEN

1 (10-oz) bag frozen chopped spinach

PREP LIST

Up to 2 Days Ahead
- Make the Saffron Panna Cotta

Up to 1 Day Ahead
- Make the olive salad for the Steamed Whitefish

Day Of
- Make the batter for the Socca
- Roast the tomatoes for the Roasted Tomato & Halloumi Salad
- Prep the cherry tomato salad for the Roasted Tomato & Halloumi Salad
- Prep the ingredients for the Spanakorizo
- Prep the vegetables for the Steamed Whitefish

1 Hour Before Guests Arrive
- Prep the salad for the Socca
- Prep and dress the strawberries for the Saffron Panna Cotta

Right Before Guests Arrive
- Broil the halloumi for the Roasted Tomato & Halloumi Salad
- Cook the Spanakorizo
- Cook the vegetables for the Steamed Whitefish

Right Before Serving
- Cook the Socca and dress the salad for assembly
- Dress the cherry tomatoes and assemble the Roasted Tomato & Halloumi Salad
- Cook the fish for the Steamed Whitefish

Game Time Pep Talk
Everything but dessert cooks right before serving, but it's surprisingly easy since we've prepped well. The Roasted Tomato & Halloumi Salad should be assembled first. Then, cook the Socca and assemble with the salad. The Steamed Whitefish should be the recipe you're finishing with before serving, but the vegetables should be simmering in the white wine and the fish should already be seasoned, so you just need to steam it and finish with the Green Olive Salad. When it's time for dessert, the Saffron Panna Cotta just needs to be unmolded and topped with the macerated strawberries. You've got this!

Lou & Christian (and Lou's painting)

socca with artichoke & arugula salad

Socca is a thin chickpea flour pancake I first stumbled upon in the markets of Nice, though you'll find it all through Provence, as well as in Northern Italy by the name *farinata*. We're taking this simple snack and treating it like a salad pizza, topping the crispy socca base with a mix of arugula and artichoke hearts. We can throw this recipe together in a few minutes, but don't get it twisted, she reads like a fancy appetizer.

Serves 6 to 8 | Prep Time: 15 minutes | Cook Time: 10 minutes

Socca Batter
1 cup chickpea flour
1 cup water
2 tablespoons olive oil
2 teaspoons minced fresh rosemary
1 teaspoon lemon zest
1 teaspoon kosher salt
2 garlic cloves, finely grated

Cooking
¼ cup olive oil

Salad
3 cups arugula
1 (15-ounce) can artichokes hearts, drained
2 tablespoons olive oil
1 tablespoon freshly squeezed lemon juice
KS&P

1. Make the socca batter: In a medium bowl, whisk together the chickpea flour, water, olive oil, rosemary, lemon zest, salt, and garlic until smooth.

2. Cook the socca: Set an oven rack to the top position and turn on the broiler.

3. Place a 12-inch cast-iron pan over medium-high heat. Add the olive oil, swirling to coat the pan, then pour in the batter. Immediately transfer the pan to the top rack of the oven and broil until golden and crisp, 5 to 6 minutes. Transfer the socca to a platter.

4. Make the salad: In a medium bowl, toss the arugula and artichokes with the olive oil, lemon juice, and a heavy pinch each of salt and pepper to coat. Taste and adjust the seasoning with salt and pepper. Pile the salad over the socca, then slice and serve.

Make Ahead Batter (step 1) can be made a few hours in advance. Cook the socca right before serving—it's so much better fresh. Arugula and artichokes can be combined in a bowl, but do not dress and season until right before serving!

Leftovers Doesn't hold well!

Roasted Tomato & Halloumi Salad

I'm constantly in awe of my chef friends, and lucky enough to get to be inspired by them constantly. This salad was influenced by a dish I had at super-mensch Mike Solomonov's restaurant Zahav in Philadelphia. Mike brought over a plate of slow-roasted tomatoes with chunks of feta that just blew my mind, like a Middle Eastern caprese singing with concentrated tomato flavor. That very moment I pulled out the Notes app on my phone where I jot down ideas and wrote out the concept for this exact recipe, which I can safely say is my favorite salad in this entire book. We're roasting tomatoes with honey and oregano to layer with broiled halloumi before topping it all with a cherry tomato salad. You get the contrast of the tender, sweet roasted tomatoes with the bright burst of fresh ones, balanced with the salty richness of the crispy halloumi. It's no replacement for a meal at Zahav, but definitely easier than scoring a reservation.

Serves 6 to 8 | Prep Time: 20 minutes | Cook Time: 1 hour

Roasted Tomatoes and Halloumi
- ¼ cup olive oil
- 2 tablespoons honey
- 2 teaspoons dried oregano
- KS&P
- 2 pounds (8 medium) plum tomatoes, halved
- 1 pound halloumi cheese, sliced ¼ inch thick

Cherry Tomato Salad
- 2 pounds (2 pints) cherry tomatoes, halved
- ½ cup minced fresh parsley leaves and tender stems
- ¼ cup olive oil
- 3 tablespoons balsamic vinegar
- 1 garlic clove, finely grated
- KS&P

1. Roast the tomatoes and halloumi: Set an oven rack to the top position and preheat the oven to 400°F.
2. In a small bowl, stir together the olive oil, honey, oregano, and 2 heavy pinches each of salt and pepper. On a sheet pan, toss the tomatoes with half of the olive oil mixture, then arrange cut side up.
3. Roast for 45 to 55 minutes, until softened and lightly browned. Transfer to a platter.
4. Turn on the broiler. To the sheet pan, add the halloumi and toss with the remaining half of the olive oil mixture.
5. Broil on the top rack for 2 to 3 minutes on each side, until golden. Transfer to the platter with the roasted tomatoes.
6. Make the cherry tomato salad: In a medium bowl, toss the cherry tomatoes, parsley, olive oil, vinegar, garlic, and 2 heavy pinches each of salt and pepper to combine. Taste and adjust the seasoning with salt and pepper, then spoon over the roasted tomatoes and halloumi and serve.

Make Ahead Roasted tomatoes (steps 1, 2, and 3) can be made a few hours in advance and held at room temperature. Halloumi can be broiled (steps 4 and 5) right before your guests arrive. Cherry tomato salad (step 6) can be prepped a few hours in advance and held at room temperature with the tomatoes and parsley in one bowl and the olive oil, vinegar, and garlic in another, only dressing the salad shortly before serving.

Leftovers 3 days in the refrigerator.

spanakorizo (Greek spinach and Feta Rice)

We're going Greek for our side dish and making spanakorizo, a pilaf packed with chopped spinach and feta. It's the smallest switch from a simple pot of rice that makes a world of difference by adding some freshness from the greenery and brininess from the cheese. There's something magical about a warm pot of freshly fluffed rice, especially this variation, so try to cook this recipe as close to serving as possible to keep things hot and steamy. Luckily, it's a side that can be thrown together quickly as long as we remembered to thaw our frozen spinach!

Serves 6 to 8 | Prep Time: 15 minutes | Cook Time: 25 minutes

- 3 tablespoons olive oil
- 1 medium yellow onion, finely chopped
- 1½ cups long-grain white rice, rinsed
- 2¼ cups water
- 1½ teaspoons kosher salt
- 1 (10-ounce) bag frozen chopped spinach, thawed and squeezed
- 8 ounces feta cheese, crumbled
- ½ cup fresh minced dill

1. In a medium saucepan, heat the olive oil over medium-high heat. Add the onion and cook until softened, 2 to 3 minutes. Stir in the rice and cook for 1 minute, then stir in the water and salt, followed by the spinach. Bring to a simmer, then reduce the heat to medium-low. Cover and cook for 15 minutes. Remove from the heat and let sit for 5 minutes.

2. Add the feta and dill over the rice, then fluff the rice with a fork to incorporate and serve.

Make Ahead Rice can be cooked (through step 1) right before guests arrive and kept warm. Fluff rice with feta and dill (step 2) right before serving.

Leftovers 3 days in the refrigerator.

steamed whitefish with caramelized fennel & green olive salad

This is my take on a dish Katie Couric taught me in the Mediterranean spa–adjacent location of her Hamptons home. We were cooking a casual dinner, and she pulled out one of her summer specialties: simply grilled whitefish topped with a bright olive and red onion salad to spoon on top. The salad added the perfect briny acidity to the delicate fish, while only taking a few minutes to stir together. I knew I wanted to re-create it here to spoon over our stovetop version, where we first cook a base of fennel and onions to bathe in white wine, which steams our fish. It's a modest meal that satisfies and still packs a punch.

Serves 6 to 8 | Prep Time: 20 minutes | Cook Time: 20 minutes

Olive Salad
- 1 cup pitted Castelvetrano olives, finely chopped
- ½ cup minced fresh parsley leaves and tender stems
- ¼ cup olive oil
- 2 tablespoons white wine vinegar
- 1 tablespoon honey
- Pinch of crushed red pepper
- ½ medium red onion, finely chopped
- KS&P

Fish
- 3 tablespoons olive oil
- 2 medium fennel bulbs, halved and thinly sliced
- 2 garlic cloves, smashed and peeled
- ½ medium red onion, thinly sliced
- KS&P
- 1¼ cups white wine
- 2 pounds whitefish fillets, such as halibut, cod, or haddock, cut into 3-inch pieces, skins removed

1. Make the olive salad: In a medium bowl, stir together the olives, parsley, olive oil, vinegar, honey, crushed red pepper, red onion, and a heavy pinch each of salt and pepper. Set aside.

2. Cook the fish: In a wide, high-sided skillet or braiser, heat the olive oil over medium-high heat. Add the fennel, garlic, onion, and 2 heavy pinches each of salt and pepper. Cook, stirring occasionally, until softened and beginning to caramelize, 6 to 8 minutes. Stir in the white wine and let simmer for 2 minutes.

3. Meanwhile, season the fish with 2 heavy pinches each of salt and pepper. Add the fish in a single layer over the fennel. Reduce the heat to medium-low, then cover and cook until the fish is fully opaque, 8 to 10 minutes. Spoon the olive salad over the fish, then serve.

Make Ahead Olive salad (step 1) can be made up to 1 day in advance and stored in an airtight container in the refrigerator. Vegetables for the fish can be cooked (step 2) right before your guests arrive, only cooking the fish (step 3) before serving.

Leftovers 3 days in the refrigerator.

saffron panna cotta

We're making a fancy yogurt Jell-O! I wanted to end our spa meal with a lightened version of panna cotta, an Italian pudding made of cream set with gelatin. So instead of heavy cream, we're using yogurt flavored with saffron and rose water to thicken up and cover with honey-macerated strawberries. It's tart and sweet and creamy, so you'd never know this dessert was pretty much just a yogurt parfait. You can use any fat percentage of yogurt, and while full-fat is beyond decadent, I often make it with fat-free yogurt and it's just as satisfying. Just don't be afraid of the rose water! While it's optional, since we're only using a tiny splash, I find that it brings out the floral sweetness of the strawberries and pairs so perfectly with the golden swirls of saffron. The best part is you can just throw some granola on the leftovers and breakfast is served!

Serves 6 to 8 | Prep Time: 15 minutes, plus overnight chilling | Cook Time: 5 minutes

Panna Cotta
3 tablespoons water
½ teaspoon rose water (optional)
1 (¼-ounce) package gelatin
½ cup whole milk
½ cup honey
½ teaspoon kosher salt
¼ teaspoon saffron threads, finely ground with a mortar and pestle
3 cups plain Greek yogurt (any fat %)

Strawberries
1 pound strawberries, hulled and quartered
3 tablespoons honey
½ teaspoon rose water (optional)
Pinch of kosher salt

1. Make the panna cotta: Line a 7 by 11-inch (2-quart) baking pan or serving dish with plastic wrap. (Alternatively, you can skip this step and just scoop the panna cotta out of the dish instead of flipping it out for ease.)

2. In a small bowl, combine the water and rose water, if using. Sprinkle the gelatin on top and let sit for 5 minutes, or until all the liquid is absorbed.

3. In a medium saucepan, combine the milk, honey, salt, and saffron. Bring to a simmer over medium heat, whisking to dissolve the honey, then remove from the heat and whisk in the gelatin mixture until smooth. Whisk in the yogurt until smooth. Pour into the prepared pan and spread in an even layer. Cover with plastic wrap and refrigerate overnight.

4. About 1 hour before serving, prepare the strawberries: In a medium bowl, toss the strawberries with the honey, rose water, if using, and salt to coat.

5. Unwrap the top layer of plastic wrap. Place a large platter over the pan and invert them together quickly, with confidence. Remove the pan and plastic wrap lining to reveal the panna cotta. Spoon the strawberries on top, then serve.

Make Ahead Panna cotta (steps 1, 2, and 3) can be made up to 2 days in advance and held in the refrigerator, ready to invert. Strawberries (step 4) can be prepared up to 1 hour in advance of serving.

Leftovers 5 days in the refrigerator.

Mediterranean Spa Food

A monochromatic **green dinner** for whenever you're craving something light and bright.

GREEN MACHINE

MENU

Avocado-Cucumber Cups | Cabbage & Farro Salad with Roasted Broccoli & Tahini Dressing | Beans & Greens | Yogurt-Roasted Salmon with Leeks | Honey-Lime Fruit Salad

GROCERY LIST

PANTRY
1½ c dried farro
1 c white wine
¾ c olive oil
⅓ c tahini
¼ c wildflower honey
1 tbsp maple syrup
2 (15-oz) cans cannellini beans

SPICES, SEASONINGS, AND FLAVORINGS
½ tsp crushed red pepper
KS&P (at least 2 c kosher salt and 1 jar whole black peppercorns to be safe)

SEAFOOD
1 (3½-lb) whole side of salmon

PRODUCE
2 lb (2 bunches) broccoli
1½ lb (3 bunches) Swiss chard
2 c green grapes
5 lemons
4 kiwis
4 medium (about 2 lb) leeks
3 celery stalks
2 English cucumbers
2 medium avocados
2 jalapeños
1 medium Honeycrisp apple
1 small daikon radish
1 honeydew melon
1 lime
1 (3-in) piece ginger
1 bunch chives
1 bunch parsley
1 bunch dill
1 small bunch thyme (or substitute 1 tsp dried)
1 small bunch mint
1 head garlic (8 cloves)
½ medium head (1¼ lb) green cabbage

REFRIGERATED
¾ c plain low-fat Greek yogurt

PREP LIST

Up to 2 Days Ahead
- Roast the broccoli for the Cabbage & Farro Salad
- Cook the farro for the Cabbage & Farro Salad

Up to 1 Day Ahead
- Make the cucumber cups for the Avocado-Cucumber Cups
- Make the dressing for the Cabbage & Farro Salad
- Prep the cabbage and herbs for the Cabbage & Farro Salad
- Make the leek yogurt for the Yogurt-Roasted Salmon
- Make the dressing for the Honey-Lime Fruit Salad

Day Of
- Prep the fruit for the Honey-Lime Fruit Salad and assemble on a platter

1 Hour Before Guests Arrive
- Make the avocado mash for the Avocado-Cucumber Cups
- Cook the vegetables and beans for the Beans & Greens
- Toss the Cabbage & Farro Salad
- Assemble the salmon to roast for the Yogurt-Roasted Salmon
- Preheat the oven to 425°F

Right Before Guests Arrive
- Assemble the Avocado-Cucumber Cups
- Cook the greens to finish the Beans & Greens
- Roast the salmon for the Yogurt-Roasted Salmon
- Assemble the Honey-Lime Fruit Salad

Game Time Pep Talk
Have the Avocado-Cucumber Cups assembled and already on the table, or even wherever your guests will congregate as they come in to start noshing. Give the Cabbage & Farro Salad one final toss and place on the table. The Beans & Greens should be done and on very low heat to just stay warm. You should be waiting on the Yogurt-Roasted Salmon in the oven since it only takes 15 minutes, which when done is your sign to sit down and eat. The fruit salad should already be assembled and held in the refrigerator, then just dress it right before serving. You've got this!

Darling Isaac!

avocado-cucumber cups

This recipe began as my ode to the avocado lettuce cups from abcV in NYC, balancing creamy avocado into a fresh finger food to start the meal off on a cool and refreshing note. After playing with both butter lettuce and endive, I remembered a canape I'd prep when I worked at Daniel that used little cucumber cups to hold tuna tartare for an appetizer so memorable that I still think about it quite often. We mash avocado with fresh ginger and jalapeño for a little bite, before folding in diced radish and apple for some crunch and sweetness. The result is a crunchy, pop-able, and simple kickoff to this meal that holds up surprisingly well, which is an important quality so we can pre-assemble our cups before our guests arrive. Don't sleep on the leftover cucumber balls you scoop out. Throw them in a large pitcher of ice water with sliced lime for a little spa-water action to keep all your thirsty friends hydrated!

Serves 6 to 8 | Prep Time: 20 minutes

Cucumber Cups
2 English cucumbers, ends trimmed
KS&P

Avocado Mash
2 medium avocados, halved and scooped
2 teaspoons finely grated ginger
1 lemon, zested and juiced
1 jalapeño, stemmed, seeded, and minced

KS&P
1 small daikon radish, peeled and diced (about 1 cup)
1 medium Honeycrisp apple, peeled and diced
Minced fresh chives, for garnish

1. Prepare the cucumber cups: Cut the cucumber crosswise into 1-inch pieces. Using a teaspoon or the small side of a melon baller, scoop 1 teaspoon of the flesh to form a cup. Assemble on a sheet pan or platter and cover with damp paper towels. Cover and chill until ready to serve.

2. About 30 minutes before your guests arrive, prepare the avocado mash: In a medium bowl, mash the avocados with the ginger, lemon zest and juice, minced jalapeño, and 2 heavy pinches each of salt and pepper until relatively smooth. Stir in the radish and apple to combine. Taste and adjust the seasoning with salt and pepper.

3. When ready to serve, season the cucumber cups with a heavy pinch each of salt and pepper. Spoon the avocado mash into the cups. Garnish with minced chives, then serve.

Make Ahead Cucumber cups can be made up to 1 day in advance, covered with damp paper towels and sealed tightly with plastic wrap in the refrigerator. Avocado mash can be made up to 1 hour before serving.

Leftovers Try to finish, as it doesn't hold well!

Cabbage & Farro Salad with Roasted Broccoli & Tahini Dressing

Rarely do you meet a salad that stays good in the fridge for DAYS and can be as satisfying as a supportive side while still holding potential to be the main event. This is that salad. The two non-negotiables are cabbage for crunch and farro for chew, while the rest can change with the seasons and your mood. That could be sauteed peas and asparagus in the spring, cherry tomatoes in the summer, and roasted butternut squash in the fall with an array of dressings spanning pesto to Caesar. But more often than not, I gravitate toward this version using roasted broccoli and a quick, rich tahini dressing to bring it all together. What makes it so magical is that everything can be prepped days in advance, from the cabbage and the farro to the dressing and the roasted broccoli. We just need to toss the salad and serve, making this dish a dream whenever life gets in the way of dinner.

Serves 6 to 8 | Prep Time: 20 minutes, plus cooling time | Cook Time: 45 minutes

Roasted Broccoli
- 2 pounds (2 bunches) broccoli, cut into small florets, stems peeled and thinly sliced
- 2 tablespoons olive oil
- 2 tablespoons water
- KS&P

Farro
- KS
- 1½ cups dried farro

Tahini Dressing
- ½ cup freshly squeezed lemon juice
- ⅓ cup tahini
- ¼ cup olive oil
- 1 tablespoon maple syrup
- 2 garlic cloves, finely grated
- KS&P

Cabbage Salad
- ½ medium head (1¼ pounds) green cabbage, cored and shredded
- ¼ cup minced fresh parsley leaves and tender stems
- ¼ cup minced fresh dill
- KS&P

1. Roast the broccoli: Preheat the oven to 450°F.
2. On a sheet pan, combine the broccoli, olive oil, water, and 2 heavy pinches each of salt and pepper. Toss to combine. Roast for 20 minutes, or until tender and golden. Let cool completely on the pan.
3. Cook the farro: Bring a medium saucepan of salted water to a boil. Add the farro and simmer until tender, about 25 minutes. Drain and rinse with cold water to cool the farro, then set aside.

4. Make the tahini dressing: In a medium bowl, whisk the lemon juice, tahini, olive oil, maple syrup, garlic, and 2 heavy pinches each of salt and pepper until smooth.

5. Assemble the salad: In a large bowl, toss the cabbage, parsley, and dill with the roasted broccoli, farro, and dressing until well coated. Taste and adjust the seasoning with salt and pepper, then serve.

Make Ahead Broccoli can be roasted up to 2 days in advance. Farro can be cooked up to 2 days in advance. Dressing can be made up to 1 day in advance. Cabbage and herbs can be prepped up to 1 day in advance. Store all separately in airtight containers in the refrigerator. Salad can be fully made and dressed up to 1 hour before serving.

Leftovers 3 days in the refrigerator.

Beans & Greens

I'm always going to be that person who orders a side of sauteed spinach at a restaurant but never the one looking to cook down 2 pounds of it to yield a half cup to share with my guests. This is the substantial side we're going to make to get our greens, a little protein, and a whole lot of flavor. I wanted this menu to be a flex for any mixed table combining vegetarians, pescatarians, and/or omnivores, offering enough options for anyone to leave satiated, even if they're skipping the salmon. A base of celery, garlic, lemon, and white wine stews with canned white beans and Swiss chard stems before wilting down the leaves to complete this beans and greens fantasy.

Serves 6 to 8 | Prep Time: 15 minutes | Cook Time: 15 minutes

- 3 tablespoons olive oil
- 1½ pounds (3 bunches) Swiss chard, stalks thinly sliced and leaves torn
- 2 teaspoons fresh thyme leaves (or 1 teaspoon dried)
- ½ teaspoon crushed red pepper
- 3 celery stalks, finely chopped
- 3 garlic cloves, thinly sliced
- 1 lemon, zested with a peeler, zest julienned
- KS&P
- 1 cup white wine
- 2 (15-ounce) cans cannellini beans, drained

1. In a medium pot or Dutch oven, heat the olive oil over medium-high heat. Add the Swiss chard stems, thyme, crushed red pepper, celery, garlic, lemon zest, and 2 heavy pinches each of salt and pepper. Cook, stirring often, until the vegetables are soft, about 5 minutes. Stir in the wine and beans and cook until reduced slightly, about 5 minutes more.

2. Add the torn leaves with a heavy pinch each of salt and pepper, then cover and cook until wilted, 3 to 4 minutes. Stir to combine, then taste and adjust the seasoning with salt and pepper. Serve immediately.

Make Ahead Cooked vegetables and beans (step 1) can be done right before your guests arrive. Remove the pot from the heat and then return to a simmer before completing step 2 right before you serve.

Leftovers 3 days in the refrigerator.

Yogurt-Roasted Salmon with Leeks

My intention with this dish was to create a flavor-packed sauce that you can just spread on salmon before popping it in the oven for a main that will stun without a headache or a kitchen that reeks of fish. This yogurt sauce laced with a mixture of caramelized leeks, garlic, and jalapeño balances tang, sweetness, and heat in a foolproof cooking method for tender, juicy salmon. Feel free to switch up the leeks with onions or scallions, triple the garlic, or keep in the jalapeño seeds for some extra heat. There's no blank canvas like a whole side of salmon!

Serves 8 | Prep Time: 10 minutes, plus cooling time | Cook Time: 25 minutes

Leek Yogurt
- 3 tablespoons olive oil
- 4 medium (about 2 pounds) leeks, light and green parts only, halved, rinsed, and thinly sliced
- 3 garlic cloves, thinly sliced
- 1 jalapeño, stemmed, seeded, and minced
- KS&P
- ¾ cup plain low-fat Greek yogurt

Roasted Salmon
- 1 (3½-pound) whole side of salmon
- KS&P
- Fresh dill, for garnish

1. Make the leek yogurt: In a large skillet, heat the olive oil over medium-high heat. Add the leeks, garlic, jalapeño, and a heavy pinch each of salt and pepper. Cook, stirring often, until softened and beginning to caramelize, 5 to 7 minutes. Transfer to a medium heatproof bowl and let cool slightly, then stir in the yogurt. Taste and adjust the seasoning with salt and pepper. If not using immediately, transfer to an airtight container and refrigerate for up to 5 days.

2. Roast the salmon: Preheat the oven to 425°F. Line a sheet pan with parchment paper.

3. Place the salmon skin-side down on the prepared pan on the diagonal to fit. Season with 2 heavy pinches each of salt and pepper. Spread the leek yogurt over the salmon in an even layer.

4. Roast for 15 to 20 minutes, until the salmon is golden at spots and reaches an internal temperature of 145°F. (If desired, broil the salmon for 2 to 3 minutes to get more color.)

5. Transfer the salmon to a platter and garnish with dill, then serve.

Make Ahead Leek yogurt (step 1) can be made up to 1 day in advance. Salmon can be prepped to roast (through step 3) up to an hour before cooking and serving.

Leftovers 3 days in the refrigerator.

Honey-Lime Fruit Salad

Fruit salad, yummy, yummy! At my family gatherings, there's always someone designated to bring a fruit salad as an option for those trying to avoid the more decadent desserts (though everyone will usually also have a sliver . . . or three . . . of that, too). I wanted to make a fruit salad that satisfies everyone who wants to end the meal with a sweet note while not overindulging. The result was a simple dressing of honey, lime, and ginger that brings the perfect zing to our trio of green fruits and stays on brand to this monochromatic menu. If you want to taste the rainbow, this dressing pairs beautifully with whatever fruit might be in season, especially peaches and cherries in the summer and apples and pears in the fall. Just make sure we're dressing the fruit shortly before serving; we want the dressing to pull out all those delicious fruit juices, but we're making salad not soup.

Serves 6 to 8 | Prep Time: 20 minutes

Fruit
1 honeydew melon, halved, seeded, peeled, and cut into 1-inch chunks

4 kiwis, peeled and sliced

2 cups green grapes, halved

Dressing
¼ cup wildflower honey

1 teaspoon finely grated ginger

¼ teaspoon kosher salt

1 lime, zested and juiced

¼ cup fresh mint leaves, roughly torn

1. Assemble the fruit: On a platter, arrange the honeydew, kiwi, and grapes. Cover with damp paper towels and refrigerate until ready to serve.

2. Make the dressing: In a small bowl, whisk together the honey, ginger, salt, and lime zest and juice until smooth.

3. When ready to serve, drizzle the dressing over the fruit, then garnish with the mint and serve.

Make Ahead Fruit can be assembled (through step 1) any time the day of serving, covered with plastic wrap if assembling more than 1 hour before serving. Dressing can be made up to 1 day in advance, stored in an airtight container in the refrigerator.

Leftovers 3 days in the refrigerator.

Everything you need to fill **fluffy pitas** with falafel and all the fixings.

pita party

MENU

Brown Butter Tehina
Spicy Cauliflower & Celery Pickles

Charred Cabbage Salad
Amba-ish Mango Relish
Za'atar Roasted Eggplant & Tomato Salad

Hot Honey Labneh
Pitas
Falafel

Lemon-Almond Blondies with Sumac Glaze (Platinum Blondies)

GROCERY LIST

PANTRY

2 lb dried chickpeas
1 lb confectioners' sugar
4¾ c (642g) bread flour
2 c (270g) all-purpose flour

1½ c (300g) granulated sugar
1½ c olive oil
1 c (214g) packed light brown sugar

1 c (140g) whole wheat flour
1 c tahini
¾ c distilled white vinegar
½ c (56g) finely ground almond flour

¼ c honey
2 tbsp baking powder
1 (¼-oz) package active dry yeast
Vegetable oil, for frying

SPICES, SEASONINGS, AND FLAVORINGS

2 tbsp ground sumac
2 tbsp ground coriander
1 tbsp za'atar

1 tbsp ground cumin
1 tbsp almond extract
1 tsp ground ginger

½ tsp ground turmeric
½ tsp cayenne pepper
Flaky sea salt

KS&P (at least 2 c kosher salt and 1 jar whole black peppercorns to be safe)

PRODUCE

½ large head (2 lb) green cabbage
2 lb (2 medium) eggplant
1 lb (1 small head) cauliflower
2 pints cherry tomatoes

9 lemons
2 large slightly underripe mangoes
3 serrano chiles
1 medium red onion

1 head garlic (5 cloves)
1 bunch celery (6 stalks and ½ c leaves)
2 bunches fresh cilantro (½ c minced)

2 bunches fresh parsley (½ c minced)
1 bunch dill (¼ c minced)
1 bunch (6 stalks) scallions

REFRIGERATED

1 pound labneh

10 oz (2½ sticks) unsalted butter

2 large eggs

PREP LIST

Up to 1 Week Ahead
- Make the Spicy Cauliflower & Celery Pickles

Up to 2 Days Ahead
- Make the Lemon-Almond Blondies

Up to 1 Day Ahead
- Prep the vegetables for the Charred Cabbage Salad
- Make the dressing for the Charred Cabbage Salad
- Make the Amba-ish Mango Relish
- Roast the eggplant for the Za'atar Roasted Eggplant & Tomato Salad
- Make the Pitas

Day Of
- Make the mixture and shape the balls for the Falafel

1 Hour Before Guests Arrive
- Toss the Charred Cabbage Salad
- Assemble the Za'atar Roasted Eggplant & Tomato Salad
- Fry the Falafel
- Preheat the oven to 400°F

Right Before Guests Arrive
- Assemble the Hot Honey Labneh
- Make the Brown Butter Tehina
- Reheat the Pitas (covered with foil on a sheet pan for about 5 minutes)
- Reheat the Falafel, if needed (5 to 10 minutes)

Game Time Pep Talk
The Spicy Cauliflower & Celery Pickles, Charred Cabbage Salad, Za'atar Roasted Eggplant & Tomato Salad, Hot Honey Labneh, and Brown Butter Tehina (make this as close to serving as possible) should all be ready, plated, and on the table. Really the only thing you should be doing is waiting on the pitas and falafel to reheat before plating and digging in. The blondies should be ready to slice and serve when it's time for dessert. You've got this!

Ben, Zikki & Tami

Brown Butter Tehina

Good tahini is liquid gold, so it doesn't take a lot to dress up this rich sesame paste. Whisk it up with a little water, lemon juice, garlic, and salt and you're ready to party. But what if we didn't stop there? I started throwing in little bit of brown butter to fortify this sauce with even more nuttiness and have never looked back. The only catch is it's one of the few recipes in this book that shouldn't be made in advance. Luckily, we can easily whip it up in minutes before dunking and drizzling!

Makes about 2 cups | Prep Time: 10 minutes | Cook Time: 5 minutes

1 cup tahini
¼ cup freshly squeezed lemon juice
1 garlic clove, finely grated
KS
4 tablespoons (2 ounces) unsalted butter
¾ to 1 cup warm water

1. In a medium heatproof bowl, whisk together the tahini, lemon juice, garlic, and a heavy pinch of salt to combine.

2. In a small saucepan, melt the butter over medium-high heat. Cook, stirring continuously, until browned and nutty in aroma, 3 to 4 minutes. Whisk into the tahini mixture. Slowly whisk in the water until a smooth, creamy sauce forms. (It will split and look as if you've done something wrong before it emulsifies.) Taste and adjust the seasoning with salt. Keep at room temperature until ready to serve. This is best prepared shortly before serving.

Make Ahead Don't do it! Texture is best fresh!

Leftovers 5 days in the refrigerator.

spicy cauliflower & celery pickles

I have always been and always will be a pickle princess. We needed something in this menu to add a little briny crunch, so let it be this jar of spicy, turmeric-stained cauliflower and celery pickles. It's as easy as pouring a spiced vinegar brine over our veg and popping it in the fridge overnight. I opted for cauliflower and celery because they stay beautifully crisp-tender after pickling, but this recipe would work just as well with any combo of radishes, carrots, and/or cucumbers. There's a little bite from the serrano, though you can always seed or omit the chile for a milder experience. Be prepared for leftover pickles, which should always be seen as a blessing. They'll last in your fridge for a month, ready to be pulled out for cheese boards, grain bowls, and those random afternoon pickle cravings.

Makes 1 quart pickles | Prep Time: 15 minutes, plus cooling time and overnight chilling | Cook Time: 5 minutes

1 pound (1 small head) cauliflower, cored and cut into small florets (3 cups florets)
2 celery stalks, cut on the bias into ¼-inch pieces
1 serrano chile, thinly sliced
1 garlic clove, smashed
1 teaspoon ground coriander

1 teaspoon ground ginger
½ teaspoon ground turmeric
¾ cup distilled white vinegar
¾ cup water
¼ cup (50g) granulated sugar
2 tablespoons kosher salt

1. Put the cauliflower, celery, serrano, and garlic in a clean glass quart jar, then add the coriander, ginger, and turmeric.

2. In a small saucepan, combine the vinegar, water, sugar, and salt. Bring to a simmer over medium-high heat, then cook until the sugar and salt have dissolved, about 1 minute. Carefully pour into the jar. Seal and let cool completely, then refrigerate overnight before serving.

Make Ahead Pickles can be made up to 1 week in advance, stored in the refrigerator.

Leftovers 1 month in the refrigerator.

Charred Cabbage Salad

This little cabbage salad you'll find at every pita shop can best be described as the best supporting actress to falafel's starring role, offering a cold, refreshing crunch in every bite. Naturally, I'm her biggest fan and determined she gets the respect she deserves. To accomplish this, we're going to first char cabbage wedges until caramelized before slicing and dressing with olive oil, lemon, and dill. Throw in some sliced celery for extra crispness and we've got a simple side that's giving main-character energy.

Serves 8 to 10 | Prep Time: 20 minutes, plus cooling time | Cook Time: 10 minutes

Salad
- ¼ cup olive oil
- ½ large head (2 pounds) green cabbage, stem intact and cut into 4 large wedges
- 4 celery stalks, thinly sliced on a bias
- ½ cup chopped celery leaves
- ¼ cup minced fresh dill

Dressing
- 3 tablespoons olive oil
- 3 tablespoons freshly squeezed lemon juice
- 1 tablespoon granulated sugar
- 1 garlic clove, finely grated
- KS&P

1. Make the salad: Turn on the vent and open a window. In a cast-iron pan, heat 2 tablespoons of the olive oil over high heat. Add 2 wedges of the cabbage and cook, flipping once, until charred, about 2 minutes per side. Transfer to a sheet pan to cool. Repeat with the remaining olive oil and cabbage wedges. Once the cabbage wedges have cooled, transfer to a cutting board to core and thinly slice each.

2. Transfer the sliced cabbage to a large bowl and add the celery, celery leaves, and dill.

3. Make the dressing: In a small bowl, whisk together the olive oil, lemon juice, sugar, garlic, and 2 heavy pinches each of salt and pepper to combine.

4. About 1 hour before serving, toss the salad with the dressing until well coated. Taste and adjust the seasoning with salt and pepper. Cover and refrigerate until ready to serve.

Make Ahead Salad (steps 1 and 2) can be prepared up to 1 day in advance, stored in an airtight container in the refrigerator. Dressing (step 3) can be made up to 1 day in advance, stored in an airtight container in the refrigerator. Salad can and should be fully made 1 hour before serving.

Leftovers 5 days in the refrigerator.

Amba-ish Mango Relish

If you're unfamiliar with amba, which is maybe the best condiment in the world, let's start at the beginning, because I love to geek out on foodways. The Jews of Iraq predominantly managed the Middle East's spice trade with India in the eighteenth and nineteenth centuries, with a large community eventually settling there, and all the while absorbing techniques and ingredients from Indian cuisine into their own culinary lexicon. A perfect example is amba, an Iraqi-Jewish mango sauce that spawns from Indian mango pickles. You take green mangoes, pickle them with salt, cook them down with spices, and puree them into a lip-smacking, spicy, tangy sauce that should be drizzled on everything. It was the condiment of choice for the Sabbath breakfast of hard-boiled eggs, fried eggplant, and chopped salad, typically eaten with flatbread. When Iraqi Jews made their way to Israel, it all got stuffed into a pita with tahini and zhug, and sabich was born! While I always have a jar in my fridge, it's a specialty item you'll have to go to a Middle Eastern market for or order online or even make if you have the time. This recipe is the solution for when you can't find a jar but quickly need a flavor bomb on the table. We take slightly underripe mangoes and chop them up into a relish that still packs in heat and acidity, with the welcome addition of some texture. It's far from the original, all while honoring my favorite Jewish tradition of continuing to adapt our recipes as we move throughout the Diaspora.

Makes about 1 quart | Prep Time: 15 minutes

2 large slightly underripe mangoes, peeled, seeded, and finely chopped
½ cup minced fresh cilantro leaves and tender stems
3 tablespoons freshly squeezed lemon juice
2 tablespoons olive oil
2 teaspoons ground sumac
1 serrano chile, stemmed, seeded, and minced
½ medium red onion, finely chopped
KS

In a medium bowl, toss the mango with the cilantro, lemon juice, olive oil, sumac, serrano, red onion, and 2 heavy pinches of salt to combine. Taste and adjust the seasoning with salt, then transfer to an airtight container. Refrigerate for at least 2 hours before serving.

Make Ahead Relish can be made up to 1 day in advance.

Leftovers 5 days in the refrigerator.

Za'atar Roasted Eggplant & Tomato Salad

Since I hyped up sabich in the Amba-ish Mango Relish (page 176), I should add that it's not uncommon to find pita shops that sneak in a couple of falafel balls as a little bonus. I wanted to do the opposite and give eggplant a cameo into our falafel-stuffed pitas. We're going to make that happen by roasting chunks of eggplant with earthy za'atar before tossing with cherry tomatoes, red onion, olive oil, and lemon into a juicy, summery salad. It's definitely going to steal some love from the falafel, but luckily there's room for everyone . . . in our pitas, at least.

Serves 8 to 10 | Prep Time: 20 minutes, plus cooling time | Cook Time: 30 minutes

Roasted Eggplant
- 2 pounds (2 medium) eggplant, stemmed and cut into 1-inch pieces
- 2 tablespoons olive oil
- 1 tablespoon za'atar
- KS&P

Salad
- ½ medium red onion, thinly sliced
- 3 tablespoons freshly squeezed lemon juice
- 3 tablespoons olive oil
- 1 tablespoon honey
- 2 garlic cloves, finely grated
- KS&P
- 2 pints cherry tomatoes, halved
- ½ cup minced fresh parsley leaves and tender stems

1. Roast the eggplant: Preheat the oven to 450°F.
2. On a sheet pan, toss the eggplant with the olive oil, za'atar, and 2 heavy pinches each of salt and pepper to coat. Roast for 30 minutes, or until tender and golden. Let cool on the pan.
3. Transfer the cooled eggplant to a large bowl, then toss with the red onion, lemon juice, olive oil, honey, garlic, and 2 heavy pinches each of salt and pepper to combine. Right before serving, add the tomatoes and parsley and toss to combine. Taste and adjust the seasoning with salt and pepper, then serve.

Make Ahead Eggplant can be roasted (steps 1 and 2) up to 1 day in advance, stored in an airtight container in the refrigerator.

Leftovers 5 days in the refrigerator.

Hot Honey Labneh

This is more of a serving suggestion than a recipe, but it still deserves the full-page treatment. It's becoming more and more common to find labneh, a super thick and creamy strained yogurt perfect for swooping and scooping with warm pitas, in the grocery store (and you'll definitely find it at any Middle Eastern market). Here, we're just lightly zhuzhing it up with olive oil, honey, minced chile, and flaky salt to round out the tang of the labneh with a sweet and spicy kick. It takes all of five minutes to make, and maybe even less time to finish.

Serves 8 to 10 | Prep Time: 5 minutes

1 pound labneh
1 serrano chile, minced
3 tablespoons honey

3 tablespoons olive oil
Flaky sea salt, for garnish

In a wide serving bowl, spread the labneh in an even layer across the bottom and up the sides. Top with the minced chile, followed by the honey and olive oil. Garnish with a heavy pinch of flaky salt, then serve.

Make Ahead Don't do it! It's too easy and best assembled fresh!

Leftovers 5 days in the refrigerator.

I've been beyond blessed with personal pita lessons from my culinary bestie Ben Gingi, who makes the fluffiest pockets out there. He's shared all his tips with me, and I shall pass them on to you! To start, and I can't stress this enough, USE A SCALE. It's so crucial to make sure we measure our flours correctly and get a consistent dough, while making it easy to double the recipe so we can freeze the second dozen for a rainy day. Once our dough has doubled in size, that scale also makes it easy to evenly divide into balls we will roll out into our pitas. Ben's first tip was to proof the rolled-out pita dough between two kitchen towels, which both prevents the dough from drying out and makes it easier to transfer when time to cook. Now here comes the craziest part: We're not going to need a pizza stone or even an oven to make it. Ben's preferred method is having two skillets side-by-side on medium heat to cook the pitas, flipping often, until they puff up after a few minutes (be patient!). Then just slice and stuff and let the pita party begin! I will say if you can get your hands on good-quality, fluffy pitas, I give you permission to skip this recipe in an emergency. Just be ready to show a doctor's note to your guests.

Makes 12 pitas | Prep Time: 30 minutes, plus 1½-hour proofing time | Cook Time: 25 minutes

2 cups (453g) water, heated to 115°F
1 tablespoon (13g) granulated sugar
1 (¼-ounce) package active dry yeast
¼ cup (53g) olive oil, plus more for greasing

4¾ cups (642g) bread flour
1 cup (140g) whole wheat flour
2 teaspoons (7g) kosher salt

1. In the bowl of a stand mixer fitted with the whisk attachment, mix the warm water and sugar to dissolve, then sprinkle the yeast over the top. Let stand until foamy, 5 to 10 minutes.

2. Switch to the dough hook. Add the olive oil followed by the flours and salt and, beginning on low speed and gradually increasing to medium, knead until a smooth, elastic dough forms, 3 to 4 minutes.

3. Grease a medium bowl with about 1 tablespoon olive oil and add the dough from the mixer, turning gently to coat. Cover with plastic wrap or a kitchen towel and set aside in a warm place until doubled in size, 1 to 1½ hours.

4. Transfer the dough to a clean work surface. Using a bench scraper, divide the dough into 12 equal pieces (about 105g each). Cup your hand and fingers around each piece of dough and roll on the work surface into a tight ball. Cover the balls with a kitchen towel and let rise for 15 minutes.

5. Roll out each ball of dough into a 6-inch circle. Place each pita on a kitchen towel, spacing them 1 inch apart, then cover with another towel and let rise for 15 minutes.

6. Meanwhile, heat 1 or 2 medium skillets over medium heat for 5 minutes (use 2 skillets if you'd like to cook all the pitas twice as fast). Transfer one pita to the hot pan. Using a spatula, flip the pita every

10 seconds until it puffs up (keep the faith, it takes time to puff) and is golden on both sides, 3 to 4 minutes total. Transfer to a sheet pan and cover with a kitchen towel. Repeat with the remaining dough, stacking the cooked pitas under the towel.

7. Half each pita for stuffing, then serve.

Make Ahead Pitas can be made up to 1 day in advance, stored in an airtight container or sealable plastic bags at room temperature. Reheat on a sheet pan in a 400°F oven for a few minutes, until warm.

Leftovers 3 days at room temperature or 1 month in the freezer.

Falafel

You might think we're making too much falafel, but is that really a thing? I originally was making a half batch of this recipe, but that was just barely enough for six people, without any leftovers. And if we're throwing a pita party, we need to be budgeting at least six balls per person. It's simple math, I don't make the rules. Luckily, we're just dumping everything into a food processor, so it can be scaled up and down easily depending on the vibe and headcount. Just make sure you're checking that the mixture holds together when squeezed with your hands, adding a little extra water one tablespoon at a time if needed. Once it's time to fry, we're going to make sure we're monitoring the oil temp so our falafel is fully cooked by the time it's golden brown. Just don't ask me about baking or air-frying this recipe. That's your journey to go on and I wish you well, but these balls are to fry for!

Makes 64 falafel balls | Prep Time: 30 minutes, plus overnight soaking and 30 minutes resting time | Cook Time: 15 minutes

- 2 pounds dried chickpeas, soaked overnight
- 1 bunch (2 cups) fresh parsley leaves and tender stems
- 1 bunch (2 cups) fresh cilantro leaves and tender stems
- 1 bunch (6 stalks) scallions, ends trimmed and roughly chopped
- ¼ cup freshly squeezed lemon juice
- ¼ cup water
- 2 tablespoons kosher salt
- 1 tablespoon ground cumin
- 1 tablespoon ground coriander
- 1 tablespoon baking powder
- ½ teaspoon cayenne pepper
- Vegetable oil, for frying

1. You obviously didn't forget to soak your chickpeas overnight, since this step is CRUCIAL. Drain the soaked chickpeas.

2. In the bowl of a food processor and working in two batches, combine half of the parsley, cilantro, and scallions. Pulse until finely chopped. Add half of the drained chickpeas, lemon juice, water, salt, cumin, coriander, baking powder, and cayenne pepper. Pulse, scraping the sides as needed, until the chickpeas are very finely chopped and the mixture holds together when squeezed with your hands, then transfer to a large bowl. Repeat with the remaining ingredients, then mix both batches by hand to combine. Cover with plastic wrap and let rest at room temperature for 15 minutes.

3. Line a sheet pan with parchment paper. Using a 2-tablespoon-sized scoop, scoop the falafel mixture into balls onto the prepared sheet pan, rolling and squeezing gently with your hands to shape.

4. In a large Dutch oven, heat 2 inches of vegetable oil to 350°F. Line another sheet pan with a wire rack.

5. Working in 4 batches, add the falafel balls to the oil. Fry, turning as needed with a metal spider or slotted spoon, until golden brown, about 3 minutes per batch. Once golden, transfer to the wire rack to drain, then repeat. Once all the falafel balls are fried, transfer to a platter and serve.

Make Ahead Falafel can be fried up to 1 hour before serving. Cooked falafel can be held on a wire rack–lined sheet pan and reheated in a 400°F oven for 5 to 8 minutes, until warm.

Leftovers 5 days in the refrigerator.

Lemon-Almond Blondies with Sumac Glaze (Platinum Blondies)

Sometimes my best recipes are born out of limited time and the compulsive need to never show up empty-handed. I was on my way to a Jewish Christmas party (naturally), and needed to throw something together that was fast, easy to transport, and made of ingredients I already had in my pantry. I pulled up my recipe for Pumpkin Pie Blondies (page 311) and adapted the blondie base to focus on my favorite flavor combo of almond and lemon, topping it with a sumac-speckled glaze for an iced sugar cookie vibe. It couldn't have been easier to throw together, and I can't express how feral people go for this recipe. When we photographed this menu, my food stylist Barrett Washburne was so obsessed that he anointed them with the title of *platinum blondies*. Though I might argue that most of the marvel comes from the extra-thick layer of glaze on top. I'm too lazy to measure confectioners' sugar, so I just use an entire box for ease. The result is a fudgy layer that's surprisingly not overly sweet since it's balanced by a good amount of salt and a pucker of tang from lemon juice and sumac. It's the Christmas miracle that keeps on giving.

Makes 24 blondies | Prep Time: 25 minutes, plus cooling and setting time | Cook Time: 25 minutes

Blondies

- 8 ounces (2 sticks) unsalted butter, melted
- 1 cup (200g) granulated sugar
- 1 cup (214g) packed light brown sugar
- 2 teaspoons lemon zest
- 2 teaspoons almond extract
- 2 large eggs
- 2 cups (270g) all-purpose flour
- ½ cup (56g) finely ground almond flour
- 1½ teaspoons kosher salt
- 1 teaspoon baking powder

Glaze

- 1 pound confectioners' sugar
- ¼ cup freshly squeezed lemon juice
- 3 to 4 tablespoons water
- 1 tablespoon ground sumac
- 1 teaspoon almond extract
- 1 teaspoon kosher salt

1. Bake the blondies: Preheat the oven to 350°F. Line a 9 by 13-inch baking pan with parchment paper, leaving overhang on at least 2 sides.

2. In a large bowl, whisk together the melted butter, sugars, lemon zest, almond extract, and eggs until very smooth. Add the flours, salt, and baking powder. Using a rubber spatula, gently stir together the dry ingredients piled above the wet ingredients a few times before folding together until incorporated. Transfer to the prepared pan and spread in an even layer.

3. Bake for 20 to 25 minutes, until golden with a matte top. Let cool completely in the pan.

4. Meanwhile, make the glaze: In a large bowl, whisk together the confectioners' sugar, lemon juice, water, sumac, almond extract, and salt until a smooth, thick glaze forms.

5. Pour the glaze over the blondies, using an offset spatula to spread in an even layer. Let the blondies sit at room temperature for at least 30 minutes to set, then slice and serve.

Make Ahead Blondies can be baked and glazed up to 2 days in advance, stored in the pan, unsliced and covered in plastic wrap, at room temperature.

Leftovers 5 days at room temperature.

The Eastern European flavors of my ancestors **zhuzhed** up for the modern table.

shtetl chic

MENU

Kielbasa in a Blanket
Caraway-Roasted Beets

Unstuffed Cabbage

Zaftig Honey Cake (Medovik-ish)

GROCERY LIST

PANTRY
4 c chicken stock
2 c long-grain white rice
2 c (270g) all-purpose flour
¾ c wildflower honey
½ c Dijon mustard
½ c olive oil
½ c (107g) packed light brown sugar
½ c (60g) confectioners' sugar
3 tbsp red wine vinegar
1 tbsp vodka
2 tsp hot sauce
1 tsp baking soda
1 (28-oz) can whole peeled tomatoes
1 (6-oz) can tomato paste

SPICES, SEASONINGS, AND FLAVORINGS
¼ c poppy seeds
1½ tsp smoked paprika
1 tsp caraway seeds
1 tsp ground cinnamon
1 tsp vanilla extract
KS&P (at least 2 c kosher salt and 1 jar whole black peppercorns to be safe)

MEAT
2 lb ground beef (preferably 80% lean)
2 (14-oz) kielbasas

PRODUCE
4 lb (10 medium) beets
1 head garlic (2 cloves)
2 medium yellow onions
1 medium head (2½ lb) green cabbage
1 bunch dill (½ c minced)

REFRIGERATED
4 oz (1 stick) unsalted butter
3 c (24 oz) full-fat sour cream
2 c heavy cream
1 (6-oz) jar prepared horseradish (1 tbsp drained)
4 large eggs

FROZEN
2 sheets store-bought puff pastry (from one 17.3-oz package)

PREP LIST

Up to 3 Days Ahead
- Roast the beets for the Caraway-Roasted Beets

Up to 2 Days Ahead
- Make the dipping sauce for the Kielbasa in a Blanket
- Make the Zaftig Honey Cake

Up to 1 Day Ahead
- Assemble the Kielbasa in a Blanket
- Prep and dress the roasted beets for the Caraway-Roasted Beets

2 Hours Before Guests Arrive
- Bake the Kielbasa in a Blanket
- Bake the Unstuffed Cabbage
- Season the sour cream for the Caraway-Roasted Beets

1 Hour Before Guests Arrive
- Preheat the oven to 350°F

Right Before Guests Arrive
- Reheat the Kielbasa in a Blanket (about 10 minutes)
- Reheat the Unstuffed Cabbage (about 20 minutes)
- Assemble the Caraway-Roasted Beets

Game Time Pep Talk
Do we even need to talk? The Caraway-Roasted Beets should be assembled and on the table. The Kielbasa in a Blanket should be warmed through and transferred to a platter with the dipping sauce, served either as an appetizer while the Unstuffed Cabbage is reheating or with the full spread. And the Zaftig Honey Cake just needs to be sliced and served when it's time for dessert. You've got this!

The Mother of Disco, Emil!

Kielbasa in a Blanket

I can't write a cookbook without including at least one pig-in-a-blanket, whether knish-wrapped like in *Jew-ish*, or coiled with challah like in *I Could Nosh*. For this book, we're rolling Polish kielbasa in puff pastry and slicing them into coins, since they've got a bit more girth than your average Hebrew National. They bake up into flaky, meaty chips that you won't be able to stop popping into your mouth. Well, that's after you've scooped up a quick honey mustard spiked with vodka and horseradish for a little kick.

Serves 8 to 10 | Prep Time: 30 minutes | Cook Time: 20 minutes

Kielbasa in a Blanket
- 2 sheets store-bought puff pastry (from one 17.3-ounce package), thawed
- 1 large egg, lightly beaten
- 2 (14-ounce) kielbasas, halved crosswise at the bend
- Poppy seeds, for garnish

Dipping Sauce
- ½ cup Dijon mustard
- 1 tablespoon drained prepared horseradish
- 1 tablespoon vodka
- 1 tablespoon honey
- 2 teaspoons hot sauce
- KS&P

1. Make the kielbasa in a blanket: Preheat the oven to 400°F. Line 2 sheet pans with parchment paper.

2. On a cutting board, unfold 1 sheet of puff pastry with the creases running horizontally. Cut the sheet in half lengthwise and brush the bottom 1 inch of each half with beaten egg. Place 1 half of kielbasa horizontally at the top of each half of puff pastry, then roll the top of each piece of puff pastry toward you to wrap the kielbasa entirely. Set the 2 rolls aside, seam-side down, and repeat with the remaining sheet of puff pastry and kielbasa.

3. Once you have 4 rolls of puff pastry–wrapped kielbasa, brush each roll with the remaining beaten egg and sprinkle liberally with poppy seeds. Trim and discard the ends of each roll up to where the kielbasa begins, then slice each roll into ¼-inch disks. Arrange on the prepared sheet pans, spacing each ½ inch apart.

4. Bake, flipping halfway, until golden and crisp, 16 to 20 minutes.

5. Meanwhile, make the dipping sauce: In a medium bowl, stir together the mustard, horseradish, vodka, honey, and hot sauce to combine. Taste and adjust the seasoning with salt and pepper.

6. Transfer the kielbasa in a blanket to a platter, then serve alongside the dipping sauce.

Make Ahead Kielbasa can be assembled (through step 3) up to 1 day in advance, stored on sheet pans covered in plastic wrap in the refrigerator. Dipping sauce (step 5) can be made up to 2 days in advance, stored in an airtight container in the refrigerator. Kielbasa in a blanket can be baked up to 2 hours before serving, reheating in the oven as needed.

Leftovers 5 days in the refrigerator.

Shtetl Chic

caraway-roasted beets

We're done with the beet slander. If you can't get behind the earthy sweetness of these roasted ruby wedges, it's time to grow up! They don't need much accompaniment to shine on your table, so we're dressing them with a simple caraway seed and garlic-infused olive oil and spooning them over a bed of tangy sour cream. The beet-stained vinaigrette swirls into the sour cream for a vibrant pink tie-dye effect that adds some welcomed color to this delicious-yet-heavily-beige menu. It's just as lovely warm as it is room temperature or cold, which comes in handy since you can have your beets marinating in the fridge up to a day in advance.

Serves 8 to 10 | Prep Time: 20 minutes | Cook Time: 1 hour 15 minutes

Roasted Beets
4 pounds (10 medium) beets, scrubbed
2 tablespoons water
¼ cup olive oil
1 teaspoon caraway seeds

2 garlic cloves, thinly sliced
1 tablespoon red wine vinegar
1 tablespoon honey
KS&P

Serving
2 cups (16 ounces) full-fat sour cream
KS&P

Dill fronds, for garnish

1. Roast the beets: Preheat the oven to 400°F.
2. Place a sheet of foil on a sheet pan and add the beets, then drizzle with the water. Place another sheet of foil on top and pinch the edges to seal into a pouch.
3. Roast for 1 hour to 1 hour 15 minutes, or until tender. Remove from the oven and let cool completely in the pouch.
4. Transfer the cooled beets to a cutting board (place a sheet of parchment on the board to prevent staining). Peel and discard the skins, then slice each into 12 wedges. Transfer the beets to a large heatproof bowl.
5. In a small saucepan, combine the olive oil, caraway seeds, and garlic over medium heat. Cook until the garlic begins to brown, about 2 minutes. Pour the oil mixture over the beets with the vinegar, honey, and 2 heavy pinches each of salt and pepper. Toss until well coated, then taste and adjust the seasoning with salt and pepper. Cover and keep in the refrigerator until ready to serve.
6. To serve: In a medium bowl, whisk the sour cream with 2 heavy pinches each of salt and pepper, then taste and adjust the seasoning. Spread in an even layer on a platter. Spoon the marinated beets on top, then garnish with dill and serve.

Make Ahead Beets can be roasted (through step 3) up to 3 days in advance, stored in an airtight container in the refrigerator. Beets can be peeled, cut, and dressed (steps 4 and 5) up to 1 day in advance, stored in an airtight container in the refrigerator.

Leftovers 5 days in the refrigerator.

unstuffed cabbage

Sometimes laziness pays off. I love cabbage in every form: roasted, boiled, shaved, and, of course, stuffed. This recipe was born out of a little too much ambition, ordering all the ingredients for stuffed cabbage and then having absolutely no interest in doing the work to make it. While I may be lazy, I certainly am not wasteful, so I pivoted and chopped up the cabbage to stir into a giant meaty, tomato-tinted rice pilaf that gets covered in chopped dill for a little bit a greenery. Immediate culinary canon. It's a hearty porridge that has all your food groups, leftovers only get better for days, and it can be enjoyed with a spoon, which personally are my three priorities for any main. And you can obviously customize! The beef can be swapped with ground chicken or turkey, or even made vegetarian with a combo of crumbled tofu and sliced mushrooms. Any way you make it, while the cabbage may be unstuffed, you certainly will be.

Serves 8 to 10 | Prep Time: 20 minutes | Cook Time: 1 hour 30 minutes

4 tablespoons olive oil
1 medium head (2½ pounds) green cabbage, cut into 1-inch pieces
KS&P
2 medium yellow onions, finely chopped
2 pounds ground beef (preferably 80% lean)
2 cups long-grain white rice, rinsed

1 (6-ounce) can tomato paste
1½ teaspoons smoked paprika
1 (28-ounce) can whole peeled tomatoes, coarsely crushed by hand
4 cups chicken stock
2 tablespoons red wine vinegar
½ cup minced fresh dill

1. Preheat the oven to 350°F.

2. In a Dutch oven or large oven-safe pot with a lid, heat 2 tablespoons of the olive oil over medium-high heat. Add the cabbage with 2 heavy pinches each of salt and pepper. Cook, stirring often, until the cabbage has softened and begins to brown, 6 to 8 minutes. Transfer to a large bowl.

3. Add the remaining 2 tablespoons of olive oil to the pot. Add the onions and cook, stirring occasionally, until softened and beginning to brown, 6 to 8 minutes. Add the beef with 2 heavy pinches each of salt and pepper. Cook, using a wooden spoon or spatula to break the meat into crumbles, until the meat is no longer pink and beginning to brown, 4 to 5 minutes. Stir in the rice, followed by the tomato paste and smoked paprika and cook until fragrant and the tomato paste begins to caramelize, about 2 minutes. Stir in the canned tomatoes, stock, vinegar, and 2 teaspoons of salt. Bring to a simmer, then spread the softened cabbage in an even layer on top of the rice mixture and cover.

4. Bake for 1 hour, or until all the liquid has been absorbed and the rice is tender. Remove from the oven and let sit, covered, for 5 minutes, then add the dill and fluff it into the rice with the cabbage. Taste and adjust the seasoning with salt and pepper, then serve.

Make Ahead Unstuffed cabbage can be made up to 2 hours before serving, reheating in the oven as needed.

Leftovers 5 days in the refrigerator.

Zaftig Honey Cake (Medovik-ish)

Many of the dessert recipes in this book are inspired by my pastry chef besties who supply me with an endless stream of sweets and inspiration. This one is dedicated to my friend Jessica Quinn, who, with her wife, Trina, runs Dacha 46, an Eastern European–queer–Jewish popup in NYC that is luckily soon to be a brick-and-mortar. Jess's medovik is easily in the top five best desserts I've ever had, and I don't throw around that kind of praise lightly. Medovik is a Soviet honey cake that's made up of many, many layers of thin rounds of cake sandwiched with a sour cream–laced whipped filling. It's an insanely time-consuming dessert, requiring each cake layer be individually spread by hand on sheet pans before baking. Before you get ready to bail on this, I'm not going to have you do that. I've taken inspiration from the original and transformed it into an extremely manageable medovik-adjacent baking project. Instead of individual layers, I spread batter (packed with brown butter for richness and wildflower honey for floral sweetness) evenly on a sheet pan to bake, so it can easily be divided into four rectangles for stacking. The layers are thicker than traditional, which is why I've bestowed it with my favorite Yiddish word: *zaftig* (full, rounded figure/plump). After assembling, the cake is chilled overnight to let the filling soak in to give an almost ice-box cakelike softness—my ideal kind of dessert that frees you up to focus on the rest of the menu when entertaining. I'm still going to encourage you to pick up a Dacha 46 cake, but this recipe will hold you over until then.

Serves 8 to 10 | Prep Time: 40 minutes, plus cooling time and overnight chilling | Cook Time: 20 minutes

Cake

- 4 ounces (1 stick) unsalted butter
- ½ cup wildflower honey
- ½ cup (107g) packed light brown sugar
- ½ cup full-fat sour cream
- 3 large eggs
- 1 teaspoon vanilla extract
- 2 cups (270g) all-purpose flour
- 1 teaspoon baking soda
- 1 teaspoon ground cinnamon
- 1 teaspoon kosher salt

Frosting

- 2 cups heavy cream
- ½ cup (60g) confectioners' sugar
- ½ teaspoon kosher salt
- ½ cup sour cream
- 2 tablespoons wildflower honey

(cont.)

1. Bake the cake: Preheat the oven to 350°F. Line a sheet pan with parchment paper.

2. In a medium saucepan, melt the butter over medium-high heat. Cook, stirring continuously, until browned and nutty in aroma, 4 to 6 minutes. Transfer to a large heatproof bowl.

3. To the brown butter, whisk in the honey, brown sugar, and sour cream until smooth. Whisk in the eggs, one at a time, followed by the vanilla. Add the flour, baking soda, cinnamon, and salt. Gently stir together the dry ingredients piled above the wet ingredients a few times before folding together into a smooth batter. Pour onto the prepared sheet pan and spread in an even layer.

4. Bake for 10 to 12 minutes, until lightly golden. Let cool completely on the pan.

5. Once cooled, make the frosting: In the bowl of a stand mixer fitted with the whisk attachment or in a large bowl with an electric hand mixer, combine the heavy cream, confectioners' sugar, and salt. Whip until soft peaks form, then add the sour cream and honey and whip until medium-stiff peaks form.

6. To assemble, run an offset spatula around the edges of the cake, then invert it onto a cutting board. Remove and discard the parchment paper, then slice the cake down the middle both lengthwise and crosswise to form 4 equal pieces.

7. To hold the cake in place, schmear 1 tablespoon of the frosting in the center of a platter. Place one piece of cake on top. Spread 1 heaping cup of the frosting over that piece, then repeat 3 more times with the remaining cake and frosting. Run an offset spatula along the sides of the cake to even any frosting sticking out. Cover with plastic wrap and refrigerate overnight.

8. When ready to serve, remove and discard the plastic wrap and smooth the frosting with an offset spatula, if necessary, then slice and serve.

Make Ahead Cake can be made up to 2 days in advance, covered in plastic wrap and stored in the refrigerator.

Leftovers 5 days in the refrigerator.

An Italian American red sauce dinner to ball out on, **literally.**

meatballs to the wall

MENU

Focaccia with Whipped Ricotta & Peppadew Honey

Chopped Salad with Pepperoncini Dressing

Caesar Cabbage

Fresh Cavatelli & Fennel-y Meatballs

Tiramisu Cake

GROCERY LIST

PANTRY

- 4 c (540g) semolina flour
- 4 c (540g) bread flour
- 1 c (135g) all-purpose flour
- 2 c olive oil
- 2 c (400g) granulated sugar
- 1½ c panko bread crumbs
- 1 c dry red wine
- ¾ c coffee liqueur
- ¾ c honey
- ½ c (60g) confectioners' sugar
- ¼ c red wine vinegar
- ¼ c (25g) cocoa powder
- 2 tsp Dijon mustard
- 1 tsp (3g) active dry yeast
- 1 tsp Worcestershire sauce
- 2 anchovy fillets
- 1 (14-oz) jar peppadew peppers (1 c drained)
- 1 (12-fl oz) jar pepperoncini (¼ c minced, plus 2 tbsp brine)
- 1 (28-oz) can crushed tomatoes

SPICES, SEASONINGS, AND FLAVORINGS

- 2 tsp dried oregano
- 1 tsp fennel seeds
- 1 tsp crushed red pepper
- 2 tsp instant espresso powder
- 1 tsp vanilla bean paste (or vanilla extract)
- Flaky sea salt
- KS&P (at least 2 c kosher salt and 1 jar whole black peppercorns to be safe)

MEAT

- 2 lb ground beef (preferably 80% lean)
- 3 oz hot soppressata salami (optional)

PRODUCE

- 2 medium fennel bulbs
- 2 medium vine-ripe tomatoes
- 2 lemons
- 2 heads garlic (15 cloves)
- 1 medium head iceberg lettuce
- 1 medium red onion
- 1 English cucumber
- 1 medium head (2½ lb) green cabbage
- 1 medium yellow onion
- 1 bunch parsley (½ c minced)

REFRIGERATED

- 1 lb full-fat ricotta
- 1 lb mascarpone cheese
- 4 oz (1 stick) unsalted butter, melted
- 1½ c heavy cream
- 1 c finely grated Parmesan cheese
- 7 large eggs

PREP LIST

Up to 2 Days Ahead
- Make the peppadew honey for the Focaccia
- Make the dressing for the Chopped Salad
- Make the dressing for the Caesar Cabbage
- Make the meatballs and sauce for the Fresh Cavatelli & Fenne-y Meatballs
- Make the Tiramisu Cake

Up to 1 Day Ahead
- Make the whipped ricotta for the Focaccia
- Make the dough for the Focaccia
- Make the topping for the Caesar Cabbage
- Make the pasta dough for the Fresh Cavatelli & Fenne-y Meatballs

Day Of
- Bake the Focaccia
- Prep the Chopped Salad
- Shape the cavatelli for the Fresh Cavatelli & Fenne-y Meatballs (optional to do this with your guests)

1 Hour Before Guests Arrive
- Roast the Caesar Cabbage
- Keep the oven at 400°F

Right Before Guests Arrive
- Reheat the Focaccia (about 5 minutes)
- Reheat the Caesar Cabbage (8 to 10 minutes)
- Reheat the meatballs in the sauce for the Fresh Cavatelli & Fenne-y Meatballs (simmer for 5 minutes)
- Get a pot of salted water boiling for the Fresh Cavatelli & Fenne-y Meatballs

Right Before Serving
- Dress the Chopped Salad
- Cook the cavatelli and assemble the Fresh Cavatelli & Fenne-y Meatballs
- Dust cocoa powder on the Tiramisu Cake

Game Time Pep Talk
The Focaccia should be reheated and on a board alongside the Whipped Ricotta and Peppadew Honey (you can pre-slice, but I like to do that tableside). The Chopped Salad should be dressed and on the table. The Caesar Cabbage should be reheated and assembled on a platter with the garlic breadcrumbs (this is a great dish because it's just as good hot as it is room temperature). The meatballs should be simmering in their sauce, so really you are just waiting on the cavatelli to cook to combine and serve. The Tiramisu Cake should be ready in the refrigerator, freshly dusted with cocoa and ready to be scooped into. You've got this!

Miz Cracker & Brian

Focaccia with Whipped Ricotta & Peppadew Honey

A little warm bread for the table is always encouraged, especially when it can be slathered with whipped ricotta and drizzled with hot honey. We're making fresh bread and pasta for this menu, but don't be frightened, since our focaccia dough comes together quickly in the mixer (especially since we ALWAYS use a kitchen scale when preparing bread!) and we can make it the night before to chill out in the fridge and go through its first rise. The next day we'll bake it off to be sliced and served with simply whipped ricotta and a spicy honey infused with peppadew peppers and garlic. Just make sure to save a piece of bread to scrape all the red sauce off your plate.

Serves 6 to 8 | Prep Time: 30 minutes, plus cooling time, overnight refrigerating, and 3 hours proofing time | Cook Time: 25 minutes

Dough
1¾ cups (385g) warm water
1 teaspoon granulated sugar
1 teaspoon (3g) active dry yeast
4 cups (540g) bread flour
2 teaspoons (6g) kosher salt
¼ cup (45g) olive oil, plus more for greasing

Peppadew Honey
1 cup drained peppadew peppers, finely chopped
½ cup honey
1 garlic clove, finely grated
KS

Whipped Ricotta
1 pound full-fat ricotta
KS&P

Baking
4 tablespoons olive oil
Flaky sea salt, for garnish

1. **Make the dough:** In the bowl of a stand mixer fitted with the dough hook attachment, add the warm water and sugar and stir with a spatula to dissolve, then sprinkle the yeast over the top. Let stand until foamy, 5 to 10 minutes. Add the flour, salt, and the ¼ cup olive oil to the mixture in the bowl and, beginning on low speed and gradually increasing to medium, knead until a smooth, elastic dough forms, 3 to 4 minutes.

(cont.)

2. Grease a bowl at least twice the size of your dough with about 1 tablespoon of olive oil. Dip your hands in the oil to grease them before transferring the dough to the bowl. Cover with plastic wrap or a lid and refrigerate overnight. (Alternatively, you could let the dough rise at room temperature until it has doubled in size, 1½ to 2 hours.)

3. Make the peppadew honey: In a small saucepan, combine the peppers, honey, garlic, and a heavy pinch of salt. Bring to a simmer over medium-high heat, then remove from the heat and let cool completely. Store in an airtight container in the refrigerator until ready to serve.

4. Make the whipped ricotta: In a food processor, combine the ricotta with a heavy pinch each of salt and pepper. Pulse until smooth. Taste and adjust the seasoning with salt and pepper, then store in an airtight container in the refrigerator until ready to serve.

5. Bake the focaccia: About 4 hours before serving, grease a 12-inch cast-iron pan with 2 tablespoons of the olive oil. Dip your hands in the oil and pick up the dough to stretch it into a smooth ball. Transfer to the prepared pan and rub the top with 1 tablespoon of the remaining olive oil, using your hands to spread the dough gently. Let sit for 2 to 3 hours, until the dough has filled out the pan and is puffy.

6. One hour before baking, preheat the oven to 450°F.

7. Drizzle the remaining 1 tablespoon olive oil on top of the dough and use your fingers to make a series of dimples in the dough. Garnish with a heavy pinch of flaky salt. Bake for 20 to 25 minutes, until golden brown. Carefully transfer to a wire rack to cool slightly, then slice and serve warm with whipped ricotta for schmearing and the peppadew honey for drizzling.

Make Ahead Peppadew honey (step 3) can be made up to 2 days in advance, stored in an airtight container in the refrigerator. Whipped ricotta (step 4) can be made up to 1 day in advance, stored in an airtight container in the refrigerator. Focaccia should be baked (steps 6 and 7) the same day as serving for the best results but can be baked a few hours in advance of your guests arriving. Keep on a wire rack–lined sheet pan, and when your guests arrive, reheat in a 400°F oven until warm.

Leftovers Bread for 3 days at room temperature, but please toast or pan-fry to refresh. Peppadew honey for 1 week in the refrigerator. Whipped ricotta for 4 days in the refrigerator.

chopped salad with pepperoncini dressing

We've got a lot of richness happening in this menu, so we're going to balance it out with a fresh chopped salad that gives Olive Garden vibes in the best way possible. Naturally, that means we're starting with a head of iceberg, the crunchy, hydrating king of all lettuces, and tossing it with our veggies in a tangy, zesty red wine vinaigrette that's packed with pepperoncini for some extra bite. And since we're worth it, some spicy salami couldn't hurt. This salad not only stands on its own surrounded by all the comfort classics on the table, but, in my experience, it's often the first dish cleaned off.

Serves 6 to 8 | Prep Time: 20 minutes

Dressing
- ½ cup olive oil
- ¼ cup red wine vinegar
- ¼ cup pickled pepperoncini, drained and minced
- 2 tablespoons pepperoncini brine
- 1½ tablespoons honey
- 2 teaspoons dried oregano
- 1 teaspoon Dijon mustard
- 1 garlic clove, finely grated
- KS&P

Salad
- 1 medium head iceberg lettuce, chopped
- 2 medium vine-ripe tomatoes, chopped
- 1 English cucumber, chopped
- ½ medium red onion
- 3 ounces hot soppressata salami, chopped (optional)
- KS&P

1. **Make the dressing:** In a pint jar or container, combine the olive oil, vinegar, pepperoncini and brine, honey, oregano, mustard, garlic, and 2 heavy pinches each of salt and pepper. Seal closed and shake vigorously until smooth. Makes about 1 cup. Set aside.

2. **Make the salad:** In a large bowl, toss the lettuce, tomatoes, cucumber, and red onion to combine. Right before serving, toss with the soppressata, if using, and dressing until well combined. Taste and adjust the seasoning with salt and pepper, then serve.

Make Ahead Salad dressing (step 1) can be made up to 2 days in advance. Salad (step 2) can be prepped (but kept undressed) a few hours before serving, covered and stored in the refrigerator.

Leftovers Doesn't hold well!

caesar cabbage

Here's the dilemma—we already had our chopped salad, but in what world could Caesar salad not make an appearance on our red sauce menu? The solution is quite simple and doesn't require us to serve two salads: We're going to be rubbing a homemade Caesar dressing over wedges of cabbage to roast in the oven until golden before covering them with garlicky bread crumbs for a veg side that gives us the same fantasy. The dressing melts into the tender leaves of cabbage so the whole dish tastes like a warm Caesar but in a mind-blowingly good way. It's my new favorite way to prepare roasted cabbage, and honestly maybe Caesar salad, too.

Serves 6 to 8 | Prep Time: 20 minutes | Cook Time: 50 minutes

Dressing
1 teaspoon finely grated lemon zest
¼ cup freshly squeezed lemon juice
1 teaspoon Dijon mustard
1 teaspoon Worcestershire sauce
3 garlic cloves, finely grated
2 anchovy fillets, mashed into a paste
1 large egg yolk
½ cup olive oil
⅓ cup finely grated Parmesan cheese
KS&P

Cabbage
1 medium head (2½ pounds) green cabbage, cut into 12 wedges

Topping
½ cup panko bread crumbs
2 tablespoons olive oil
2 garlic cloves, finely grated
KS&P

1. Make the dressing: In a medium bowl, whisk together the lemon zest and juice, mustard, Worcestershire sauce, garlic, anchovies, and egg yolk until smooth. Slowly whisk in the olive oil until emulsified, followed by the Parmesan. Taste and adjust the seasoning with salt and pepper. Makes about 1 cup dressing.

2. Roast the cabbage: Preheat the oven to 400°F. Line a sheet pan with parchment paper.

3. Add the cabbage to the pan and rub the dressing liberally over all sides of each wedge. Arrange the cabbage wedges, cut side down. (It's okay if they overlap slightly.)

4. Roast for 45 minutes, or until golden and tender.

5. Meanwhile, make the topping: In a medium skillet, combine the bread crumbs, olive oil, garlic, and a heavy pinch each of salt and pepper. Cook over medium heat, stirring continuously, until golden and crisp, 4 to 5 minutes.

6. Transfer the roasted cabbage to a platter and top with the bread crumbs, then serve.

Make Ahead Dressing (step 1) can be made up to 2 days in advance, stored in an airtight container in the refrigerator. Cabbage can be fully roasted (steps 2, 3, and 4) up to 1 hour before serving, held on the sheet pan to reheat. Topping (step 5) can be made up to 1 day in advance, stored in an airtight container at room temperature.

Leftovers 5 days in the refrigerator.

Fresh Cavatelli & Fennel-y Meatballs

Naturally, I know my way around some balls, and I can assure you these won't disappoint. We start by seasoning ground beef with ground fennel seeds, garlic, and herbs to be rolled and seared before getting simmered in a red sauce flavored with a heavy glug of wine and caramelized onions and fennel. Once our meatballs are ready, we puree the sauce, creating a velvety orange vodka-sauce-like texture that perfectly coats fresh cavatelli. (Everything also doubles beautifully if you have a bigger crowd coming or just want ample leftovers!) Yes, we're going to tackle fresh pasta together. Both because I believe in you, but also, we only need flour and water, and we're rolling out one of the easiest shapes possible. And if you're wondering, why not the classic choice of spaghetti? Well, my controversial opinion of the day is that spaghetti is the worst possible pasta shape for meatballs, requiring excessive gymnastics with my fork and always leaving me splattered with tomato sauce. And while I can recognize that that is a me problem, my dream is a world in which we normalize serving meatballs with a short pasta shape so we can scoop it all up with a spoon. Together, we can make this dream a delicious reality, one bowl of cavatelli and meatballs at a time!

Serves 6 to 8 | Prep Time: 1 hour, plus 1 hour resting time | Cook Time: 1 hour 15 minutes

Cavatelli
3½ cups (560g) semolina flour, plus more for dusting
1¼ cups (275g) water
KS, for boiling

Balls
1 tablespoon kosher salt
1 teaspoon fennel seeds
1 cup panko bread crumbs
4 garlic cloves, finely grated
½ medium yellow onion, coarsely grated
2 pounds ground beef (preferably 80% lean)
½ cup minced fresh parsley leaves and tender stems
½ cup minced fennel fronds, plus more for garnish
½ cup finely grated Parmesan cheese (optional)
½ teaspoon crushed red pepper

Sauce
3 tablespoons olive oil
2 medium fennel bulbs, diced
½ medium yellow onion, diced
KS&P
¼ teaspoon crushed red pepper
4 garlic cloves, thinly sliced
1 cup dry red wine
1 (28-ounce) can crushed tomatoes
2 teaspoons granulated sugar

(cont.)

1. Make the cavatelli: On a clean work surface, place the flour in a pile and make a large well in the center. (Alternatively, you can add the flour to a large bowl.) Add the water to the well. Using a fork, whisk, slowly incorporating the flour. Once a shaggy dough forms, switch to using your hands to knead it together until you have a very smooth ball of dough. (If you started in a bowl, once the dough is shaggy, transfer to a clean work surface to knead.) This typically takes 8 to 10 minutes. (If your dough isn't getting smooth, cover and let rest for 5 minutes, then return to kneading.) Press the ball of dough into a disk, then cover with plastic wrap and let rest at room temperature for 1 hour.

2. Meanwhile, make the balls: Using a mortar and pestle, grind the salt and fennel seeds until coarsely ground. Transfer to a large bowl with the bread crumbs, garlic, and onion and mix until well combined. Add the beef, parsley, fennel fronds, Parmesan, if using, and crushed red pepper. Using your hands, mix until well combined. Scoop the meat mixture into ¼-cup-sized balls, rolling with your hands to smooth.

3. Make the sauce: In a large pot or Dutch oven, heat the olive oil over medium-high heat. Add the balls and cook, turning as needed, until golden brown, 6 to 8 minutes. (All the balls should fit in a large Dutch oven, but if too crowded, sear the balls in 2 batches.) Transfer the seared balls to a platter or sheet pan.

4. Add the fennel, onion, and 2 heavy pinches each of salt and pepper and cook until softened and beginning to caramelize, 5 to 6 minutes. Stir in the crushed red pepper and garlic and cook for 1 minute. Slowly pour in the wine, scraping up any browned bits on the bottom of the pot with a wooden spoon, then stir in the crushed tomatoes, sugar, and 2 heavy pinches each of salt and pepper. Carefully add the meatballs to the sauce with any drippings. Bring to a simmer, then cover and cook, reducing the heat to maintain a light simmer, for 1 hour.

5. Transfer the balls from the sauce to a bowl. Using an immersion blender or working in batches in a standard blender, puree the sauce until smooth and return to the pot. Taste and adjust the seasoning with salt and pepper, then return the meatballs to the sauce. Keep warm.

6. Line a sheet pan with parchment paper and dust liberally with semolina flour. Cut the pasta dough into 1-inch-thick strips. Take one strip at a time, keeping the rest covered in plastic wrap, and use your hands to roll into a ½-inch-thick rope. Using a bench scraper or knife, cut into ½-inch pieces. One at a time, use your thumb to press and roll each piece of dough away from you to indent and curl into cavatelli. (If desired, do this against a pasta board or the back of the tines of a fork to make ridges on the cavatelli, which helps pick up the sauce.) Transfer to the prepared sheet pan, tossing gently with the flour to prevent sticking. Repeat this process of rolling, cutting, and shaping until all the cavatelli are formed.

7. Bring a large pot of salted water to a boil. Add the cavatelli and cook, stirring occasionally, until al dente, 4 to 5 minutes. Using a large metal spider or slotted spoon, transfer the cavatelli directly to the pot with the meatballs. Gently stir to coat, then garnish with fennel fronds and serve.

Make Ahead Pasta dough (step 1) can be made up to 1 day in advance, letting it come to room temperature before rolling and shaping. Cavatelli can be fully made (step 6) and frozen on the sheet pan (transferring to a sealable plastic bag once frozen) up to 1 month in advance and can be boiled from frozen. Meatballs and sauce (steps 2, 3, 4, and 5) can be made up to 2 days in advance.

Leftovers 5 days in the refrigerator.

Tiramisu Cake

Let it be known, this is the best dessert in this book. (Okay, I know I say that a lot, but it's definitely top three.) I kept seeing these viral videos online of restaurants with giant tiramisu drawers to scoop from and I became low-key obsessed with finding a way to bring that same energy to my dinner parties. My tableside-tiramisu fantasy quickly turned into this tiramisu–tres leches cake hybrid, and from the first test I knew we were on to something! Instead of using ladyfingers to dip in coffee, we bake an espresso sponge cake to soak in coffee syrup and cover in mascarpone frosting. Popped in the fridge overnight, the cake becomes saturated with the syrup for the softest texture, which makes it just as easy to scoop as it does to slice. Plus, you get the perfect balance of cream to cake for a rich dessert that still feels surprisingly light, making it beyond easy to go for a second scoop. The true stamp of approval is that it has become the go-to birthday cake request from many of my friends. Luckily, it's one of the easiest desserts to prep ahead and even transfer, requiring just a dusting of cocoa powder before digging in.

Serves 6 to 8 | Prep Time: 30 minutes, plus cooling and soaking time, and overnight chilling | Cook Time: 30 minutes

Sponge
6 large eggs, separated
1 cup (200g) granulated sugar
1 tablespoon coffee liqueur
1 teaspoon instant espresso powder
1 teaspoon kosher salt
4 ounces (1 stick) unsalted butter, melted
1 cup (135g) all-purpose flour

Syrup
¾ cup (150g) granulated sugar
¾ cup water
2 teaspoons instant espresso
½ teaspoon kosher salt
½ cup coffee liqueur

Frosting
1½ cups heavy cream
½ cup (60g) confectioners' sugar
1 teaspoon vanilla bean paste (or vanilla extract)
½ teaspoon kosher salt
1 pound mascarpone cheese
Cocoa powder, for garnish

(cont.)

1. Make the sponge: Preheat the oven to 350°F.

2. In a large bowl, whisk the egg yolks and ½ cup (100g) of the granulated sugar until pale yellow in color. Whisk in the coffee liqueur, instant espresso, and salt, followed by the butter and flour.

3. Put the egg whites in the bowl of stand mixer fitted with the whisk attachment. Whip on medium speed, slowly adding the remaining ½ cup (100g) granulated sugar. Once all the sugar is added, increase the speed to medium-high and whip until stiff peaks form. Working in 3 additions, fold the whipped egg whites into the batter until fully incorporated. Pour the batter into an ungreased 9 by 13-inch baking pan and spread in an even layer.

4. Bake for 25 to 30 minutes, until golden and puffed with no jiggle. Let cool completely in the pan.

5. Meanwhile, make the syrup: In a small saucepan, combine the granulated sugar, water, instant espresso, and salt. Bring to a simmer over medium-high heat and cook, stirring continuously, until the sugar has dissolved, about 1 minute. Remove from the heat and stir in the coffee liqueur.

6. Using a paring knife, poke holes in the cooled cake, then pour the syrup over to coat the entire cake. Let soak for 30 minutes.

7. Meanwhile, make the frosting: In the bowl of stand mixer fitted with the whisk attachment, combine the heavy cream, confectioners' sugar, vanilla bean paste, and salt. Whip on medium speed until soft peaks form. Add the mascarpone, then continue to whip until medium-stiff peaks form. Spoon the frosting over the soaked cake and spread in an even layer. Cover and refrigerate overnight.

8. The next day, before serving, dust the top of the cake with cocoa powder, then scoop or slice and serve.

Make Ahead Full cake can be made up to 2 days in advance, but only dusted with cocoa before serving.

Leftovers 5 days in the refrigerator.

A winning roast chicken menu of classic crowd-pleasers.

winner winner, chicken dinner

MENU

Green Goddess Wedge Salad with Radishes & Crispy Capers

Scallion-Horseradish Smashed Potatoes

Roasted Broccoli with Buffalo Beurre Blanc

Roast Chicken with Lemony Sauce Soubise

Tarte Tatin

GROCERY LIST

PANTRY

- 2 c (270g) all-purpose flour, plus more for dusting
- ½ c neutral oil, such as vegetable, avocado, or sunflower
- 1 c plus 2 tablespoons olive oil
- 1 c (200g) granulated sugar
- 1¼ c dry white wine
- ¼ c hot sauce
- 2 tbsp apple cider vinegar
- 2 tbsp maple syrup
- 1 tsp baking powder
- 1 jar capers (enough for ¼ c drained)

SPICES, SEASONINGS, AND FLAVORINGS

- 1 tsp ground cinnamon
- 1 tsp vanilla extract
- ¼ tsp crushed red pepper
- KS&P (at least 2 c kosher salt and 1 jar whole black peppercorns to be safe)

MEAT

- 2 (4- to 5-lb) whole chickens

PRODUCE

- 4 lb baby golden potatoes
- 3 lb broccoli
- 3 lb (about 8 medium) Honeycrisp apples
- 2 c mixed herbs, such as basil, chives, dill, parsley, and tarragon
- 4 medium scallions
- 2 medium yellow onions
- 2 medium radishes (preferably watermelon or green daikon)
- 2 medium shallots
- 2 small heads iceberg lettuce
- 2 lemons
- 1 orange
- 1 head garlic (5 cloves)
- 1 small bunch chives

REFRIGERATED

- 12 oz (3 sticks) unsalted butter
- 1 c plain Greek yogurt (any fat %)
- ½ c heavy cream
- 1 jar prepared horseradish (enough for 2 tbsp drained)

FROZEN

- 2 pints vanilla ice cream

Dad, Jamie & Bubbles ♡

PREP LIST

Up to 2 Days Ahead
- Boil the potatoes for the Scallion-Horseradish Smashed Potatoes

Up to 1 Day Ahead
- Make the crispy capers for the Green Goddess Wedge Salad
- Make the dressing for the Green Goddess Wedge Salad
- Make the dressing for the Scallion-Horseradish Smashed Potatoes
- Make the dough for the Tarte Tatin
- Bake the apples for the Tarte Tatin

Day Of
- Prep the lettuce and radishes for the Green Goddess Wedge Salad
- Smash and roast the potatoes for the Scallion-Horseradish Smashed Potatoes
- Roast the broccoli for the Roasted Broccoli with Buffalo Beurre Blanc
- Prep chickens to be roasted for the Roast Chicken with Lemony Sauce Soubise
- Bake the Tarte Tatin

1 Hour Before Guests Arrive
- Make the buffalo beurre blanc for the Roasted Broccoli with Buffalo Beurre Blanc
- Roast the chickens for the Roast Chicken with Lemony Sauce Soubise
- Make the sauce for the Roast Chicken with Lemony Sauce Soubise
- Lower the oven to 400°F

Right Before Guests Arrive
- Assemble the Green Goddess Wedge Salad
- Reheat the potatoes for the Scallion-Horseradish Smashed Potatoes (10 to 15 minutes)
- Reheat the broccoli and sauce for the Roasted Broccoli with Buffalo Beurre Blanc (about 10 minutes for the broccoli)
- Reheat the chicken and sauce for the Roast Chicken with Lemony Sauce Soubise, if needed (10 to 15 minutes)

Right Before Dessert
- Reheat the Tarte Tatin (5 to 10 minutes)

Game Time Pep Talk
The chicken is the star, so everything else should be handled! The Green Goddess Wedge Salad can be dressed and on the table. The potatoes for the Scallion-Horseradish Smashed Potatoes should be warm and ready to be transferred to a platter and topped with the dressing. The broccoli for the Roasted Broccoli with Buffalo Beurre Blanc should be warm and ready to be transferred to a platter. Whisk the beurre blanc over medium heat for about 2 minutes to warm through and re-emulsify before spooning over the broccoli. The Roast Chicken should be rested and ready to be carved. If you just roasted them, blend and season the Lemony Sauce Soubise to have at the base of the platter to shingle the chicken over. If you prepared it in advance, warm in a saucepan over medium heat for 2 to 3 minutes before plating. The Tarte Tatin should be already baked but still in the pan ready to reheat before flipping and serving. You've got this!

Green Goddess Wedge Salad with Radishes & Crispy Capers

A chunky wedge always looks good, whether on your feet or dinner table. It satisfies all my requirements for an entertaining salad: quick and easy to assemble, holds up when dressed throughout the meal, and features iceberg, the superior lettuce choice. A superior lettuce requires a superior dressing! We're going to bury every wedge in a creamy, tangy green goddess packed with yogurt and herbs. But the secret to its punch of flavor is frying capers until crispy for garnish and reserving the resulting caper-infused oil for this dressing. You really don't need much more to round out this salad, so I just add some extra crunch with sliced radishes. It's just the light and bright way to kick off this meal, while leaving ample room in your stomach for chicken and potatoes . . . and probably a second serving of salad.

Serves 6 to 8 | Prep Time: 20 minutes, plus cooling time | Cook Time: 10 minutes

Crispy Capers
- ½ cup neutral oil, such as vegetable, avocado, or sunflower
- ¼ cup drained capers, patted dry with paper towels

Dressing
- 2 cups mixed herbs, such as basil, chives, dill, parsley, and tarragon
- 1 cup plain Greek yogurt (any fat %)
- 1 teaspoon finely grated lemon zest
- 2 tablespoons freshly squeezed lemon juice
- 1 tablespoon maple syrup
- 1 garlic clove, finely grated
- KS&P
- 1 to 2 tablespoons water

Salad
- 2 small heads iceberg lettuce, cut into wedges
- 2 medium radishes (preferably watermelon or green daikon), trimmed and thinly sliced

1. Make the crispy capers: Place a fine-mesh sieve over a small heatproof bowl. Line a plate with paper towels. In a small saucepan, combine the oil and capers over medium-high heat. Cook, stirring occasionally, until the bubbling dissipates and the capers are crisp, 8 to 10 minutes. Pour the mixture into the sieve to strain, reserving the oil, then transfer the fried capers to the paper towels to drain. Let the oil cool completely. Once the capers are completely cooled, store in an airtight container lined with paper towels at room temperature until ready to serve.

2. Make the dressing: In a food processor, combine the cooled oil with the herbs, yogurt, lemon zest and juice, maple syrup, garlic, and 2 heavy pinches each of salt and pepper. Pulse, scraping the sides as needed, until a smooth dressing forms. Thin out with water, if needed. Taste and adjust the seasoning

with salt and pepper. Transfer to an airtight container and refrigerate until ready to serve. Makes about 1½ cups of dressing.

3. Make the salad: Arrange the wedges of iceberg on a platter, then spoon the dressing liberally over the wedges. Top with the radishes and crispy capers, then serve.

Make Ahead Crispy capers (step 1) can be made up to 1 day in advance, stored in an airtight container lined with paper towels at room temperature. Dressing (step 2) can be made up to 1 day in advance, stored in an airtight container in the refrigerator.

Leftovers 1 day in the refrigerator.

scallion-horseradish smashed potatoes

There's a time and a place for silky, soft potatoes and one for shatteringly crisp potatoes. With roast chicken, it's crispy or bust. And while I won't make you get out the pot of oil for fries, a giant platter of smashed potatoes is absolutely required. If you're new to this preparation, we just boil baby potatoes until tender, then drain and lightly smash them on a sheet pan before roasting until crispy on the outside and fluffy on the inside. From years of personal experience, I can promise you even simply seasoned with only salt and pepper, smashed potatoes will always be the star of the show. But I love to be a little extra, and so do my potatoes. A quick dressing of scallions and horseradish adds a bit of bite to the crunch, taking this simple side to the next level. To describe it in one word: *smash*.

Serves 6 to 8 | Prep Time: 15 minutes | Cook Time: 1 hour 15 minutes

Smashed Potatoes
4 pounds baby golden potatoes
KS&P
½ cup olive oil

Dressing
¼ cup olive oil
2 tablespoons drained prepared horseradish
2 tablespoons apple cider vinegar
1 tablespoon maple syrup
¼ teaspoon crushed red pepper
4 medium scallions, roots trimmed and thinly sliced
2 garlic cloves, finely grated
KS&P

1. Make the smashed potatoes: Preheat the oven to 450°F.

2. In a medium pot, cover the potatoes with 2 inches of cold water and 2 heavy pinches of salt. Bring to a simmer over medium-high heat. Cook, reducing the heat to maintain a simmer, until the potatoes are tender, 15 to 20 minutes, then drain.

3. Transfer the potatoes to a sheet pan and toss with the olive oil to coat. Using a measuring cup or glass, smash the potatoes until ½ inch thick.

4. Bake for 45 to 55 minutes, until golden and crisp.

5. Meanwhile, make the dressing: In a bowl, stir together the olive oil, horseradish, vinegar, maple syrup, crushed red pepper, scallions, garlic, and 2 heavy pinches each of salt and pepper. Taste and adjust the seasoning with salt and pepper.

6. Transfer the smashed potatoes to a platter and spoon on the dressing, then serve.

Make Ahead Potatoes can be boiled and drained (step 2) up to 2 days in advance, stored in an airtight container in the refrigerator. Dressing (step 5) can be made up to 1 day in advance, stored in an airtight container in the refrigerator. Potatoes can be smashed and roasted (steps 3 and 4) up to 2 hours before serving, then reheated in the oven as needed.

Leftovers 5 days in the refrigerator.

Roasted Broccoli with Buffalo Beurre Blanc

My last restaurant job was working the line at ABC Kitchen in NYC under the brilliant chef Dan Kluger. While so many of his creations are burned into my memory, today we're focusing on his hot sauce butter. Always pooled under crispy fried chicken, this fine-dining buffalo sauce was spicy and citrusy and still ridiculously luscious. It was my blueprint for developing this recipe, which features an adaptation of those flavors transformed into a classic French beurre blanc. It adds fat, acid, heat, and sweetness to simply roasted broccoli, giving your veg side the love and attention it deserves!

Serves 6 to 8 | Prep Time: 15 minutes | Cook Time: 35 minutes

Roasted Broccoli
- 3 pounds broccoli, cut into large florets, stems peeled and roughly chopped
- 2 tablespoons olive oil
- KS&P
- ½ cup water

Buffalo Beurre Blanc
- ½ cup dry white wine
- ¼ cup hot sauce
- 1 teaspoon finely grated orange zest
- ¼ cup freshly squeezed orange juice
- 2 medium shallots, minced
- KS&P
- 4 ounces (1 stick) unsalted butter, cubed

1. Roast the broccoli: Preheat the oven to 450°F.

2. On a sheet pan, toss the broccoli with the olive oil and 2 heavy pinches each of salt and pepper. Pour the water into the pan, but not directly over the broccoli.

3. Roast for 25 minutes, or until the broccoli is golden and tender.

4. Meanwhile, make the buffalo beurre blanc: In a small saucepan, combine the wine, hot sauce, orange zest and juice, shallots, and a heavy pinch each of salt and pepper. Bring to a simmer and cook until almost all the liquid has evaporated, 6 to 8 minutes. Remove from the heat and whisk in the butter, a few cubes at a time, until fully emulsified. Taste and adjust the seasoning with salt and pepper.

5. Transfer the roasted broccoli to a platter and spoon the buffalo beurre blanc on top, then serve.

Make Ahead Broccoli can be roasted (through step 3) a few hours before your guests arrive, kept on the sheet pan to reheat in the oven once the chicken comes out. Buffalo beurre blanc (step 4) can be made up to 1 hour before your guests arrive, kept in the saucepan off the heat ready to be whisked over medium heat to warm through and re-emulsify.

Leftovers 5 days in the refrigerator.

Roast Chicken with Lemony Sauce Soubise

Let me take a minute to extend some gratitude that I get to live out my Ina Garten fantasy. I write cookbooks. I use the good vanilla. All my friends are gay. But most importantly, there is no shortage of meals I host surrounding a gorgeous roast chicken. This is my quintessential recipe for a simple, perfect chicken that stretches every ounce of flavor possible. To start, we need two birds. Just by myself, I can pick apart half a chicken (and I have), so there's no world in which I'm roasting only one and risking either not having enough food or—possibly even worse—forgoing the chance for leftovers. We're spatchcocking our chickens to ensure even cooking and crispy skin, plus it cuts down on oven time to leave room for the other dishes on your menu. The seasoning is simple (as it should be), rubbing a mixture of olive oil and garlic all over before liberally sprinkling a combo of salt, pepper, and lemon zest. But the real witchcraft happens in the oven. Our chickens are roasting on a wire rack nestled over sliced onions and lemon that get to cook in a combo of wine and schmaltzy pan drippings. Once they're out of the oven, we puree that onion mixture with a little cream into an easy, sunny take on soubise, a rich French onion sauce that you'll want slathered on every bite. While Ina has yet to try my chicken, I'm just going to assume game recognizes game!

Serves 6 to 8 | Prep Time: 20 minutes, plus 10 minutes resting time | Cook Time: 55 minutes

2 (4- to 5-pound) whole chickens
¼ cup olive oil
2 garlic cloves, finely grated
KS&P
1 lemon, zested

2 medium yellow onions, thinly sliced
¾ cup white wine
½ cup heavy cream, at room temperature
Minced fresh chives, for garnish

1. Preheat the oven to 450°F. Place a rack in the center of the oven. Line a sheet pan with a wire rack.

2. Place the chickens on a large cutting board. Use strong kitchen shears to cut along both sides of the backbone to remove it completely. Set the chicken skin-side down, open the cavity, and make a small cut in the breastbone (you're not looking to cut through all the way). Flip the chicken over (skin-side up) and use the palm of your hand to press on the breastbone and flatten the chicken. Tuck the wing tips under so they don't burn.

(cont.)

3. Place the chickens skin-side up on the wire rack, with the legs pointing toward the corners of the pan and the breasts lined up in the center. (Though depending on size and shape, feel free to arrange chickens in any way to fit.) In a small bowl, stir together the olive oil and garlic to combine, then rub it all over the chickens. In a small bowl, stir together 2 tablespoons salt, 1 teaspoon freshly ground black pepper, and the zest of the lemon to combine, then sprinkle liberally on both sides of each chicken.

4. Lift the wire rack with the seasoned chickens and set aside. Quarter and seed the zested lemon, then thinly slice and add to the sheet pan with the onions, tossing to combine. Pour the wine over the onions, then place the wire rack with the chickens back on top.

5. Roast on the center rack for 45 to 55 minutes, until the chickens are golden and have reached an internal temperature of 165°F in both the thighs and breasts.

6. Transfer the chickens to a cutting board and let rest for 10 minutes. Transfer the onions and lemon with any pan drippings to a blender with the cream. Puree the soubise sauce until smooth, then taste and adjust the seasoning with salt and pepper.

7. Carve the chickens. Spread the sauce on a platter and top with the roasted chicken. Garnish with minced chives, then serve.

Make Ahead Roast chicken with lemony sauce soubise (through step 5) can be made up to 30 minutes before serving, though is best served as close to roasting as possible. The soubise sauce can be held in a saucepan ready to reheat over medium heat. The chicken can remain on the wire rack–lined sheet pan to reheat in the oven as needed.

Leftovers 5 days in the refrigerator.

Tarte Tatin

There was no other way to end a menu of crowd-pleasers than with this classic French tart of glossy, caramel-soaked apples perched on a crisp yet tender crust. It's also one of those desserts that isn't very complicated to make, yet when done well, makes you seem like a master pastry chef. So, let's set you up for success. We'll start with a quick pie dough, but then halve, stack, and press it onto itself eight times to create many little pockets of butter for peak flakiness. Plus, a little baking powder in the mix adds a hint of lift in the crust to prevent any toughness. Don't be fooled by fruit tart recipes that call for store-bought puff pastry! I find they never stay crisp, quickly turning into a soggy mess. We're not about to take a shortcut and serve up a soggy bottom, are we? For our apples, par-baking Honeycrisps in a little cinnamon sugar ensures they're nice and jammy when serving, while also creating the option to prep this step ahead. Then when it's time to bake, we'll master caramel with confidence. Remember, we are just stirring the sugar until it's all liquid (no lumps!) and dark amber in color (not pale amber!), which I promise will happen with a bit of heat and patience. Throw it all together and we're a bake away from flipping out this tart. Of course, everyone else will be flipping out, too.

Serves 6 to 8 | Prep Time: 20 minutes, plus chilling and cooling time | Cook Time: 1 hour 15 minutes

Dough
- 2 cups (270g) all-purpose flour, plus more for dusting
- 1 teaspoon kosher salt
- 1 teaspoon baking powder
- 6 ounces (1½ sticks) unsalted butter, cold and cubed
- ½ cup ice water

Apples
- 3 pounds (about 8 medium) Honeycrisp apples, peeled, quartered, and cored
- ¼ cup (50 g) granulated sugar
- 1 teaspoon ground cinnamon
- ½ teaspoon kosher salt

Caramel
- ¾ cup (150g) granulated sugar
- 4 tablespoons (2 ounces) cold unsalted butter
- 1 teaspoon vanilla extract
- ½ teaspoon kosher salt

Serving
Vanilla ice cream

(cont.)

1. Make the dough: In a large bowl, stir the flour, salt, and baking powder to combine. Add the butter and, using your fingers, pinch the butter into the flour mixture until pea-sized crumbles form. Using your hand, knead in the water until a shaggy dough forms. Transfer to a clean work surface. Using a bench scraper, cut the dough in half, then stack the two halves and press down with your hands to flatten into a disk. Repeat this cut and press process, dusting with flour as needed to prevent sticking, for a total of 8 times. Cover in plastic wrap and refrigerate the dough for 1 hour.

2. Cook the apples: Preheat the oven to 400°F. Line a sheet pan with parchment paper.

3. On the prepared sheet pan, toss the apples with the sugar, cinnamon, and salt to coat. Arrange the apples cut-side down. Roast for 25 to 30 minutes, until just tender. Let cool on the pan.

4. Make the caramel: In a 10-inch ovenproof skillet, heat the sugar over medium-high heat. Cook, stirring often, until amber in color, 4 to 6 minutes. Working quickly, remove from the heat and stir in the butter, followed by the vanilla and salt. Arrange the roasted apples in concentric circles cut-side up over the caramel in the skillet, shingling to fit.

5. Transfer the chilled dough to a lightly dusted surface. Roll into a 12-inch circle, dusting with more flour as needed. Drape over the apples, tucking the edges of the dough into the pan.

6. Bake for 35 to 40 minutes, until golden and bubbling. Remove from the oven and let cool for 10 minutes. (If making in advance, see note below.)

7. Serve the tarte tatin: Place a large plate over the top of the pan and use a kitchen towel or oven mitts to invert together. Carefully remove the pan to reveal the tarte tatin, then slice and serve with vanilla ice cream.

Make Ahead Dough (step 1) can be made up to 1 day in advance of baking, stored in the refrigerator. Apples (steps 2 and 3) can be made up to 1 day in advance of baking, stored in an airtight container in the refrigerator. Tarte tatin (through step 6) can be made any time the day of serving, kept in the pan. Reheat in a 400°F oven for 5 to 10 minutes to warm through before serving (step 7).

Leftovers 5 days in the refrigerator.

steak 'n' cake

MENU

Brown Butter Parker House Rolls

Blue Cheese Ranch

Bloody Mary Shrimp Cocktail

Deviled Potatoes

Garlic-Parmesan Brussels Sprouts Gratin

Filet Mignon au Poivre

The Perfect Chocolate Cake with Ganache Frosting & Raspberry Filling

GROCERY LIST

PANTRY

- 4 c (540g) bread flour
- 2 c (270g) all-purpose flour
- 18 oz (3 c) dark chocolate chips
- 2¼ c (450g) granulated sugar
- 1½ c dry white wine
- 1 o olive oil
- 1 c (214g) packed light brown sugar
- ½ c plus 2 tbsp mayonnaise
- ½ c ketchup
- ½ c panko bread crumbs
- ½ c chicken stock
- ½ c (50g) cocoa powder
- ⅓ c vodka
- ⅓ c cognac
- 2 tbsp honey
- 2 tbsp Dijon mustard
- 2 tbsp neutral oil, such as vegetable, avocado, or sunflower
- 2 tsp Worcestershire sauce
- 2 tsp baking soda
- 1 tsp hot sauce
- 1 (¼-oz) package active dry yeast
- Nonstick cooking spray

SPICES, SEASONINGS, AND FLAVORINGS

- 4 tsp vanilla extract
- 1 tsp instant espresso
- ½ tsp smoked paprika
- 2 dried bay leaves
- Flaky sea salt
- KS&P (at least 2 c kosher salt and 1 jar whole black peppercorns to be safe)

MEAT

- 6 to 8 (8-oz) filet mignon steaks (depending on how many guests you have)

SEAFOOD

- 1 lb 16–20 shrimp, peeled and deveined with tails on

PRODUCE

- 4 lb (6 medium) russet potatoes
- 2 lb Brussels sprouts (pre-shredded if available)
- 1½ lb raspberries
- 4 medium shallots
- 1 lemon
- 2 heads garlic (10 cloves)
- 1 bunch chives
- 1 bunch dill
- 1 bunch parsley
- 1 small bunch thyme
- Assorted crudités, such as carrots, celery, radishes, cucumber, and kohlrabi

REFRIGERATED

- 1½ lb (6 sticks) unsalted butter
- 16 oz full-fat sour cream
- 4 oz blue cheese
- 2 c heavy cream
- 1 c plus 2 tablespoons buttermilk
- 1 c whole milk
- ¾ c finely grated Parmesan cheese
- 1 jar prepared horseradish (2 tbsp drained)
- 8 large eggs

♡Alex♡

PREP LIST

Up to 1 Week Ahead
- Brown the butter for the Parker House Rolls

Up to 3 Days Ahead
- Make the whipped honey butter for the Parker House Rolls
- Make the cocktail sauce for the Bloody Mary Shrimp Cocktail

Up to 2 Days Ahead
- Make the raspberry filling for the Perfect Chocolate Cake

Up to 1 Day Ahead
- Make the dough for the Parker House Rolls
- Make the Blue Cheese Ranch
- Poach the shrimp for the Bloody Mary Shrimp Cocktail
- Roast and assemble the Deviled Potatoes
- Cook the Brussels sprouts for the Brussels Sprouts Gratin
- Bake the cakes for the Perfect Chocolate Cake
- Make the ganache frosting for the Perfect Chocolate Cake
- Assemble the Perfect Chocolate Cake

Day Of
- Bake the Parker House Rolls
- Prep the crudités for the Blue Cheese Ranch
- Bake the Deviled Potatoes
- Parcook the steaks for the Filet Mignon au Poivre

1 Hour Before Guests Arrive
- Take out the whipped butter for the Parker House Rolls
- Assemble and bake the Brussels Sprouts Gratin
- Make sure the parcooked steaks are taken out to come to room temperature for the Filet Mignon au Poivre
- Keep the oven at 425°F

Right Before Guests Arrive
- Warm the Parker House Rolls (6 to 8 minutes at 425°F)
- Reheat the Deviled Potatoes (10 to 15 minutes at 425°F)
- Reheat the Brussels Sprouts Gratin (10 to 15 minutes at 425°F)
- Have a cast-iron pan preheating over low heat and have everything prepped to make the au poivre sauce

Game Time Pep Talk
Your Bloody Mary Shrimp Cocktail and Blue Cheese Ranch with crudités should both be plated and on the table. I made sure everything should be reheating in the oven because it's steak time! Feel free to put out the Parker House Rolls once warm alongside the whipped brown butter. Crank up the temperature on the cast iron and sear the steaks, then make the au poivre sauce while they rest. Transfer the Deviled Potatoes to a platter and put on the table with the Brussels Sprouts Gratin. For the Steak Au Poivre, you can either serve a platter of the steaks with the sauce on the side or you can slice the steaks and arrange on a platter with the sauce and chives. The Perfect Chocolate Cake should be already ready to slice and serve for dessert. You've got this!

Brown Butter Parker House Rolls

In our senior year at the Culinary Institute of America, my peers and I were able to enjoy a cute three-course repast at the student-run restaurants as part of our meal plan if it was a slow day, helping add a little extra hustle and bustle to the learning chefs-in-training. I've always identified as a lady who lunches, and this was the first time I got to live out my truth, gabbing with my friends at the American Bounty Restaurant over a cast-iron tray of glistening Parker House rolls that just popped out of the oven. It was the first moment on my journey to realizing that there's no faster way to make people feel loved than starting a meal with warm, freshly baked bread. And since this is a celebration menu, I want my guests to feel nothing but gushy feelings of love, and maybe an overwhelming need to lie down after dessert. These Parker House rolls get the slightest zhuzh by browning the butter that enriches and glosses the dough to add subtle notes of nuttiness. And since subtleness isn't the name of the game at a party, we might as well brown extra butter to whip up with honey for schmearing. It's the only way to roll up to the party!

Make 12 rolls | Prep Time: 45 minutes, plus cooling time and lots of proofing time | Cook Time: 30 minutes

Brown Butter
12 ounces (3 sticks) unsalted butter

Dough
1 cup whole milk, heated to 115°F
¼ cup brown butter, melted, but not hotter than 115°F
¼ cup (50g) granulated sugar
1 (¼-ounce) package active dry yeast

3 large eggs
4 cups (540g) bread flour
1½ teaspoons kosher salt
2 tablespoons olive oil, for greasing

Whipped Brown Honey Butter
1 cup brown butter, at room temperature
2 tablespoons honey

1 teaspoon kosher salt

Baking
2 tablespoons olive oil, for greasing
1 large egg, lightly beaten
Flaky sea salt

¼ cup brown butter, melted

(cont.)

1. Make the brown butter: In a medium saucepan, melt the butter over medium-high heat. Cook, stirring continuously, until browned and nutty in aroma, 8 to 10 minutes. Transfer to a heatproof bowl and let cool completely. If you're in a rush to cool, place the bowl over ice and whisk the brown butter until cooled. Store in an airtight container in the refrigerator for up to 1 week.

2. Make the dough: In the bowl of a stand mixer fitted with the whisk attachment, mix the warm milk, ¼ cup of the brown butter, and the sugar to dissolve, then sprinkle the yeast over the top. Let stand until foamy, 5 to 10 minutes. Add the eggs, then whisk on medium speed until incorporated.

3. Switch to the dough hook. Add the flour and salt to the mixture in the bowl and, beginning on low speed and gradually increasing to medium, knead until a smooth, elastic dough forms, 3 to 4 minutes.

4. Grease a bowl at least twice the size of your dough with the olive oil. Dip your hands in the oil to grease them before transferring the dough to the bowl. Cover with plastic wrap or a lid and refrigerate overnight. (Alternatively, you could let the dough rise at room temperature until it has doubled in size, 1½ to 2 hours.)

5. Meanwhile, make the whipped brown honey butter: Clean out the bowl of the stand mixer and the whisk attachment and return both to the mixer. Add 1 cup of the brown butter, the honey, and salt. Whip until light and fluffy, about 2 minutes. Transfer to an airtight container, then refrigerate until ready to serve. The whipped butter lasts in the refrigerator for up to 5 days.

6. Prepare the rolls for baking: The next day, punch down the dough to release any air bubbles, then transfer to a clean work surface. Using a bench scraper, divide the dough into 12 equal pieces. Cup your hand and fingers around each piece of dough and roll on the work surface into a tight ball.

7. Grease a 12-inch cast-iron pan (or 9 by 13-inch baking pan) with the olive oil. Arrange the balls of dough in the pan, spacing each 1 inch apart. Cover with plastic wrap and refrigerate until 1 hour before your guests arrive/baking. (Alternatively, you could let the dough rise at room temperature until the rolls fill up the pan, about 1 hour.)

8. At least 45 minutes before baking, preheat the oven to 425°F. Take the whipped brown honey butter out of the refrigerator to soften.

9. Brush the rolls with the beaten egg and sprinkle a heavy pinch of flaky salt on top. Bake for 15 to 18 minutes, until golden brown. Immediately when the rolls come out of the oven, brush with the remaining brown butter. Let cool for 10 minutes, then serve alongside a bowl of the whipped brown honey butter for schmearing.

Make Ahead Brown butter can be made up to 1 week in advance, stored in an airtight container in the refrigerator, or 1 month in advance, stored in an airtight container in the freezer. Whipped honey butter (step 5) can be made up to 3 days in advance, stored in an airtight container in the refrigerator. Rolls can be baked anytime the day of serving, reheating in the oven as needed to warm.

Leftovers Rolls for 5 days at room temperature. Whipped honey butter for 5 days in the refrigerator.

blue cheese ranch

Nothing could stop my mother from ruining her appetite at any steakhouse like a tray of crudités on ice with a bowl of blue cheese dressing. Since I'm my mother's son, I proudly continue the tradition. The cold, crisp crunch of the veggies balanced by the creamy tang of the dressing adds the exact contrast I want to any warm breadbasket, so I can volley back and forth until it's time for steak. I may get some hate from this, but I kind of feel like blue cheese dressing is just ranch with blue cheese instead of herbs, and vice versa. Since I love shoveling both options into my mouth with a celery stick, it was an easy choice to combine the two into an herby, funky dip that turns even the saddest bowl of baby carrots into a spectacle.

Makes 1¾ cups ranch | Prep Time: 10 minutes

Ranch
8 ounces (1 cup) full-fat sour cream
4 ounces blue cheese, crumbled (1 cup)
¼ cup minced fresh chives
¼ cup minced fresh dill
¼ cup minced fresh parsley
2 tablespoons mayonnaise
2 tablespoons buttermilk
1 teaspoon finely grated lemon zest
1 garlic clove, finely grated
KS&P

Serving
Crushed ice
Assorted crudités, such as carrots, celery, radishes, cucumber, and kohlrabi

1. Make the ranch: In a medium bowl, whisk together the sour cream, blue cheese, chives, dill, parsley, mayonnaise, buttermilk, lemon zest, garlic, and a heavy pinch each of salt and pepper until well combined. Taste and adjust the seasoning with salt and pepper, then store in the refrigerator in an airtight container until ready to serve. The ranch keeps in the refrigerator for up to 5 days.

2. To serve: Cover a platter with crushed ice, then arrange the crudités over top. Nestle a bowl of the ranch into the ice, then serve.

Make Ahead Ranch can be made up to 1 day in advance.

Leftovers 5 days in the refrigerator.

BLOODY MARY SHRIMP COCKTAIL

I hate shrimp. Whew, I feel so much lighter now that I got that off my chest. Maybe it's the texture? Or maybe it's the flavor (or lack thereof)? Maybe it's the trickle down of generations of kosher homes and only relatively recent introduction of treif into our family's culinary lexicon? Whatever it is, in my best *Shark Tank* voice, *I'm out*. But much to my chagrin, it's not all about me. I have many family members who love nothing more than to take down a shrimp cocktail, so you better believe I still know how to turn it out. We're going to poach the shrimp in a delicate broth of white wine and aromatics until just tender and quickly shock them in ice water to ensure they don't overcook into curls of rubber. We'll also whip up a punchy cocktail sauce that's very much a mashup of a cocktail (Bloody Mary) and a sauce (vodka sauce). By simmering horseradish and shallots in vodka until it's mostly evaporated, you cook off most of the alcohol, leaving only trace amounts, which amplify all the flavors so even a simple ketchup concoction really POPS. Put the two together and you have an upgraded classic that will blow away the shrimp lovers in your life and make even a stubborn shellfish hater like me feel like I'm missing out.

Serves 6 to 8 | Prep Time: 20 minutes | Cook Time: 20 minutes

Bloody Mary Cocktail Sauce
⅓ cup vodka
2 tablespoons drained prepared horseradish
½ teaspoon freshly ground black pepper
½ medium shallot, minced

½ cup ketchup
2 teaspoons Worcestershire sauce
1 teaspoon hot sauce
KS

Poached Shrimp
4 cups water
1 cup dry white wine
2 teaspoons kosher salt
1 teaspoon whole black peppercorns
4 thyme sprigs

2 dried bay leaves
2 garlic cloves, smashed
1 pound 16–20 shrimp, peeled and deveined with tails on

Serving
1 tablespoon olive oil
1 tablespoon freshly squeezed lemon juice

Minced fresh dill, for garnish
Flaky sea salt, for garnish

1. Make the Bloody Mary cocktail sauce: In a small saucepan, combine the vodka, horseradish, black pepper, and shallot. Bring to a simmer and cook until almost all of the liquid has evaporated, 3 to 4 minutes. Transfer to a bowl and stir in the ketchup, Worcestershire sauce, hot sauce, and a heavy pinch

of salt. Taste and adjust the seasoning with salt, then store in an airtight container in the refrigerator until ready to serve. This cocktail sauce lasts in the refrigerator for up to 5 days.

2. Poach the shrimp: In a medium saucepan, combine the water, wine, salt, peppercorns, thyme, bay leaves, and garlic. Bring to a boil, then reduce the heat to maintain a simmer and cook for 10 minutes. Meanwhile, fill a medium bowl with ice and water.

3. After 10 minutes, remove the poaching liquid from the heat and add the shrimp. Let poach from the residual heat until fully cooked, about 3 minutes. Using a slotted spoon, transfer the shrimp to the ice bath to chill. Drain the shrimp and pat dry with paper towels. Transfer to a bowl and refrigerate until ready to serve.

4. Serve the shrimp cocktail: Toss the chilled shrimp with the olive oil and lemon juice to coat. Transfer to a platter and garnish with dill and flaky sea salt, then serve alongside a bowl of the Bloody Mary cocktail sauce.

Make Ahead Cocktail sauce can be made (step 1) up to 3 days in advance, stored in an airtight container in the refrigerator. Shrimp can be poached (steps 2 and 3) up to 1 day in advance, stored in an airtight container in the refrigerator.

Leftovers 3 days in the refrigerator.

Deviled Potatoes

What is a steak dinner without a potato on the side? This recipe gives the humble spud a deviled-egg-meets-potato-skin treatment to scratch every kind of starchy itch you could crave. You start with baked potatoes, then halve and scoop them to whip up with sour cream, mayo, and Dijon for a creamy mash to refill the skins before baking until golden. The result is a crispy golden potato skin that, when cut into, reveals a fluffy mashed potato filling that's both rich and just a bit tangy in the best way possible. Past the obvious goal of everyone losing their minds over these potatoes, this recipe can be fully prepped or even finished in advance, so you have one less thing to worry about while you focus on not overcooking the steak. Leave it to the most devilish dishes to give you a little taste of heaven!

Serves 6 to 8 | Prep Time: 15 minutes, plus cooling time | Cook Time: 1 hour and 30 minutes

4 pounds (6 medium) russet potatoes, scrubbed
2 tablespoons olive oil
KS&P
½ cup sour cream

½ cup mayonnaise
2 tablespoons Dijon mustard
½ teaspoon smoked paprika
Minced fresh parsley, for garnish

1. Preheat the oven to 425°F. Line a sheet pan with parchment paper.

2. Place the potatoes on the prepared sheet pan. Using a fork, poke a few holes into each potato, then rub with the olive oil and a heavy pinch each of salt and pepper.

3. Bake for 50 minutes to 1 hour, until tender. Let cool.

4. Transfer the potatoes to a cutting board. Slice each potato in half lengthwise. Scoop most of the flesh out of each half and transfer to a medium bowl. Return the potato skins back to the sheet pan, skin-side down. Season each with a pinch of salt and pepper.

5. Using a potato masher, mash the scooped-out flesh until mainly smooth. Stir in the sour cream, mayonnaise, mustard, paprika, and 2 heavy pinches each of salt and pepper until well incorporated. Taste and adjust the seasoning with salt and pepper, then spoon into the potato skins, dividing evenly.

6. Bake for 25 to 30 minutes, until golden and crisp. Serve immediately or keep warm. Garnish with the minced parsley right before serving.

Make Ahead Potatoes can be roasted and filled (through step 5) up to 1 day in advance, stored on a sheet pan covered in plastic wrap in the refrigerator. Potatoes can be finished (step 6) a few hours before serving, reheating in the oven as needed.

Leftovers 5 days in the refrigerator.

Garlic-Parmesan Brussels Sprouts Gratin

Here's the dilemma: We need a vegetable on the table that can add a touch of levity to a heavy-ish spread while still hitting all the cozy feelings of comfort to stay on theme. Creamed spinach? Too rich and no texture. Sauteed spinach? Too much of a headache since pounds of spinach wilt to nothing and must be cooked right before serving. Roasted asparagus? Too basic and it fades into the background. That's not to say I don't love these sides when I'm dining out, but a celebration menu you're cooking deserves only the best! With these concerns in mind, we're going to turn to the hearty Brussels sprout to save the day. Shredded sprouts (I encourage you to buy the pre-shredded bags at the store) are sauteed with garlic and white wine before getting hit with just a bit of cream and Parm for richness and baked in a cheesy bread crumb crust. It's the lightest gratin you'll ever make and will stand up to our steak and potatoes with as much ease as it takes to throw together. And since I'm unwell and focus on these things, it's always the first dish my guests reach back to for seconds (the highest compliment!).

Serves 6 to 8 | Prep Time: 15 minutes | Cook Time: 30 minutes

Sprouts
2 tablespoons olive oil
2 pounds Brussels sprouts, shredded
2 teaspoons thyme leaves, finely chopped
4 garlic cloves, thinly sliced
1 medium shallot, thinly sliced
KS&P
½ cup white wine (or water)
½ cup heavy cream
½ cup finely grated Parmesan cheese

Topping
½ cup panko bread crumbs
¼ cup finely grated Parmesan cheese
2 tablespoons olive oil
1 garlic clove, finely grated
Pinch kosher salt

1. Prepare the Brussels sprouts: Preheat the oven to 425°F.

2. In a large pot or Dutch oven, heat the olive oil over medium-high heat. Add the Brussels sprouts, thyme, garlic, shallot, and 2 heavy pinches each of salt and pepper. Cook, stirring often, until softened and lightly golden, 4 to 5 minutes. Stir in the wine and cook until all the liquid has evaporated and the sprouts are just tender, about 2 minutes more. Add the cream and Parmesan and cook, stirring to coat the sprouts, for 1 minute more. Transfer to a 9 by 13-inch baking dish.

3. Make the topping: In a small bowl, toss together the bread crumbs, Parmesan, olive oil, garlic, and salt to combine. Sprinkle evenly over the sprouts.

4. Bake for 20 minutes, or until golden, then serve or keep warm.

Make Ahead Sprouts can be prepared (steps 1 and 2) up to 1 day in advance, stored in the refrigerator. Gratin can be assembled and baked up to 1 hour before serving, reheating in the oven as needed.

Leftovers 5 days in the refrigerator.

FILET MIGNON AU POIVRE

This entire menu was inspired by the fact that I've been raised to celebrate all joyous occasions at a steakhouse. Since cooking for others is my love language, I think there is no better way to express my feelings than turning my kitchen into Keens (my family's preferred purveyor of porterhouses) for the evening. Of course, in my NYC apartment that meant running the vent fan, opening all windows, cracking the door, and having a towel ready to wave at the fire alarm that would always go off without fail. And while I think it's all part of the steak-night experience, I've turned to reverse-searing the steaks to make sure any smoke or screeching noises are coming exclusively from my guests. Reverse-searing just means we're going to cook the steaks low-and-slow on a wire rack in the oven until almost ready and then quickly sear them in the pan before serving. This way you can finish your steaks on the stovetop without smoking out your kitchen or disappearing for too long. While ideally you would pop your steaks in the oven as close to searing as possible, I've found that you even can bake them off in the morning to be extra prepped. Just keep them covered in the fridge once cooled and let them sit out for an hour to come to room temperature before searing. Now that you have a flawless filet, it's time to smother it in a creamy peppercorn sauce. We're taking the au poivre route not only because it's divine and comes together in minutes, but because, according to my mother, it's a mandatory requirement, the star of any celebration, whether for her or not. She'd want me to preface that this leverage is because she now is a flexitarian, only eating meat on three occasions: a Passover brisket, a Thanksgiving turkey, and when I'm hosting steak night. It would only be fair to let her request her favorite sauce on such a special meal. Luckily, it's my favorite now, too . . . and soon to be yours!

Serves 6 to 8 | Prep Time: 20 minutes, plus resting time | Cook Time: 1 hour

Reverse-Seared Steaks
6 to 8 (8-ounce) filet mignon steaks

KS&P

Au Poivre Sauce
2 tablespoons neutral oil, such as vegetable, avocado, or sunflower
2 tablespoons unsalted butter
2 garlic cloves, smashed
2 thyme sprigs
2 teaspoons coarsely ground black pepper

2 medium shallots, minced
⅓ cup cognac
½ cup chicken stock
½ cup heavy cream
KS
Minced fresh chives, for garnish

(cont.)

1. Reverse sear the steaks: Preheat the oven to 200°F. Line a sheet pan with a wire rack.

2. Season the steaks liberally with 2 heavy pinches each of salt and pepper. Place on the wire rack, spaced 2 inches apart.

3. Bake for 45 to 55 minutes, until the steaks reach an internal temperature of 120°F. Let rest for at least 10 minutes.

4. Sear the steaks and make the au poivre sauce: In a large cast-iron pan, heat the oil over medium-high heat. Pat the steaks dry with paper towels, then add to the pan. Cook until the bottoms of the steaks are golden brown, 1 to 2 minutes. Flip and add the butter, garlic, and thyme. Cook, basting the steaks with the butter, until golden brown, another 1 to 2 minutes. Transfer the steaks to a platter to rest while you make the sauce. Discard the garlic and thyme sprigs.

5. Reduce the heat to medium and add the pepper and shallots. Cook until softened, 2 to 3 minutes. Add the cognac to the pan, followed by the stock. Bring to a simmer and cook until reduced by half, about 2 minutes. Stir in the cream and a heavy pinch of salt and simmer until slightly thickened, about 1 minute. Remove from the heat, then taste and adjust the seasoning with salt.

6. Pour the sauce over the steaks, then garnish with chives and serve.

Make Ahead Steaks can be parcooked in the oven (through step 3) anytime the day you're serving them, stored in an airtight container in the refrigerator if it will be more than 1 hour before searing and serving. If chilling the parcooked steaks, let them come to room temperature for 1 hour before searing.

Leftovers 3 days in the refrigerator.

The Perfect Chocolate Cake with Ganache Frosting & Raspberry Filling

This is the recipe that took the most amount of work and it may also be the best thing you'll make out of this book. And with the same enthusiasm as Nathan Lane in the bakery scene of *The Birdcage*, it's *a triumph*! I wanted it to be as chocolatey and moist as possible, so we're putting the work in. That means a combo of butter for flavor and olive oil for both moistness and a hint of acidity to pair with the chocolate. That means a combo of cocoa powder and melted ganache, plus some instant espresso, for an intense richness. That means a healthy glug of buttermilk for a tender crumb and fluffy rise. And that's just for the cake. In between our rounds, we're layering a bright raspberry jam that both balances the chocolatiness and soaks into the cakes to keep them extra moist for days. As for the frosting, I had tried every variation of chocolate buttercream, but all fluffy frostings faded away the second I tried a fudgy chocolate ganache to crown this masterpiece. (And while we're making a layer cake here, if you don't have round cake pans, no problem. This recipe bakes up beautifully in a 9 by 13-inch baking dish in 35 to 38 minutes.) So much love went into developing this cake and, trust me, you can taste it.

Makes 1 (9-inch) layer cake | Prep Time: 45 minutes, plus cooling time | Cook Time: 30 minutes

Chocolate Cake
Nonstick cooking spray
6 ounces (1 cup) dark chocolate chips
4 ounces (1 stick) unsalted butter
1 cup water
½ cup (50g) cocoa powder
¼ cup olive oil
1 teaspoon instant espresso
1 cup (214g) packed light brown sugar
1 cup (200g) granulated sugar
4 large eggs
1 tablespoon vanilla extract
1½ teaspoons kosher salt
2 cups (270g) all-purpose flour
2 teaspoons baking soda
1 cup buttermilk

Raspberry Filling
1 pound raspberries
½ cup (100g) granulated sugar
1 tablespoon freshly squeezed lemon juice
¼ teaspoon kosher salt

Ganache Frosting
1 cup heavy cream
½ cup (100g) granulated sugar
1 teaspoon vanilla extract
1 teaspoon kosher salt
12 ounces (2 cups) dark chocolate chips
8 tablespoons (4 ounces) unsalted butter, cold and cubed

Assembly
Fresh raspberries, for garnish

(cont.)

1. Make the chocolate cake: Preheat the oven to 350°F. Grease two 9-inch round cake pans with nonstick cooking spray and line with parchment paper.

2. In a medium saucepan, combine the chocolate chips, butter, water, cocoa powder, olive oil, and instant espresso over medium heat. Cook, whisking often, until the chocolate has melted and the mixture is smooth, 3 to 4 minutes.

3. In a large bowl, whisk together the sugars and eggs until smooth, followed by the vanilla and salt. Slowly whisk in the chocolate mixture until smooth.

4. In a medium bowl, stir together the flour and baking soda to combine. Alternate whisking in half of the flour mixture and half of the buttermilk into the chocolate mixture until all is incorporated and you have a smooth batter. Divide the batter between the prepared cake pans evenly (about 800g of batter per pan).

5. Bake for 28 to 30 minutes, until the cakes dome with no jiggle. Let cool for 20 minutes in the pan. Run a knife or offset spatula around the edge of each cake and invert them onto a wire rack, discarding the parchment. Let cool completely.

6. Meanwhile, make the raspberry filling: In a medium saucepan, combine the raspberries, sugar, lemon juice, and salt over medium-high heat. Cook until the raspberries have broken down and the mixture thickens, 15 to 18 minutes. Makes 1½ cups of filling. Transfer to a medium heatproof bowl and let cool completely.

7. Make the ganache frosting: In a medium saucepan, combine the cream, sugar, vanilla, and salt. Bring to a simmer over medium-high heat and cook until the sugar has dissolved, 1 minute. Remove from the heat and whisk in the chocolate chips and butter until a smooth ganache forms. Transfer to a medium heatproof bowl and place plastic wrap or parchment directly onto the surface of the ganache. Let cool completely. (The ganache should be firm but still spreadable.)

8. Assemble the cake: On a cake stand or platter, dollop 1 tablespoon of the ganache in the center and place one of the cakes on top to hold in place. Spoon 1 cup of the ganache around the outer border of the cake to make a 1-inch ring, smoothing with an offset spatula. Spread the raspberry filling evenly within the ring. Place the second cake over the filling, then spoon on the remaining ganache, spreading to cover the top of the cake. Run an offset spatula around the sides of the cake to smooth any ganache spilling onto the sides for a slightly-frosted-naked-cake-look.

9. Let sit for at least 1 hour to let the ganache set and the filling soak into the cake. Decorate with fresh raspberries, then slice and serve.

Make Ahead Chocolate cake (through step 5) can be made up to 1 day in advance of assembling, covering each cake with plastic wrap and storing at room temperature. Raspberry filling (step 6) can be made up to 2 days in advance, stored in an airtight container in the refrigerator. Ganache frosting (step 7) can be made up to 4 hours in advance of frosting. Cake can be assembled up to 1 day in advance of serving, stored under a cake dome or large pot at room temperature.

Leftovers 5 days at room temperature.

A springy **Passover** Seder menu to remind us of days long ago.

Let My People Nosh

MENU

Garlic Matzo
Ashkenazi Charoset
Jammy Eggs with Horseradish Mayo
Rainbow Gefilte Fish
Brighter Chicken Soup
Garlicky Matzo Balls
Crunch Salad Supreme
Paprika Potatoes
Celery-Heavy Brisket with Caramelized Lemon & Leeks
Apricot Chicken with Roasted Asparagus
Matzo & Almond Strawberry Cobbler
Charoset Truffles

GROCERY LIST

PANTRY

12 oz (2 c) dark chocolate chips
12 oz (2 packed cups) pitted Medjool dates
6 oz (1 packed cup) dried apricots
10 c chicken stock
3¾ c matzo meal
2½ c olive oil
2 c white wine
2 c walnuts
2 c (224g) finely ground almond flour
2½ c neutral oil, such as vegetable, avocado, or sunflower
1¼ c (250g) granulated sugar
1 c potato starch
1 c Castelvetrano olives
1 c toasted pistachios
½ c Manischewitz wine
½ c golden raisins
½ c seltzer
½ c honey
⅓ c apricot preserves
¼ c date syrup (or honey)
2 tbsp balsamic vinegar
2 tsp coconut oil
¾ c mayonnaise
2 boxes matzo
2 jars prepared beet horseradish
6 in butcher's twine

SPICES, SEASONINGS, AND FLAVORINGS

2 tbsp garlic powder
1 tbsp onion powder
1 tbsp plus ½ tsp smoked paprika
1½ tsp ground cinnamon
1 tsp almond extract (or the seeds scraped from 1 vanilla bean)
4 dried bay leaves
Flaky sea salt
KS&P (at least 2 c kosher salt and 1 jar whole black peppercorns to be safe)

MEAT

5 to 6 lb bone-in, skin-on chicken thighs and drumsticks
1 (6-lb) whole chicken
1 (6-lb) beef brisket

SEAFOOD

3 lb whitefish, such as haddock or cod

PRODUCE

5 lb red potatoes
4 lb strawberries
3 lb asparagus
1½ lb (about 5 medium) Honeycrisp apples
1 lb cremini mushrooms
7 lemons
1 lime
4 medium fennel bulbs
7 medium carrots
4 medium parsnips
4 medium yellow onions
3 heads romaine lettuce
2 medium daikon radishes
4 heads garlic (39 cloves)
3 bunches fresh parsley
2 bunches fresh dill
2 bunches celery
1 bunch chives
1 bunch scallions
1 bunch thyme (10 sprigs)
1 bunch leeks
1 jalapeño (optional)
1 (2-in) piece ginger
1 (2-in) piece horseradish

REFRIGERATED

2 dozen large eggs

Judy! (Jew-dy)

PREP LIST

Up to 5 Days Ahead
- Make the Garlic Matzo

Up to 3 Days Ahead
- Make the Ashkenazi Charoset
- Make the Mock Chopped Liver
- Make the Charoset Truffles

Up to 2 Days Ahead
- Boil the eggs for the Jammy Eggs
- Make the Gefilte Fish
- Make the Brighter Chicken Soup
- Cook the Celery-Heavy Brisket

Up to 1 Day Ahead
- Make the horseradish mayo for the Jammy Eggs
- Make the mixture for the Matzo Balls
- Make the dressing for the Crunch Salad Supreme
- Slice the Celery-Heavy Brisket
- Marinate the Apricot Chicken

Day Of
- Peel the eggs and prep the chives for the Jammy Eggs
- Prep the vegetables for the Crunch Salad Supreme
- Roast the Paprika Potatoes
- Prep the asparagus and assemble the Apricot Chicken
- Bake the Matzo & Almond Strawberry Cobbler

1 Hour Before Guests Arrive
- Reheat the Brighter Chicken Soup
- Cook the Matzo Balls
- Reheat the Celery-Heavy Brisket
- Roast the Apricot Chicken
- Reduce the oven to 350°F

Right Before Guests Arrive
- Reheat the Paprika Potatoes (10 to 15 minutes)
- Reheat the Apricot Chicken, if needed (10 to 15 minutes)

Right Before Serving
- Assemble the Jammy Eggs with Horseradish Mayo
- Assemble the Crunch Salad Supreme

Right Before Dessert
- Reheat the Matzo & Almond Strawberry Cobbler, if desired (10 to 15 minutes)

Game Time Pep Talk
The Garlic Matzo and Mock Chopped Liver should be ready and put out. The Ashkenazi Charoset and Jammy Eggs with Horseradish Mayo should be on the table, ready to be incorporated into Seder. The Brighter Chicken Soup and Matzo Balls should each be kept warm on the stovetop ready to serve during the meal. The Crunch Salad Supreme should be dressed and ready. The Celery-Heavy Brisket should be warm on the stovetop. The Apricot Chicken and Paprika Potatoes should be warm in the oven, so once you plate them it's time to serve dinner. Remember to reheat the Matzo & Almond Strawberry Cobbler before dessert, which is optional but a lovely touch. The Charoset Truffles should be ready in the refrigerator to serve with dessert. You've got this! Chag sameach!

GARLIC MATZO

To be totally honest, matzo is a wonderful blank canvas. While it lacks seasoning on its own, we're tossing shards of matzo with oil, salt, and spices to toast in the oven until golden and crisp. These crackers become the ideal crunchy nosh to scoop up some chopped liver, whether real or mock. The magic is in the salt, so feel free to go as heavy or light with the spices as your heart desires!

Serves 8 to 10 | Prep Time: 10 minutes, plus soaking and cooling time | Cook Time: 10 minutes

½ cup neutral oil, such as vegetable, avocado, or sunflower

2 teaspoons garlic powder

1 teaspoon kosher salt

½ teaspoon smoked paprika

1 box matzo, broken into 3-inch pieces

1. Preheat the oven to 400°F.

2. In a small bowl, stir together the oil, garlic powder, salt, and paprika. Place the matzo in a large sealable plastic bag, then pour in the oil mixture. Seal the bag closed and gently shake to coat the matzo well. Let sit for 30 minutes, shaking every 10 minutes, for the oil mixture to soak into the matzo.

3. Divide the matzo pieces between 2 sheet pans in an even layer. Bake for 8 to 10 minutes, until golden and crisp. Let cool completely on the pans. Store in an airtight container.

Make Ahead Garlic matzo can be made up to 5 days in advance, stored in an airtight container at room temperature.

Leftovers 8 days at room temperature.

ashkenazi charoset

The queen of Jewish cookbooks (and my dear friend and mentor) Joan Nathan has put in the hard work to document the variations of Passover charoset from across the Diaspora. And while Joan loves to put out a flight of different recipes for representing various Jewish communities around the world, today we're just going to perfect the classic Ashkenazi charoset that I've been making since Hebrew school. We're starting by rehydrating golden raisins in a sweet mixture of honey, Manischewitz wine, and cinnamon to toss with a combo of chopped and grated Honeycrisp apples (the combo provides both body and texture!) and chopped walnuts. It's just sweet enough, while still packing a pop of acidity from the apples and lemon. Let this recipe be your starting point, and then feel free to hit up my girl Joan for extra credit.

Makes about 4 cups | Prep Time: 15 minutes, plus overnight chilling | Cook Time: 5 minutes

½ cup Manischewitz wine
½ cup golden raisins
2 tablespoons honey
½ teaspoon ground cinnamon
½ teaspoon kosher salt

1 lemon, zested and juiced
1½ pounds (about 5 medium) Honeycrisp apples, peeled and cored
1 cup toasted walnuts, finely chopped

1. In a small saucepan, combine the wine, raisins, honey, cinnamon, salt, and lemon zest and juice. Bring to a simmer over medium-high heat and cook for 2 minutes, then remove from the heat.
2. Coarsely grate 2 of the apples, and finely chop the others. Add both to a medium bowl with the walnuts and pour the raisin mixture over the top, stirring until well combined.
3. Transfer to an airtight container and refrigerate overnight before serving.

Make Ahead Charoset can be made up to 3 days in advance, stored in an airtight container in the refrigerator.

Leftovers 5 days in the refrigerator.

Jammy Eggs with Horseradish Mayo

While my Seders always include a plate of plain hard-boiled eggs to be passed around and dipped in saltwater before the meal, I can't give up an opportunity to zhuzh up a little edible symbolism. Instead of a full hard-boil, we're cooking our eggs until the yolks are jammy before halving them to be topped with a spoonful of beet horseradish–tinted mayo. The pink dollop paired with the soft yolk creates the same vibe as a deviled egg, but is so much easier to throw together. It's the chicest beitzah you've ever seen!

Serves 8 to 10 | Prep Time: 20 minutes | Cook Time: 10 minutes

10 large eggs, at room temperature
¾ cup mayonnaise
3 tablespoons drained jarred beet horseradish
1 teaspoon finely grated lemon zest

1 garlic clove, finely grated
KS&P
Minced fresh chives, for garnish

1. Bring a medium pot of water to a boil and fill a medium bowl with ice and water. Using a slotted spoon, lay the eggs carefully on the bottom of the pot of boiling water. Reduce the heat to maintain a simmer and cook for 8 minutes. Using the slotted spoon, transfer the eggs to the ice bath and let cool for 5 minutes, then drain.

2. In a medium bowl, whisk together the mayonnaise, beet horseradish, lemon zest, garlic, and a heavy pinch each of salt and pepper to combine. Taste and adjust the seasoning with salt and pepper.

3. Peel the eggs and slice each in half. Arrange them on a platter, cut-side up. Spoon dollops of the mayo over the eggs, then garnish with chives and serve.

Make Ahead Eggs can be boiled up to 2 days in advance, stored in an airtight container in the refrigerator. They can be peeled anytime the day you are serving, stored in an airtight container in the refrigerator. Horseradish mayo can be made up to 1 day in advance, stored in an airtight container in the refrigerator. Assemble right before serving.

Leftovers Doesn't hold well but can be saved and chopped into egg salad!

Mock Chopped Liver

If you want the real stuff, you can head over to *Jew-ish* and find my decadent Salted Honey Chopped Liver recipe. But most of the time, my family, who naturally has a history of high cholesterol, always requests the mock version. (Though it won't stop them from telling you their latest LDL numbers!) For this vegan version, we're cooking down mushrooms, walnuts, fennel, and onions for all that earthy richness before pulsing it all in the food processor into a chunky dip. This is hands down my favorite recipe from this menu and should not be slept on. Just don't fill up on it, since we worked hard on the full meal ahead!

Serves 8 to 10 | Prep Time: 20 minutes, plus cooling time | Cook Time: 25 minutes

3 tablespoons olive oil
1 pound cremini mushrooms, thinly sliced
1 cup toasted walnuts, roughly chopped
8 garlic cloves, smashed and peeled
2 medium fennel bulbs, diced
2 medium yellow onions, thinly sliced

KS&P
2 tablespoons balsamic vinegar
2 tablespoons honey
Minced fresh chives, for garnish
Garlic Matzo (page 265), for serving
Celery sticks, for serving

1. In a large skillet or braiser, heat the olive oil over medium-high heat. Add the mushrooms, garlic, fennel, onions, and 2 heavy pinches each of salt and pepper. Cook, stirring often, until softened and lightly golden, about 20 minutes. Stir in the vinegar and honey and cook for another 5 minutes, or until lightly caramelized.

2. Transfer to a food processor and pulse until coarsely chopped, with the consistency of chopped liver. Taste and adjust the seasoning with salt and pepper. Let cool slightly, then transfer to a serving bowl. Serve warm or at room temperature, garnishing with chives and serving with garlic matzo and celery sticks.

Make Ahead Mock chopped liver can be made up to 3 days in advance, stored in an airtight container in the refrigerator.

Leftovers 5 days in the refrigerator.

Rainbow Gefilte Fish

While you can always outsource your gefilte fish needs to Costco, like my family often does, this is a stunning shortcut recipe to shock your family with your commitment to tradition. Tradition!!! Now that I have *Fiddler* stuck in your head, we're making rainbow cookie–inspired loaves, splitting our fish to make three layers: one colored orange with carrots, one plain with onion, and one colored green with fresh herbs. The concept came from my friend Michael Kleinmann, and it's pure genius. Baked in the oven, this gefilte fish luckily doesn't require any fish bones for a gelatinous stock or live carp in the bathtub. But it still tastes like you tried, so eat your heart out, Kirkland!

Makes 2 (9-inch) loaves | Prep Time: 30 minutes | Cook Time: 55 minutes

Carrot Layer

- 8 ounces (3 medium) carrots, peeled and cut into 2-inch pieces
- ⅓ medium yellow onion
- 1 pound whitefish, such as haddock or cod, cut into 2-inch pieces
- ¼ cup matzo meal
- 1 tablespoon granulated sugar
- 2 teaspoons kosher salt
- 1 large egg

Plain Layer

- ⅓ medium yellow onion
- 1 pound whitefish, such as haddock or cod, cut into 2-inch pieces
- ¼ cup matzo meal
- 1 tablespoon granulated sugar
- 2 teaspoons kosher salt
- 1 large egg

Herbed Layer

- 1 bunch (2 cups) parsley, leaves and tender stems
- ½ bunch (1 cup) dill, fronds and tender stems
- ⅓ medium yellow onion
- 1 pound whitefish, such as haddock or cod, cut into 2-inch pieces
- ¼ cup matzo meal
- 1 tablespoon granulated sugar
- 2 teaspoons kosher salt
- 1 large egg

1. Preheat the oven to 325°F. Line 2 (9 by 5-inch) loaf pans with parchment paper.

2. Make the carrot layer: In a food processor, combine the carrots and onion and pulse until minced. Add the whitefish, matzo meal, sugar, salt, and egg, then pulse, scraping the sides of the bowl as needed, until relatively smooth with speckles of carrot and onion. Divide between the 2 prepared pans, spreading in an even layer.

3. Make the plain layer: Wipe out the food processor, then add the onion and pulse until minced. Add the whitefish, matzo meal, sugar, salt, and egg, then pulse, scraping the sides of the bowl as needed,

until relatively smooth with speckles of onion. Divide between the 2 prepared pans, spreading in an even layer over the carrot layer.

4. Make the herbed layer: In the food processor (no need to wipe out), combine the parsley, dill, and onion and pulse until minced. Add the whitefish, matzo meal, sugar, salt, and egg, then pulse, scraping the sides of the bowl as needed, until relatively smooth with speckles of herbs and onion. Divide between the 2 prepared pans, spreading in an even layer over the plain layer.

5. Bake for 45 to 55 minutes, until the gefilte fish reaches an internal temperature of 145°F. Let cool completely in the pan. Cover and refrigerate for at least 4 hours, then slice and serve.

Make Ahead Gefilte fish can be made up to 2 days in advance, stored in an airtight container in the refrigerator.

Leftovers 3 days in the refrigerator or 3 months in the freezer.

Brighter Chicken Soup

A new chicken soup! I've tackled every version, from homemade stock with roasted legs to fortified broth with a whole simmered chicken, and this recipe is just the way I've been making it as of late, pairing a streamlined process with some unexpected twists. We're popping a whole bird into our pot and roasting it in the oven before adding all our stock and vegetables to simmer away. To brighten things up, ginger, a squeeze of lime juice, tons of fresh herbs, and sliced jalapeños make a cameo in our cozy soup. It's just enough change to make people notice the zing, but without causing any uproar, since we know every Jewish family LOVES a change from tradition. TRADITION!!!

Serves 8 to 10 | Prep Time: 30 minutes, plus cooling time | Cook Time: 1 hour 30 minutes

Soup
- 1 (6-pound) whole chicken
- 2 tablespoons olive oil
- KS&P
- 8 cups chicken stock
- 6 cups water
- 4 medium carrots, peeled and sliced
- 4 medium parsnips, peeled and sliced
- 4 celery stalks, sliced
- 2 garlic cloves, thinly sliced
- 1 medium yellow onion, diced
- 1 (2-inch) piece ginger, peeled and minced
- 6 thyme sprigs
- 4 dried bay leaves
- ½ bunch parsley
- ½ bunch dill

Finishing
- 1 bunch scallions, thinly sliced
- ½ bunch parsley, leaves and tender stems minced
- ½ bunch dill, fronds and tender stems minced
- 1 lime, zested and juiced
- 1 jalapeño, thinly sliced (optional)
- KS&P
- Garlicky Matzo Balls (page 277)

1. Make the soup: Preheat the oven to 425°F.

2. Place the chicken in a large ovenproof pot or Dutch oven and rub with the olive oil and 2 heavy pinches each of salt and pepper. Roast for 30 minutes, then transfer to the stovetop over medium-high heat.

3. To the pot, add the chicken stock, water, carrots, parsnips, celery, garlic, onion, and ginger. Tie together the thyme, bay leaves, parsley, and dill tightly with butcher's twine. Nestle in the soup.

(cont.)

4. Bring the soup to a simmer, then cook, reducing the heat to maintain a low simmer, for 1 hour. Carefully transfer the chicken to a sheet pan and let cool slightly. Remove and discard the herb bundle.

5. Once the chicken is cool enough to handle, roughly shred the meat, discarding the skin and bones. Return the shredded meat to the soup.

6. Finish the soup: Stir in the scallions, parsley, dill, lime zest and juice, and jalapeño, if using. Taste and adjust the seasoning with salt and pepper. Divide among bowls and serve with matzo balls.

Make Ahead Soup can be made up until finishing (through step 5) up to 2 days in advance, stored in the covered pot in the refrigerator. Finish the soup (step 6) right before serving.

Leftovers 5 days in the refrigerator or 3 months in the freezer.

Garlicky Matzo Balls

This matzo ball variation was born out of a two-birds situation, because I both had a vegetarian coming for Seder and I couldn't get my hands on schmaltz (my preferred fat). Instead, we're frying garlic in neutral oil to add an extra layer of flavor to our balls. This is a bulked-up version of my other recipes to ensure you have enough balls for any last-minute additions to your table as well as plenty extra for the annual division of leftovers between the matriarchs!

Makes about 20 balls | Prep Time: 25 minutes, plus 1 hour chilling time | Cook Time: 1 hour 20 minutes

1 cup neutral oil, such as vegetable, avocado, or sunflower
6 garlic cloves, finely grated
1 tablespoon kosher salt, plus more for boiling
8 large eggs
3 cups matzo meal
1 tablespoon onion powder
½ cup minced fresh dill
½ cup seltzer

1. In a small saucepan, combine ¼ cup of the oil with the grated garlic over medium heat. Bring to a simmer and cook, stirring constantly, until the garlic is lightly golden and fragrant, about 1 minute. Transfer to a large, heatproof bowl, then stir in the remaining ¾ cup oil to cool it down.

2. To the garlic oil, whisk in the 1 tablespoon salt and eggs until smooth. Stir in the matzo meal, onion powder, and dill until smooth, followed by the seltzer until incorporated. Cover and refrigerate for 1 hour.

3. Bring a large, wide pot of salted water to a boil. Scoop the chilled matzo mixture into ¼-cup balls, using wet hands to roll them until smooth. You should have about 20 matzo balls. Gently add the matzo balls, one at a time, to the boiling water. Reduce the heat to maintain a simmer, cover, and cook until tender, about 1 hour. Remove from the heat, cover, and let sit for 15 minutes, then keep warm until the soup is ready.

Make Ahead Matzo ball mixture (step 1) can be made up to 1 day in advance, stored in an airtight container in the refrigerator. Balls can be cooked (step 2) up to 1 hour before serving, kept warm in the cooking liquid until serving.

Leftovers 5 days in the refrigerator.

Crunch Salad Supreme

We can't let our Seder plate get all the chazeret! While the hearty romaine leaf no longer tastes like a bitter herb, we can still toss it with sliced fennel and radishes for a textural trio that will give matzo a run for its money. Tossed with a lemony dressing studded with smashed Castelvetrano olives (the gateway olive for picky eaters!), this crunchy salad is the simplest way to add brightness to a typically heavy meal.

Serves 8 to 10 | Prep Time: 25 minutes

Dressing
- 1 cup Castelvetrano olives, smashed and pitted
- ⅓ cup freshly squeezed lemon juice
- ⅓ cup olive oil
- 1 tablespoon honey
- 2 garlic cloves, finely grated
- KS&P

Salad
- 3 heads romaine, thinly sliced
- 2 medium fennel bulbs, thinly sliced
- 2 medium daikon radishes, peeled, halved lengthwise, and thinly sliced
- KS&P

1. Make the dressing: In an airtight container, combine the olives, lemon juice, olive oil, honey, garlic, and 2 heavy pinches each of salt and pepper. Seal the container and shake to combine. Refrigerate until ready to dress the salad.

2. Make the salad: In a large bowl, toss the romaine, fennel, and daikon with the dressing to coat. Taste and adjust the seasoning with salt and pepper, then serve.

Make Ahead Dressing (step 1) can be made up to 1 day in advance, stored in an airtight container in the refrigerator. Salad (step 2) can be prepped and undressed any time the day of serving, stored in a covered bowl in the refrigerator. Salad should be dressed only right before serving.

Leftovers 2 days in the refrigerator.

paprika potatoes

A Jewish gathering without some form of potatoes might as well be a Christmas party. You need something to soak up all that brisket sauce, and it isn't going to be matzo! My mother always had a tray of simply roasted red potatoes for every holiday, and I'm continuing the tradition. (TRADITION!!!!) All done on one sheet pan, our quartered potatoes are just tossed with olive oil and spices to roast up until golden on the outside and fluffy on the inside. A humble potato side that never fails to stun.

Serves 8 to 10 | Prep Time: 15 minutes | Cook Time: 50 minutes

5 pounds red potatoes, scrubbed and quartered
½ cup olive oil
1 tablespoon smoked paprika
2 teaspoons garlic powder
KS&P

1. Preheat the oven 450°F.
2. On a sheet pan, toss the potatoes with the olive oil, smoked paprika, garlic powder, and 2 heavy pinches each of salt and pepper.
3. Roast for 40 to 50 minutes, until golden and tender, then serve.

Make Ahead Potatoes can be roasted a few hours before serving, held on the sheet pan for reheating.

Leftovers 5 days in the refrigerator.

celery-heavy brisket with caramelized lemon & leeks

Since I did a tomato brisket in my last book, I felt like it was only fitting to do a tomato-less version in this one. I'm obsessed with making this menu a true celebration of spring, so our brisket is braised with a combo of caramelized leeks (even the dark green tops) and lemon with garlic, horseradish, white wine, and an entire bunch of a celery. After a low-and-slow braise and time to chill out in the fridge, we puree half of the braising liquid and vegetables to thicken up the sauce. With intense flavors of caramelized alliums and tart lemon, it's by far the brightest brisket you'll ever try. Just remember, even my own family is divided on which brisket recipe they want me to make. Some have adopted this version as their new favorite, while others are begging for a return of the French Onion Brisket from *Jew-ish* or the Jew-mami Brisket from *I Could Nosh*. Consider your audience and adjust accordingly, because all briskets are valid, and all braises are beautiful!

Serves 8 to 10 | Prep Time: 20 minutes | Cook Time: 4 hours 20 minutes, plus cooling and overnight chilling time

1 (6-pound) beef brisket, fat cap intact
KS&P
2 tablespoons neutral oil, such as vegetable, avocado, or sunflower
12 garlic cloves, smashed and peeled
1 bunch leeks, ends trimmed, halved, thinly sliced, and rinsed
1 lemon, quartered, seeded, and thinly sliced
1 (2-inch) piece horseradish, peeled and finely chopped
2 cups white wine
2 cups chicken stock
1 bunch celery, end trimmed, cut into 1-inch pieces, and rinsed

1. Preheat the oven to 325°F.
2. Season each side of the brisket with 2 heavy pinches each of salt and pepper. In a large Dutch oven, heat the oil over medium-high heat. Sear the brisket, turning it as needed, until golden brown on all sides, 15 to 20 minutes. Transfer the brisket to a sheet pan.
3. Reduce the heat to medium, then add the garlic, leeks, lemon, and horseradish to the pot. Cook, stirring often, until softened and lightly caramelized, 8 to 10 minutes. Add the wine, then stir continuously with a wooden spoon for 1 minute to scrape up any browned bits on the bottom of the pot.
4. Stir in the stock, celery, and 2 heavy pinches each of salt and pepper, then return the brisket to the pot. Bring to a simmer, then cover the pot and transfer to the oven. Cook for 3 to 3½ hours, until the brisket is very tender when pierced with a fork. Remove from the oven and let cool completely, then refrigerate overnight.
5. The next day, skim off and discard any fat. Transfer the brisket to a cutting board and cut it across the grain (perpendicular to the fibers you'll see running through the brisket) into ¼-inch-thick slices. Transfer half of the braising liquid and solids to a blender and puree until smooth, then return to the pot

to thicken the sauce. Return the meat to the sauce and heat over medium heat until warmed through, about 20 minutes. Taste and adjust the seasoning with salt and pepper, then serve.

Make Ahead Brisket can be cooked (through step 4) up to 2 days before serving, stored in the refrigerator. It can be sliced and the sauce finished (step 5) up to 1 day in advance, stored in the refrigerator.

Leftovers 5 days in the refrigerator.

Apricot Chicken with Roasted Asparagus

Every Passover, my Aunt Susi would make her famous apricot chicken, a sweet and savory dish of baked chicken stuffed with matzo farfel and glazed with apricot preserves. And while I always thought it was Susi's genius invention, I learned a few years ago that my favorite chicken was really an iconic Joan Nathan recipe from *Jewish Cooking in America*. Nevertheless, its impact remains and my love for apricot preserves and chicken has not waned. This is my take on the beloved recipe, simplified with a springy twist. We're marinating chicken thighs and drumsticks in a combo of apricot preserves and garlic before roasting them over a bed of asparagus. In the time it takes for our chicken to get a deep golden brown, our asparagus is tender, soaking up all the schmaltzy drippings. And since we marinated our chicken the night before, the whole dish comes together quickly and easily on one sheet pan. If that isn't a Passover miracle, I don't know what is!

Serves 8 to 10 | Prep Time: 25 minutes, plus marinating time | Cook Time: 30 minutes

Marinated Chicken

- 5 to 6 pounds bone-in, skin-on chicken thighs and drumsticks
- ⅓ cup olive oil
- ⅓ cup apricot preserves
- 2 teaspoons kosher salt
- ½ teaspoon freshly ground black pepper
- 4 garlic cloves, finely grated

Roasting

- 3 pounds asparagus, ends trimmed and cut into 3-inch pieces
- ¼ cup olive oil
- 2 tablespoons freshly squeezed lemon juice
- 4 garlic cloves, smashed and peeled
- 4 thyme sprigs
- KS&P

1. Marinate the chicken: In a large bowl, toss the chicken with the olive oil, apricot preserves, salt, pepper, and garlic to coat. Cover and refrigerate for at least 2 hours, but preferably overnight.

2. Roast the chicken and vegetables: Preheat the oven to 425°F.

3. On a sheet pan, toss the asparagus, olive oil, lemon juice, garlic, thyme, and 2 heavy pinches each of salt and pepper to combine. Nestle the marinated chicken, skin-side up, into the asparagus.

4. Roast for 30 minutes, or until the chicken is golden and reaches an internal temperature of 165°F. Transfer the chicken and asparagus to a platter and serve.

Make Ahead Chicken (step 1) can be marinated up to 1 day in advance. Chicken and vegetables can be roasted (step 4) up to 1 hour before serving, held on the sheet pan for reheating.

Leftovers 5 days in the refrigerator.

Matzo & Almond Strawberry Cobbler

I'm not going to lie, there's no greater feeling that serving up a Passover dessert that blows people away without using any chametz. I will never shy away from a culinary challenge and have served everything from layer cakes and brownies to cookies and even a matzo tiramisu (you can find all these recipes in my previous books), but I've never really ventured into fruity territory. So, it only seemed appropriate that we serve a big cobbler with our extra-springy Passover menu. We're tossing strawberries (though you can sub chopped rhubarb for a pound of them for the classic combo) with potato starch and sugar to bake up under spoons of an almond and matzo topping. The result is a nutty, chewy crust that pairs perfectly with the jammy strawberries for a just-sweet-enough finish to the meal. It's an easy recipe to throw together, but the key to success is in the bubbling. We need to make sure that the potato starch has activated, creating the luscious gel of fruit juices that suspends our strawberries. Luckily, we'll be able to easily see this, as the bubbling juices will be visibly thick when the cobbler is ready. Then, just scoop into another sweet Passover success story!

Serves 8 to 10 | Prep Time: 30 minutes, plus cooling time | Cook Time: 55 minutes

Topping
- ½ cup (100 g) granulated sugar
- ½ cup neutral oil, such as vegetable, avocado, or sunflower
- 1 teaspoon almond extract (or the seeds scraped from 1 vanilla bean)
- ½ teaspoon kosher salt
- ½ teaspoon ground cinnamon
- 2 large eggs
- 2 cups (224g) finely ground almond flour
- ½ cup (96g) potato starch
- 3 sheets matzo, crumbled

Filling
- 4 pounds strawberries, hulled and quartered
- ¾ cup (150g) granulated sugar
- ⅓ cup (64g) potato starch
- 2 tablespoons freshly squeezed lemon juice
- ½ teaspoon kosher salt

1. Preheat the oven to 350°F.

2. Make the topping: In a medium bowl, whisk together the sugar, oil, almond extract, salt, cinnamon, and eggs until smooth. Add the almond flour and potato starch. Gently stir together the dry ingredients piled above the wet ingredients a few times before folding together into a smooth batter. Fold in the crumbled matzo, then set aside.

3. Make the filling: In a large bowl, toss the strawberries, sugar, potato starch, lemon juice, and salt until well coated. Transfer to a 9 by 13-inch baking dish. Spoon the topping over the filling.

4. Bake for 45 to 55 minutes, until golden and the bubbling juices have thickened. Let cool for at least 20 minutes, then serve warm.

Make Ahead Cobbler can be made and baked anytime the day of serving, reheating to warm right before serving.

Leftovers 5 days in the refrigerator.

Charoset Truffles

Omg, did Joan Nathan inspire this entire menu? As I hinted at in the Ashkenazi Charoset recipe (page 266), Joan introduced me to the magic of Moroccan charoset, which are the most divine rolled truffles made from a paste of dried fruit and nuts. These truffles are decadently simple on their own, so we're just going to lean in and cover them in chocolate with a little pinch of flaky salt to be fancy. It's a sweet reminder of the diversity of the Jewish people, since no matter what foods we use to symbolize the retelling of the Exodus, the ritual itself connects us all!

Makes about 30 truffles | Prep Time: 20 minutes, plus chilling time | Cook Time: 5 minutes

12 ounces (2 packed cups) pitted Medjool dates
6 ounces (1 packed cup) dried apricots
1 cup toasted pistachios
¼ cup date syrup (or honey)
½ teaspoon ground cinnamon
½ teaspoon kosher salt
12 ounces (2 cups) dark chocolate chips
2 teaspoons coconut oil
Flaky sea salt, for garnish

1. In a food processor, combine the dates, apricots, pistachios, date syrup, cinnamon, and salt. Pulse until finely chopped and combined. Scoop 1 tablespoon-sized balls, rolling with your hands to smooth, and place on a parchment paper–lined sheet pan.

2. Set a medium metal or heatproof glass bowl over a small pot of simmering water, making sure the bottom of the bowl doesn't touch the water. Put the chocolate and coconut oil in the bowl and heat, stirring occasionally, until completely melted and combined.

3. Using 2 forks and working one at a time, dip the charoset balls in the chocolate, letting any excess drip off before transferring back to the parchment-lined sheet pan. Once all the balls are covered in chocolate, sprinkle a pinch of flaky salt on top of each.

4. Place the sheet pan in the refrigerator until the chocolate is set, about 30 minutes. Transfer the truffles to an airtight container and refrigerate until ready to serve.

Make Ahead Truffles can be made up to 3 days in advance, stored in an airtight container in the refrigerator.

Leftovers 1 week in the refrigerator or 1 month in the freezer.

gobble, gobble

MENU

Sumac-Ginger Cranberry Sauce

Sourdough & Challah Stuffing

German Green Bean Casserole

Sour Cream & Onion Mashed Potatoes

Honey-Roasted Squash with Sunflower Seed Brittle

Spatchcocked Pastrami-Spiced Turkey & Gravy

Pumpkin Pie Blondies

Pecan Pie Brownies

GROCERY LIST

PANTRY

- 12 oz dark chocolate (70% cacao)
- 4 c (856g) packed dark brown sugar
- 3½ c (700g) granulated sugar
- 3½ c (473g) all-purpose flour
- 2 c olive oil
- 2 c chopped pecans
- 1 c shelled sunflower seeds
- ¾ c slivered almonds
- 1 c dry white wine
- ½ c honey
- 3 tbsp cornstarch
- ¼ c (25g) unsweetened cocoa powder
- 3 tbsp red wine vinegar
- 1 tsp balsamic vinegar
- 1 tbsp apple cider vinegar
- 1 tbsp sriracha
- 2 tsp Dijon mustard
- 1 tsp baking powder
- 1 (15-oz) can pumpkin puree
- 1 (5-oz) bag sour cream and onion potato chips
- Nonstick cooking spray

SPICES, SEASONINGS, AND FLAVORINGS

- 3 tbsp vanilla extract
- 1 tbsp ground cinnamon
- 1 tbsp whole coriander seeds
- 2 tsp yellow mustard seeds
- 2 tsp garlic powder
- 2 tsp onion powder
- 2 tsp smoked paprika
- 1 tsp ground ginger
- 1 tsp freshly grated nutmeg
- 1 tsp ground sumac
- 3 dried bay leaves
- Flaky sea salt
- KS&P (at least 2 c kosher salt and 1 jar whole black peppercorns to be safe)

BREAD

- 1 lb sourdough bread
- 1 lb challah bread

MEAT

- 1 (12- to 14-lb) turkey

PRODUCE

- 4 lb (6 medium) russet potatoes
- 4 lb squash, such as butternut, honeynut, and/or acorn
- 3 lb green beans
- 2 lb mixed mushrooms, such as cremini, oyster, and maitake
- 1 lb fresh cranberries
- 2 c apple cider
- 11 garlic cloves
- 5 medium shallots
- 3 medium carrots
- 5 celery stalks
- 5 medium yellow onions
- 6 medium leeks
- 2 medium parsnips
- 2 navel oranges
- 1 medium Honeycrisp apple
- 1 bunch thyme
- 1 bunch sage
- 1 bunch rosemary
- 1 bunch chives
- 1 bunch parsley
- 1 bunch dill
- 1 (2-in) knob ginger

REFRIGERATED

- 20 oz (5 sticks) unsalted butter
- 4 c heavy cream
- ½ c full-fat sour cream
- 16 large eggs

PREP LIST

Up to 3 Days Ahead
- Make the Sumac-Ginger Cranberry Sauce
- Toast the bread for the Sourdough & Challah Stuffing
- Make the brittle for the Honey-Roasted Squash
- Make the dry rub for the Pastrami-Spiced Turkey

Up to 2 Days Ahead
- Cook the vegetables for the Sourdough & Challah Stuffing
- Blanch the green beans for the German Green Bean Casserole
- Cook the mushroom mixture for the German Green Bean Casserole
- Brine the Pastrami-Spiced Turkey
- Make and reduce the turkey stock for the Pastrami-Spiced Turkey
- Bake the Pumpkin Pie Blondies
- Bake the Pecan Pie Brownies

Up to 1 Day Ahead
- Assemble Sourdough & Challah Stuffing
- Make the vinaigrette for the German Green Bean Casserole
- Make the Sour Cream & Onion Mashed Potatoes
- Roast the squash for the Honey-Roasted Squash

Day Of
- Bake the Sourdough & Challah Stuffing
- Assemble the German Green Bean Casserole
- Glaze and finish roasting the Honey-Roasted Squash
- Slice the Pumpkin Pie Blondies
- Slice the Pecan Pie Brownies

4 Hours Before Guests Arrive
- Take your Pastrami-Spiced Turkey out of the refrigerator

2 Hours Before Guests Arrive
- Roast the Pastrami-Spiced Turkey

1 Hour Before Guests Arrive
- Warm through the Sour Cream & Onion Mashed Potatoes
- Make the gravy for the Pastrami-Spiced Turkey while it rests
- Keep the oven at 350°F

The DP Animal, Himself!

Right Before Guests Arrive
- Reheat the Honey-Roasted Squash (about 15 minutes)
- Reheat the Sourdough & Challah Stuffing (20 to 30 minutes)
- Reheat the German Green Bean Casserole (about 15 minutes)

Right Before Serving
- Carve the Pastrami-Spiced Turkey

Game Time Pep Talk
The Sumac-Ginger Cranberry Sauce should already be in a bowl on the table. The Sour Cream & Onion Mashed Potatoes should be on low heat and fully warmed through, ready to be transferred to a bowl and topped with potato chips. The Honey-Roasted Squash, Sourdough & Challah Stuffing, and German Green Bean Casserole should be in the oven warming through. (If you don't have space for all at the same time, heat the squash first because it's just as good at room temperature.) Transfer the squash to a platter and top with the sunflower seed brittle. Toss the green bean casserole with the dressing, then serve it right in its baking dish like the stuffing. The gravy should be warm on the stove and the Pastrami-Spiced Turkey should be rested and carved, held covered with foil on the sheet pan. Transfer the turkey to a platter and the gravy to a boat. The Pumpkin Pie Blondies and Pecan Pie Brownies should be already sliced and on a platter. If you're serving the blondies with whipped cream, you can already have it whipped in a bowl in the refrigerator, or I typically keep some cream in a shaker bottle (like for protein drinks) to shake up when it's time for dessert. You've got this!

Sumac-Ginger Cranberry Sauce

No shade if your family is all about slices of the canned cranberry sauce—you do you! However, if you are looking for a homemade recipe, this version is my ideal, using sumac and ginger for some tartness and zing while minced shallot and rosemary add a beautiful balance of savory notes, for dolloping onto your plate. Don't sleep on leftovers—this sauce should be the base of any turkey sandwich you make or even just simply slathered on your morning buttered toast.

Makes 3 cups | Prep Time: 10 minutes, plus cooling time | Cook Time: 20 minutes

2 tablespoons olive oil
1 medium shallot, minced
1 (2-inch) knob ginger, peeled and minced
1 teaspoon minced fresh rosemary
1 pound fresh cranberries

¾ cup (150g) granulated sugar
½ cup freshly squeezed orange juice
½ cup water
1 teaspoon ground sumac
KS&P

In a medium saucepan, heat the olive oil over medium heat. Add the shallot, ginger, and rosemary and cook until softened, 3 to 4 minutes. Stir in the cranberries, sugar, orange juice, water, sumac, and 2 heavy pinches each of salt and pepper. Bring to a simmer and cook, reducing the heat to maintain a simmer, until the cranberries have broken down and the sauce has thickened, 16 to 18 minutes. Let cool completely. Taste and adjust the seasoning with salt and pepper, then serve.

Make Ahead Cranberry sauce can be made and stored in an airtight container in the refrigerator up to 3 days in advance.

Leftovers 5 days in the refrigerator.

Gobble, Gobble

Sourdough & Challah Stuffing

This is the cookbook where I give my mother her flowers as a home cook! She always crushed Thanksgiving, and especially the stuffing. Her secret was tons of cooked veggies, paired with slivered almonds for crunch and apple juice for sweetness. Now that I handle cooking for the holidays, I took her recipe and zhuzhed it up a bit. While she only used whole wheat sandwich bread (a classic almond mom move), I use a combo of toasted sourdough and challah for the perfect blend of tang and sweetness to soak up a mixture of caramelized veggies, apple cider, turkey stock, and herbs. The slivered almonds stayed in because they add the most iconic texture, though I've been known from time to time to swap them for chopped hazelnuts when I'm feeling fancy. Since we're making a turkey stock for the gravy, we'll reserve 2 cups to throw into this stuffing. (Vegetable stock can be easily swapped in if there are any vegetarians coming.) Any way we tackle this recipe, the steps can be split up across days and the whole thing can be assembled and ready to bake the night before. If you stay ready, you don't have to get ready!

Serves 8 to 10 | Prep Time: 30 minutes, plus cooling time | Cook Time: 1 hour 30 minutes

- 1 pound sourdough bread, cut into 1-inch cubes
- 1 pound challah bread, cut into 1-inch cubes
- ½ cup olive oil
- 3 medium leeks, white and light green parts only, thinly sliced
- KS&P
- 2 medium carrots, finely chopped
- 2 celery stalks, finely chopped
- 2 parsnips, finely chopped
- 1 tablespoon minced fresh sage
- 2 teaspoons minced fresh thyme leaves
- 3 garlic cloves, minced
- 2 cups turkey stock (see recipe page 307; alternatively use chicken or vegetable stock)
- 2 cups apple cider
- ¾ cup slivered almonds
- ½ cup minced parsley
- 1 tablespoon apple cider vinegar
- 4 large eggs, beaten
- 1 medium Honeycrisp apple, chopped

1. Preheat the oven to 300°F.

2. Divide the bread pieces between 2 sheet pans in an even layer. Bake for 15 to 20 minutes, until dry and crisp. Let cool completely on the pans. Raise the oven temperature to 375°F.

3. Meanwhile, in a large skillet, heat the olive oil over medium-high heat. Add the leeks with a heavy pinch each of salt and pepper and cook until jammy, 8 to 10 minutes. Stir in the carrots, celery, and parsnips and cook until softened but still slightly crisp, 6 to 8 minutes. Add the sage, thyme, and garlic and continue to cook until fragrant, about 2 minutes. Remove from the heat, then taste and adjust the seasoning with salt and pepper. Let cool.

(cont.)

4. In a large bowl, combine the toasted bread and cooked vegetables with the stock, cider, almonds, parsley, vinegar, eggs, and apple. Use your hands to mix until well incorporated and the bread soaks up all the liquid. Season with 2 heavy pinches each of salt and pepper, then transfer to a 9 by 13-inch baking dish.

5. Bake for 40 to 50 minutes, until golden and set. Remove from the oven and let cool slightly, then serve.

Make Ahead Bread can be toasted (steps 1 and 2) and stored in sealable plastic bags up to 3 days in advance. Cooked vegetables (step 3) can be made up to 2 days in advance, stored in an airtight container in the refrigerator. Stuffing can be assembled (step 4) up to 1 day in advance, covered in plastic wrap, and stored in the refrigerator. Stuffing can be baked any time the day of serving, reheating before serving.

Leftovers 4 days in the refrigerator.

German Green Bean Casserole

This is by no means a menu where we skimp on decadence, but with a plate of stuffing and mashed potatoes and gravy, it's a welcomed reprieve to have a lighter and brighter green bean casserole side. It's kind of inspired by one of my favorite snacking recipes from my second cookbook, *I Could Nosh*, called finger beans, which embraces the beauty of blanched green beans tossed with a lemony garlic vinaigrette. Instead of a rich, creamy sauce for this casserole, we're giving the ol' German potato salad treatment, tossing the green beans and sauteed mushrooms and shallots with a mustardy vinaigrette packed with fresh dill and raw garlic. The whole dish can be prepped long in advance, so you just have to reheat in the oven and toss in the dressing before serving. I opt for caramelizing shallots that melt into the green beans, but I won't say anything if you want to sprinkle some crispy onions from the jar on top for nostalgia.

Serves 8 to 10 | Prep Time: 20 minutes | Cook Time: 45 minutes

Casserole
KS&P
3 pounds green beans, stems trimmed
3 tablespoons olive oil
2 pounds mixed mushrooms, such as sliced cremini, torn oyster, and torn maitake
4 medium shallots, thinly sliced
4 thyme sprigs
¼ cup dry white wine

Vinaigrette
¼ cup olive oil
¼ cup minced fresh dill
3 tablespoons red wine vinegar
1 tablespoon honey
2 teaspoons Dijon mustard
2 garlic cloves, finely grated
KS&P

1. Make the casserole: Bring a large pot of salted water to a boil and fill a large bowl with ice and water. Add the green beans to the pot and cook for 3 to 4 minutes, until bright green and tender. Quickly transfer to the ice bath to cool. Once cooled, drain the green beans well and transfer to a 9 by 13-inch baking dish.

2. In a large, high-sided skillet, heat the olive oil over medium-high heat. Add the mushrooms, shallots, thyme, and 2 heavy pinches each of salt and pepper. Cook, stirring often, until all the moisture from the mushrooms has evaporated and the mixture is golden, 15 to 20 minutes. Stir in the wine, using a wooden spoon to scrape up any browned bits on the bottom of the pan. Remove from the heat

(cont.)

and let cool slightly in the pan. Transfer to the baking dish with the green beans and toss to incorporate. Cover with foil.

3. Make the vinaigrette: In a medium bowl, whisk together the olive oil, dill, vinegar, honey, mustard, garlic, and 2 heavy pinches each of salt and pepper.

4. An hour before serving, preheat the oven to 350°F.

5. Place the foil-covered baking dish into the oven. Bake for 20 to 25 minutes, until warmed through. Remove from the oven and discard the foil. Drizzle the vinaigrette over the casserole and toss to coat. Taste and adjust the seasoning with salt and pepper, then transfer to a platter and serve.

Make Ahead Green beans can be blanched and drained (step 1) up to 2 days in advance, stored in an airtight container in the refrigerator. Mushrooms can be cooked (step 2) up to 2 days in advance, stored in an airtight container separate from the green beans in the refrigerator. Vinaigrette (step 3) can be made up to 1 day in advance, stored in an airtight container in the refrigerator.

Leftovers 4 days in the refrigerator.

Sour Cream & Onion Mashed Potatoes

All mashed potatoes are beautiful! Whether chunky or smooth, butter-laced or olive oil–based, or packed with herbs and spiced or simply seasoned, a little TLC is all potatoes need to add extra comfort to your plate. In this recipe, a buttery base of caramelized onion, rosemary, and garlic infuses the cream that gets mashed into our tender potatoes. Finished with sour cream and fresh chives, it would be silly not to crumble potato chips of the same flavor profile right on top for a little added texture and whimsy. We're keeping it simple with yellow onions, though I've been known to swap in a couple of thinly sliced leeks, which get beautifully jammy for mashing in. Personally, I'm team chunky, which saves you some time, but if you love a super smooth mash, you can run your potatoes through a food mill or ricer and puree the onion and cream mixture for that extra silky texture. Whatever your preference, feel free to make this recipe up to a day in advance (see note below), though I'll typically make it a few hours before serving and hold it at room temperature covered with plastic, saving some fridge space and making it a bit easier and quicker to reheat.

Serves 8 to 10 | Prep Time: 20 minutes | Cook Time: 15 minutes

4 pounds (6 medium) russet potatoes, peeled and cut into 1-inch pieces
KS&P
4 ounces (1 stick) unsalted butter
1 medium yellow onion, thinly sliced
1 tablespoon minced fresh rosemary

6 garlic cloves, minced
1½ cups heavy cream
½ cup full-fat sour cream
½ cup minced fresh chives
Sour cream and onion potato chips, for garnish (optional)

1. In a large pot, add the potatoes and cover with 2 inches of cold water. Season with 2 heavy pinches of salt and bring to a boil. Reduce the heat to maintain a simmer and cook until the potatoes are tender when pierced with a fork, 12 to 15 minutes. Drain, then return to the pot.

2. Meanwhile, in a medium saucepan, melt the butter over medium-high heat. Add the onion with 2 heavy pinches each of salt and pepper and cook until softened and just beginning to caramelize, 8 to 10 minutes. Stir in the rosemary and garlic, then cook for another 2 minutes. Stir in the heavy cream and sour cream, then bring to a simmer. Remove from the heat and keep warm.

3. Using a potato masher, roughly mash the cooked, drained potatoes. Slowly add the warm cream mixture while continuing to mash until fully incorporated. Taste and adjust the seasoning with salt and pepper.

4. When ready to serve, stir in the chives and transfer to a serving bowl. Lightly crush a few handfuls of potato chips on top, if using, then serve.

Make Ahead Mashed potatoes can be made up to 1 day in advance, stored in an airtight container in the refrigerator. Reheat in a pot over medium-low heat, stirring in a little milk or cream if needed.

Leftovers 4 days in the refrigerator.

Honey-Roasted Squash with Sunflower Seed Brittle

You heard it here first, but at some point I will be writing an entire cookbook inspired by this recipe. Becoming a great home cook is all about simple preparations zhuzhed with a sauce, dressing, or topping to make it explode with flavor and texture. Here, we're roasting the humble squash with a sweet and spicy honey glaze and finishing it with an addictively crunchy sunflower seed brittle. What kind of squash you may ask? Any squash you want! When I have time to go to the farmer's market, I'll splurge on honeynuts. When I don't want to deal with peeling, I'll use acorns. But most of the time, this is my favorite way to prepare a trusty butternut. The brittle can be made days in advance and the squash can even be pre-roasted, ready to be glazed and finished in the oven before serving. Just make sure to hide the brittle before serving, since it has a tendency to disappear among a family of noshers!

Serves 8 to 10 | **Prep Time:** 20 minutes, plus cooling time | **Cook Time:** 30 minutes

Roasted Squash
- 4 pounds squash (12 small honeynut squash, halved and seeded; 2 medium butternut squash, peeled, halved, seeded, and cut into 2-inch chunks; or 3 medium acorn squash, halved, seeded, and cut into 2-inch wedges)
- 3 tablespoons olive oil
- KS&P
- ¼ cup honey
- 1 tablespoon sriracha
- 1 tablespoon apple cider vinegar (or any vinegar)

Sunflower Seed Brittle
- 2 tablespoons unsalted butter
- 2 tablespoons honey
- 1 cup shelled sunflower seeds
- ½ teaspoon smoked paprika
- ½ teaspoon kosher salt

1. Roast the squash: Preheat the oven to 450°F.

2. On a sheet pan, toss the squash with the olive oil and 2 heavy pinches each of salt and pepper. (If using honeynut squash, place cut-side down.) Roast for 20 minutes, or until just tender.

3. Meanwhile, make the brittle: Line a small tray or plate with parchment paper. In a small saucepan, melt the butter and honey over medium heat. Stir in the sunflower seeds, smoked paprika, and salt and cook, stirring continuously, until the sunflower seeds are toasted and coated in a thick glaze, 3 to 5 minutes. Transfer to the parchment-lined tray in an even layer and let cool completely.

4. In a small bowl, stir together the honey, sriracha, vinegar, and a heavy pinch each of salt and pepper. Once the squash is tender, brush the honey mixture liberally over the squash. (If using honeynut squash, flip so they are cut-side up before brushing.) Return to the oven to roast for another 10 minutes, or until lightly caramelized.

5. Transfer to a platter, then crumble the sunflower seed brittle on top and serve.

Make Ahead Brittle (step 3) can be made up to 3 days in advance, stored in an airtight container at room temperature. Squash can be roasted (steps 1 and 2) up to 1 day in advance, stored in an airtight container in the refrigerator. Roasted squash can be glazed and finished in the oven (step 4) a few hours before serving, held at room temperature until ready to reheat and serve.

Leftovers 5 days in the refrigerator.

Gobble, Gobble   305

Spatchcocked Pastrami-Spiced Turkey & Gravy

While I have no shortage of controversial opinions, my biggest one is that I truly don't see any need to make turkey on Thanksgiving. The sides are the true stars, and really, I just want to make sure I save room for dessert. Of course, I'm a walking contradiction, because I'm going to be campaigning for you to make this beast of a recipe because it's literally going to get you a juicy, perfectly seasoned bird without fail every November. This recipe is an exercise in flavor meeting function. We're going to spatchcock the turkey, which makes it cook both more evenly and faster (like a fraction of the time), while also fitting so much easier in the fridge. Since we're taking out the backbone, we're also going to cut off the wings and use them to make a turkey stock that will become our gravy, and even save some for our stuffing. Our turkey is covered with a pastrami dry brine for two days, giving ample time for the flavors to infuse while also allowing us to work in advance so the day before Thanksgiving can be dedicated to desserts and sides. Roasting happens on a wire rack–lined sheet pan, so you don't need to go out and buy a big roasting pan, plus you get more air circulation this way for extra crispy skin. And it's also all happening at one temperature, so you get golden brown perfection without having to futz with your oven throughout. Okay, wow, I take it all back, I love this turkey so much and it wouldn't be Thanksgiving without it!

Serves 8 to 10 | Prep Time: 45 minutes, plus 24 hours brining time and resting time | Cook Time: 4 hours

1 (12- to 14-pound) turkey, thawed if frozen and patted dry with paper towels

Dry Rub
1½ tablespoons whole black peppercorns
1 tablespoon whole coriander seeds
2 teaspoons yellow mustard seeds
¼ cup kosher salt
2 tablespoons dark brown sugar
2 teaspoons garlic powder
2 teaspoons onion powder
1 teaspoon smoked paprika

Turkey Stock
3 medium carrots, cut into 2-inch pieces
3 celery stalks, cut into 2-inch pieces
1 medium yellow onion, quartered
2 tablespoons olive oil
KS&P
1 teaspoon whole black peppercorns
4 thyme sprigs
3 medium leeks, dark green tops only, cut into 2-inch pieces
3 dried bay leaves
16 cups water

(cont.)

Roast Turkey

¼ cup olive oil

Gravy

3 tablespoons cornstarch
3 tablespoons water
1 teaspoon balsamic vinegar
KS&P

1. Place the turkey on a large cutting board breast-side down. Remove the neck and gizzards from the cavity, transferring the neck to a sheet pan and discarding the gizzards. Use strong kitchen shears to cut along both sides of the backbone to remove it completely and place it on the sheet pan with the neck. Open the cavity and make a small cut in the breastbone (you're not looking to cut through all the way). Flip the turkey over (skin-side up) and use the palm of your hand to press on the breastbone and flatten the turkey. Use a sharp boning knife to remove the wings where the joint connects to the top of the breast and transfer them to the sheet pan with the neck and back bone. Transfer the spatchcocked turkey to a sheet pan lined with a wire rack.

2. Make the dry rub: Using a spice grinder, mortar and pestle, or empty pepper mill, coarsely grind the peppercorns, coriander seeds, and mustard seeds. Transfer to a small bowl, add the salt, brown sugar, garlic powder, onion powder, and smoked paprika, and stir to combine.

3. Liberally season both sides of the spatchcocked turkey with the dry rub. Place skin-side up and refrigerate uncovered for at least 24 hours and up to 2 days.

4. Meanwhile, make the turkey stock: Preheat the oven to 350°F.

5. To the sheet pan with the turkey neck, backbone, and wings, add the carrots, celery, and onion, then toss with the olive oil and 2 heavy pinches each of salt and pepper. Roast for 30 minutes, or until lightly golden. Transfer the roasted turkey pieces and vegetables to a large stockpot, add the peppercorns, thyme, leek tops, and bay leaves, then cover with the water. Bring to a simmer over medium-high heat. Cook, adjusting the heat to maintain a simmer, for 2 hours. Remove from the heat and let cool slightly, then strain, discarding all solids. You should have about 10 cups of turkey stock. Reserve 2 cups of the turkey stock for the stuffing recipe (page 297).

6. Transfer the remaining 8 cups of turkey stock to a medium pot and bring to a simmer over medium-high heat. Cook, reducing the heat to maintain a simmer, until reduced to 4 cups, 30 to 40 minutes. Then let cool completely. Transfer to an airtight container and refrigerate overnight.

7. The next day, roast the turkey: Remove the turkey from the refrigerator 4 hours before your guests arrive. Let sit out, uncovered, for 2 hours to come to room temperature.

8. Meanwhile, preheat the oven to 400°F. Remove the wire rack with the turkey and set aside. Clean out the sheet pan, discarding any liquid that accumulated.

9. Line the sheet pan with foil. Place the wire rack with the turkey on top and rub it with the olive oil.

10. Roast for 1 hour 10 minutes to 1 hour 30 minutes, until an instant-read thermometer inserted in the center of the breast and thigh reads 165°F. (Don't be afraid of a deep golden color, but if you have a larger turkey that's perfectly brown and still needs longer to cook, feel free to tent with foil.) Remove from the oven and let rest for 30 minutes.

11. While the turkey rests, make the gravy: In a medium saucepan, bring the 4 cups of reduced turkey stock to a simmer. In a small bowl, stir together the cornstarch and water into a smooth slurry, then whisk into the simmering stock. Cook until thickened, about 2 minutes. Remove from the heat, then whisk in the vinegar. Taste and adjust the seasoning with salt and pepper. Keep warm.

12. Transfer the rested, cooked turkey to a large board and carve. Transfer to a platter, then serve with the gravy.

Make Ahead Dry rub (step 2) can be made up to 3 days in advance, stored in an airtight container at room temperature. Turkey can be dry brined (step 3) up to 2 days in advance, stored in the refrigerator. Turkey stock can be made (steps 4 and 5) up to 2 days in advance, stored in an airtight container in the refrigerator. Turkey stock reduction can be made (step 6) up to 2 days in advance, stored in an airtight container in the refrigerator.

Leftovers 4 days in the refrigerator.

Pumpkin Pie Blondies

Every book I write, there is a shout-out to my friend Miro Uskokovich, the insanely talented pastry chef (formerly of Gramercy Tavern in NYC, but now owner of my favorite bakery, Hani's, with his wife, Shilpa) who I couldn't be more obsessed with. One year when he was at Gramercy, he sold Thanksgiving pies, including a pumpkin custard pie with maple meringue that I swear was the best pie dessert I've ever tasted. The next year they weren't selling the pumpkin pies, but since Miro is the biggest mensch, he still made two for me. One was to be preciously served at Thanksgiving, and one was to be devoured on Black Friday in the comfort of my pajamas. Of course, I got the recipe from Miro and, of course, it is life-changing and, of course, it's a labor of love. This last Thanksgiving, tired of having to blind-bake pie crusts, I made the brave choice to pour Miro's pumpkin custard over my brown-butter blondie recipe, and all I can say is sometimes the best recipes spawn from living your truth. Fudgy blondies meeting silky pumpkin custard really is as magical as it sounds. And while these squares are perfect just as they are, I've been known to dollop on some whipped cream (typically made with a splash of almond extract).

Makes 24 blondies | Prep Time: 30 minutes, plus cooling and chilling time | Cook Time: 1 hour

Blondie Base

Nonstick cooking spray, for greasing
8 ounces (2 sticks) unsalted butter
2 cups (856g) packed dark brown sugar
2 large eggs
1 teaspoon vanilla extract

2 cups (270g) all-purpose flour
1 teaspoon kosher salt
1 teaspoon ground cinnamon
1 teaspoon baking powder

Pumpkin Pie Filling

½ cup (100g) granulated sugar
¼ cup (54g) packed dark brown sugar
3 large eggs
1 (15-ounce) can pumpkin puree
1 teaspoon vanilla extract

1 teaspoon ground cinnamon
1 teaspoon ground ginger
1 teaspoon freshly grated nutmeg
1 teaspoon kosher salt
1½ cups heavy cream

Serving

Whipped cream (optional)

(cont.)

1. Make the blondie base: Preheat the oven to 350°F. Grease a 9 by 13-inch baking pan with nonstick cooking spray and line with parchment paper, leaving overhang on all sides.

2. In a medium saucepan, melt the butter over medium-high heat. Cook, stirring continuously, until browned and nutty in aroma, 5 to 7 minutes. Transfer to a large heatproof bowl and let cool slightly.

3. To the warm browned butter, whisk in the sugar until smooth, followed by the eggs and vanilla. Add the flour, salt, cinnamon, and baking powder. Gently stir together the dry ingredients piled above the wet ingredients a few times before folding together until incorporated. Transfer to the prepared pan and spread in an even layer.

4. Bake for 20 minutes, then remove from the oven and let cool for 15 minutes. Reduce the oven temperature to 325°F.

5. Meanwhile, prepare the pumpkin pie filling: In a large bowl, whisk together the sugars and eggs until well combined. Whisk in the pumpkin puree, vanilla, cinnamon, ginger, nutmeg, and salt, followed by the heavy cream until a smooth filling forms. Gently pour the filling over the blondie layer.

6. Return the pan to the oven and bake for 35 to 40 minutes, until the pumpkin pie is just set with the faintest jiggle when you gently shake the pan. Let cool completely in the pan, then cover and chill for at least 2 hours.

7. Remove from the refrigerator 1 hour before serving. Transfer the blondies to a cutting board and cut into 24 bars (4 rows lengthwise by 6 columns). Arrange on a platter and top with whipped cream, if using, right before serving.

Make Ahead Pumpkin pie blondies can be made up to 2 days in advance, stored covered in the refrigerator.

Leftovers 4 days in the refrigerator.

Pecan Pie Brownies

To me, Black Friday isn't as much a shopping day as it is a day to be spent with a nice 10mg prize for all that hard work cooking and hosting! I was simply making my way back and forth between the trays of leftover stuffing and blondies when the idea for pecan pie brownies just hit me. If you're new to me and my recipes, my modesty falls short of my brownies, which I imagine will one day make me Tate's Cookies–rich. Until then, we're going to parbake a fudgy brownie layer to be topped with a gooey pecan pie filling that uses no corn syrup, though also no shortage of sugar. Past a perfect pairing to our blondies, this recipe has brought peace to my never-ending struggle with my mother over my brownies. In general, I'm incredibly ANTI-NUT in brownies and will not be taking any feedback or criticism at this time! My mother does not agree, going so far as to bring her own bag of walnuts with her to shove into my brownies just to spite me. A truce has been made, luckily just in time for the holidays.

Makes 24 brownies | Prep Time: 30 minutes, plus cooling and chilling time | Cook Time: 40 minutes

Brownie Base

- 8 ounces dark chocolate (70% cacao), coarsely chopped
- 4 ounces (1 stick) unsalted butter, cubed
- 1½ cups (300g) granulated sugar
- ½ cup (107g) packed dark brown sugar
- 4 large eggs
- ¼ cup (25g) unsweetened cocoa powder
- 1 tablespoon vanilla extract
- 1½ teaspoons kosher salt
- 1 cup (135g) all-purpose flour

Pecan Pie Filling

- ¾ cup (150g) granulated sugar
- ½ cup (107g) packed dark brown sugar
- 4 tablespoons (2 ounces) unsalted butter, melted
- 1 tablespoon vanilla extract
- 1 teaspoon ground cinnamon
- 1 teaspoon kosher salt
- 3 large eggs
- 4 ounces dark chocolate (70% cacao), coarsely chopped (¾ cup)
- 2 cups chopped pecans

1. Make the brownie base: Preheat the oven to 350°F. Line a 9 by 13-inch baking pan with parchment paper, leaving overhang on all sides.

2. Set a medium metal or heatproof glass bowl over a small pot of simmering water, making sure the bottom of the bowl doesn't touch the water. Add the chopped chocolate and butter and heat, stirring occasionally, until completely melted and combined, then remove the bowl from the heat.

(cont.)

3. Meanwhile, in a large bowl, whisk together the sugars and eggs until very smooth. Whisk in the cocoa powder, vanilla, and salt until smooth. Slowly whisk in the melted chocolate mixture until smooth. Fold in the flour until just incorporated. Scrape the batter into the prepared pan and spread it into an even layer.

4. Bake for 20 minutes, then remove from the oven and let cool for 15 minutes.

5. Meanwhile, prepare the pecan pie filling: In a large bowl, whisk together the sugars, melted butter, vanilla, cinnamon, and kosher salt until smooth. Whisk in the eggs until very smooth, then fold in the chopped chocolate and pecans. Gently pour the filling over the brownie layer and spread in an even layer.

6. Bake for about 20 minutes, until just set with no jiggle when you gently shake the pan. Let cool completely in the pan, then cover and chill for at least 2 hours.

7. Remove from the refrigerator 1 hour before serving. Transfer the brownies to a cutting board and cut into 24 bars (4 rows lengthwise by 6 columns). Arrange on a platter and serve.

Make Ahead Pecan pie brownies can be made up to 2 days in advance, stored covered in the refrigerator.

Leftovers 4 days in the refrigerator.

JUST THE RECIPES
A Master List by Category

When you don't want a whole menu, just the perfect recipe.

(Page references in *italics* indicate photographs.)

APPETIZERS

Ashkenazi Charoset, 266, *267*
Avocado-Cucumber Cups, *156*, 157
Bloody Mary Shrimp Cocktail, 248–49, *249*
Cacio e Pepe Cheese Twists, *64*, 65

Caramelized Onion, Date & Brie Hand Pies, *108*, 109–10
Heirloom Tomato Toasts with Goat Cheese Schmear, 88–89, *89*
Jammy Eggs with Horseradish Mayo, *268*, 269
Kielbasa in a Blanket, 194–95, *195*

Maple-Candied Nuts, 62, *63*
Marinated Party Mix, *56*, 57
Party Animal Mix, 54, *55*
Rainbow Gefilte Fish, 272–73, *273*
Spicy Cauliflower & Celery Pickles, 172, *173*

DIPS & CONDIMENTS

Au Poivre Dip, 58, *59*
Bloody Mary Cocktail Sauce, 248–49, *249*
Blue Cheese Ranch, *246*, 247

Brown Butter Tehina, *170*, 171
Hot Honey Labneh, 180, *181*
Minty Pea & White Bean Dip, *60*, 61
Mock Chopped Liver, 270, *271*

Scallion Chimichurri, *94*, 95
Sumac-Ginger Cranberry Sauce, 295, *295*
Sun-Dried Tomato & Yogurt Dip, *74*, 75

BREADS (& UNLEAVENED BREAD)

Bagels, *20*, 21–23
Brown Butter Parker House Rolls, 243–44, *245*

Garlic Matzo, *264*, 265
Focaccia with Whipped Ricotta & Peppadew Honey, 209–10, *211*

Pitas, 182–83, *183*

BREAKFAST & BRUNCH

Bagel Toppings Salad, 30, *31*
Blueberry Corn Muffins, *36*, 37
Challah French Toast Sticks, 38–39, *39*

Dirty Martini–Cured Salmon, *24*, 25
Herby Cottage Cheese Frittata, *40*, 41
Maple-Candied Bacon

Saffron Hash Browns, *44*, 45
Wasabi-Lime Tuna Salad, *26*, 27
Whipped Schmear, *28*, 29

SOUPS & SALADS

Bagel Toppings Salad, 30, *31*
Brighter Chicken Soup, *274*, 275–76 with Garlicky Matzo Balls, *276*, 277
Cabbage & Farro Salad with Roasted Broccoli & Tahini Dressing, 158–59, *159*
Caesar Cabbage, 214–15, *215*
Charred Cabbage Salad, *174*, 175
Chopped Salad with Pepperoncini Dressing, *212*, 213

Creamy Pistachio Salad, 76, *77*
Crunch Salad Supreme, *278*, 279
Farro & Cabbage Salad with Roasted Broccoli & Tahini Dressing, 158–59, *159*
Green Bean & Grilled Corn Salad with Honey-Lime Vinaigrette, 92–93, *93*
Green Goddess Wedge Salad with Radishes & Crispy Capers, 226–27, *227*
Harissa Carrot Salad, 126, *127*

Kale & Pomegranate Salad, *128*, 129
Roasted Tomato & Halloumi Salad, 144–45, *145*
Socca with Artichoke & Arugula Salad, *142*, 143
Sumac-Smashed Cucumber Salad, *124*, 125
Za'atar Roasted Eggplant & Tomato Salad, *178*, 179

SIDES

Amba-ish Mango Relish, 176, *177*
Beans & Greens, *160*, 161
Caraway-Roasted Beets, 196–97, *197*
Deviled Potatoes, *250*, 251
Garlic-Parmesan Brussels Sprouts Gratin, 252–53, *253*
German Green Bean Casserole, 299–300, *301*

Honey Mustard Potato Salad with Cornichons & Dill, *90*, 91
Honey-Roasted Squash with Sunflower Seed Brittle, 304–5, *305*
Lemony Turmeric Rice, 130, *131*
Paprika Potatoes, 280, *281*
Roasted Broccoli with Buffalo Beurre Blanc, *230*, 231

Scallion-Horseradish Smashed Potatoes, 228–29, *229*
Sour Cream & Onion Mashed Potatoes, 302–3, *303*
Sourdough & Challah Stuffing, *296*, 297–98
Spanakorizo (Greek Spinach and Feta Rice), *146*, 147

PASTA

Fresh Cavatelli & Fennel-y Meatballs, *216*, 217–18

Spicy Sausage Gnocchi Bake with Pesto Ricotta, *78*, 79

MAINS

VEGETARIAN
Falafel, 184–85, *185*
Tofu Curry with Roasted Cauliflower, Sweet Potatoes & Chickpeas, *132*, 133–34

FISH
Steamed Whitefish with Caramelized Fennel & Green Olive Salad, 148, *149*
Yogurt-Roasted Salmon with Leeks, 162, *163*

POULTRY
Apricot Chicken with Roasted Asparagus, *284*, 285
Chicken & Biscuits Pot Pie, *114*, 115–16
Honey-Balsamic Grilled Chicken & Summer Veg, 96, *97*
Roast Chicken with Lemony Sauce Soubise, 232–34, *233*
Spatchcocked Pastrami-Spiced Turkey & Gravy, *306*, 307–9

LAMB
Veg-Heavy Shepherd's Pie, 111–12, *113*

BEEF
Burgers Provençal, 98–99, *99*
Celery-Heavy Brisket with Caramelized Lemon & Leeks, 282–83, *283*
Cheeseburger Arayes Sliders, 66–67, *67*
Filet Mignon au Poivre, *254*, 255–56
Unstuffed Cabbage, 198–99, *199*

DESSERTS

Apple Pie Calzone, *100*, 101–2
Banana Cream Pie with Biscoff Crust, 117–19, *118*
Charoset Truffles, *288*, 289
Chocolate-Covered Halva-Stuffed Dates, *136*, 137
Honey-Lime Fruit Salad, *164*, 165

Lemon-Almond Blondies with Sumac Glaze (Platinum Blondies), 186–87, *187*
Matzo & Almond Strawberry Cobbler, 286–87, *287*
Peanut Butter Hot Fudge Sundaes, 80–81, *81*
Pecan Pie Brownies, 313–14, *314*
Pumpkin Pie Blondies, *310*, 311–12

Saffron Panna Cotta, 150–51, *151*
Tarte Tatin, 235–36, *237*
The Perfect Chocolate Cake with Ganache Frosting & Raspberry Filling, 257–58, *259*
Tiramisu Cake, 219–20, *221*
Raspberry Goat Cheese Bars, 68, *69*
Zaftig Honey (Medovik-ish), *200*, 201–2

DRINKS & MIXERS

Basil-Cucumber Shrub, *50*, 51

Honey-Ginger Syrup, *50*, 52

Rose Grenadine, *50*, 53

Universal Conversion Chart

Oven temperature equivalents

250°F	=	120°C
275°F	=	135°C
300°F	=	150°C
325°F	=	160°C
350°	=	180°C
375°F	=	190°C
400°F	=	200°C
425°F	=	220°C
450°F	=	230°C
475°F	=	240°C
500°F	=	260°C

Measurement equivalents

Measurements should always be level unless directed otherwise.

⅛ teaspoon	=	0.5 mL				
¼ teaspoon	=	1 mL				
½ teaspoon	=	2 mL				
1 teaspoon	=	5 mL				
1 tablespoon	=	3 teaspoons	=	½ fluid ounce	=	15 mL
2 tablespoons	=	⅛ cup	=	fluid ounce	=	30 mL
4 tablespoons	=	¼ cup	=	2 fluid ounces	=	60 mL
5⅓ tablespoons	=	⅓ cup	=	3 fluid ounces	=	80 mL
8 tablespoons	=	½ cup	=	4 fluid ounces	=	120 mL
10⅔ tablespoons	=	⅔ cup	=	5 fluid ounces	=	160 mL
12 tablespoons	=	¾ cup	=	6 fluid ounces	=	180 mL
16 tablespoons	=	1 cup	=	8 fluid ounces	=	240 mL

ACKNOWLEDGMENTS

I love gratitude! I'm a very grateful person in general, but to have the opportunity to thank everyone here is a blessing beyond words.

So, from the bottom of my heart, I love you:

The person who is reading this book, supporting my dreams.

Sarah Passick, the best literary agent/friend/neck-snapper in the game.

Sarah Pelz, my dream editor who lets me be crazy on paper and knows when to reel me back in.

Matt Taylor-Gross, my brilliant photographer who make my books stunning beyond belief.

Barrett Washburne, my food stylist who makes every recipe a work of art.

Megan Hedgpeth, my prop stylist who magically brought all of my wild ideas to life.

Bonni Leon-Berman, my designer who created my dream book with care and collaboration.

Amelia Arend, Chris Smith, Anne Eastman, John Ligenfelter, and Lorie Reilly, my team who made this crazy photoshoot possible.

Alexandra Emmerman, Megan Brown, Noah Swimmer, and the rest of my team, past and present, that help me make magic from behind the scenes.

Dr. Elizabette Cohen, Mike Cohen, Jamie Cohen, Susi Heilberg,

Annie Heilberg, and the rest of my family, my greatest supporters and toughest taste-testers.

Benj Pasek and Alex Edelman, the best roommates I could dream of.

Brian Derrick and Jason Abramson, my faygeleh sisters.

Alex Shapiro, forever my muse.

Dana Golub, my favorite recipe tester who makes me better at my job.

Benny Blanco, Taffy Brodesser-Akner, Emil Cohen, Katie Couric, Miz Cracker, Manu Diez, Dave Dreifus, Dan Geneen, Gabi Gershenson, Judy Gold, Iggy Gurin, Richie Jackson, David Jacobs, Jenji Kohan, Erin Lichy, Stephen Mack, Jess Marko, Debra Messing, Isaac Mizrahi, Joan Nathan, Barbara Nevis, Sophie Nir, Claudia Oshry, Leo Paige, Ben Picket, Modi Rosenfeld, Brian Schaeffer, Ben Siman-Tov, Ally Shapiro, Ben Soffer, Mike Solomonov, Miro Uskokovich, Lou Venturelli, Jill Zarin, and Zikki Zaryckyj, my friends who not only taste-tested all of these recipes, but took the time to come to the photoshoot to get their portraits taken.

FreshDirect, HexClad, Staub, Susan Alexandra, and Jono Pandolfi, the brands I love and live by that helped make my photoshoot possible.

Every person who sat at any of these dinner parties, you helped make me into the animal I am today.

index

Note: Page references in *italics* indicate photographs.

A

Almond(s)
- -Lemon Blondies with Sumac Glaze (Platinum Blondies), 186–87, *187*
- Maple-Candied Nuts, 62, *63*
- & Matzo Strawberry Cobbler, 286–87, *287*
- Sourdough & Challah Stuffing, *296*, 297–98

Amba-ish Mango Relish, 176, *177*

Appetizers. *See also* Dips
- Ashkenazi Charoset, 266, *267*
- Avocado-Cucumber Cups, 156, *157*
- Bloody Mary Shrimp Cocktail, 248–49, *249*
- Cacio e Pepe Cheese Twists, *64*, 65
- Caramelized Onion, Date & Brie Hand Pies, *108*, 109–10
- Cheeseburger Arayes Sliders, 66–67, *67*
- Dirty Martini–Cured Salmon, 24, *25*
- Garlic Matzo, *264*, 265
- Heirloom Tomato Toasts with Goat Cheese Schmear, 88–89, *89*
- Jammy Eggs with Horseradish Mayo, *268*, 269
- Kielbasa in a Blanket, 194–95, *195*
- Maple-Candied Nuts, 62, *63*
- Marinated Party Mix, *56*, 57
- Party Animal Mix, *54*, 55
- Socca with Artichoke & Arugula Salad, *142*, 143
- Spicy Cauliflower & Celery Pickles, 172, *173*

Apple(s)
- Ashkenazi Charoset, 266, *267*
- Avocado-Cucumber Cups, 156, *157*
- Pie Calzone, *100*, 101–2
- Sourdough & Challah Stuffing, *296*, 297–98
- Tarte Tatin, 235–36, *237*

Apricot(s)
- Charoset Truffles, *288*, 289
- Chicken with Roasted Asparagus, *284*, 285

Arayes Cheeseburger Sliders, 66–67, *67*

Artichoke(s)
- & Arugula Salad, Socca with, *142*, 143
- Marinated Party Mix, *56*, 57

Arugula & Artichoke Salad, Socca with, *142*, 143

Ashkenazi Charoset, 266, *267*

Asparagus, Roasted, Apricot Chicken with, *284*, 285

Avocado-Cucumber Cups, 156, *157*

B

Bacon, Maple-Candied, 42, *43*

Bagel Bonanza
- Bagels, 20, 21–23
- Bagel Toppings Salad, 30, *31*
- Dirty Martini–Cured Salmon, 24, *25*
- grocery list, 18
- menu, 18
- prep list, 19
- Wasabi-Lime Tuna Salad, 26, *27*
- Whipped Schmear, 28, 29

Bagels, 20, 21–23

Banana Cream Pie with Biscoff Crust, 117–19, *118*

Bars
- Lemon-Almond Blondies with Sumac Glaze (Platinum Blondies), 186–87, *187*
- Pecan Pie Brownies, 313–14, *314*
- Pumpkin Pie Blondies, *310*, 311–12
- Raspberry Goat Cheese, 68, *69*

Basil-Cucumber Shrub, *50*, 51

Bean(s). *See also* Chickpeas; Green Bean
- Chicken & Biscuits Pot Pie, 114, 115–16
- & Greens, 160, *161*
- White, and Pea Dip, Minty, *60*, 61

Beef
- Burgers Provençal, 98–99, *99*
- Celery-Heavy Brisket with Caramelized Lemon & Leeks, 282–83, *283*
- Cheeseburger Arayes Sliders, 66–67, *67*
- Filet Mignon au Poivre, *254*, 255–56
- Fresh Cavatelli & Fennel-y Meatballs, *216*, 217–18
- Unstuffed Cabbage, 198–99, *199*

Beets, Caraway-Roasted, 196–97, *197*

Biscoff Crust, Banana Cream Pie with, 117–19, *118*

Black pepper
- Au Poivre Dip, 58, *59*
- Cacio e Pepe Cheese Twists, *64*, 65
- Filet Mignon au Poivre, *254*, 255–56

Blondies
- Lemon-Almond, with Sumac Glaze (Platinum Blondies), 186–87, *187*
- Pumpkin Pie, *310*, 311–12

Bloody Mary Shrimp Cocktail, 248–49, *249*

Blueberry Corn Muffins, *36*, 37

Blue Cheese Ranch, *246*, 247

Bourbon or brandy
- Au Poivre Dip, 58, *59*

Bread
- Bagels, 20, 21–23

Brown Butter Parker House Rolls, 243–44, *245*

Challah French Toast Sticks, 38–39, *39*

Focaccia with Whipped Ricotta & Peppadew Honey, 209–10, *211*

Heirloom Tomato Toasts with Goat Cheese Schmear, 88–89, *89*

Pitas, 182–83, *183*

Socca with Artichoke & Arugula Salad, *142*, 143

Sourdough & Challah Stuffing, *296*, 297–98

Brie, Caramelized Onion & Date Hand Pies, *108*, 109–10

Brittle
- Peanut, 80, *81*
- Sunflower Seed, 304–5, *305*

Broccoli
- Roasted, & Tahini Dressing, Cabbage & Farro Salad with, 158–59, *159*
- Roasted, with Buffalo Beurre Blanc, *230*, 231

Brownies, Pecan Pie, 313–14, *314*

Brussels Sprouts Gratin, Garlic-Parmesan, 252–53, *253*

Burger Sauce, 66–67, *67*

Burgers Provençal, 98–99, *99*

Butter
- Brown, Parker House Rolls, 243–44, *245*
- Brown, Tehina, *170*, 171
- Roasted Broccoli with Buffalo Beurre Blanc, *230*, 231
- Whipped Brown Honey, 243–44, *245*

C

Cabbage
- Caesar, 214–15, *215*
- Charred, Salad, *174*, 175
- & Farro Salad with Roasted Broccoli & Tahini Dressing, 158–59, *159*
- Unstuffed, 198–99, *199*

Cacio e Pepe Cheese Twists, *64*, 65

Cakes
- Chocolate, The Perfect, with Ganache Frosting & Raspberry Filling, 257–58, *259*
- Tiramisu, 219–20, *221*
- Zaftig Honey (Medovik-ish), 200, 201–2

Calzone, Apple Pie, *100*, 101–2

Capers
- Bagel Toppings Salad, 30, *31*
- Crispy, & Radishes, Green Goddess Wedge Salad with, 226–27, *227*

Caraway-Roasted Beets, 196–97, *197*
Carrot(s)
    Rainbow Gefilte Fish, 272–73, *273*
    Salad, Harissa, 126, *127*
Cauliflower
    & Celery Pickles, Spicy, 172, *173*
    Roasted, Sweet Potatoes & Chickpeas, Tofu Curry with, *132*, 133–34
Celery
    & Cauliflower Pickles, Spicy, 172, *173*
    Charred Cabbage Salad, 174, *175*
    -Heavy Brisket with Caramelized Lemon & Leeks, 282–83, *283*
Challah
    French Toast Sticks, 38–39, *39*
    & Sourdough Stuffing, 296, *297*–98
Charoset, Ashkenazi, 266, *267*
Cheese
    Blue, Ranch, *246*, 247
    Caesar Cabbage, 214–15, *215*
    Caramelized Onion, Date & Brie Hand Pies, *108*, 109–10
    Cheeseburger Arayes Sliders, 66–67, *67*
    Cottage, Frittata, Herby, *40*, 41
    Creamy Pistachio Salad, 76, *77*
    Focaccia with Whipped Ricotta & Peppadew Honey, 209–10, *211*
    Garlic-Parmesan Brussels Sprouts Gratin, 252–53, *253*
    Goat, Raspberry Bars, 68, *69*
    Goat, Schmear, 88–89, *89*
    Roasted Tomato & Halloumi Salad, 144–45, *145*
    Spanakorizo (Greek Spinach and Feta Rice), *146*, 147
    Spicy Sausage Gnocchi Bake with Pesto Ricotta, 78, *79*
    Tiramisu Cake, 219–20, *221*
    Twists, Cacio e Pepe, *64*, 65
    Whipped Schmear, *28*, 29
Chicken
    Apricot, with Roasted Asparagus, *284*, 285
    & Biscuits Pot Pie, *114*, 115–16
    Honey-Balsamic Grilled, & Summer Veg, 96, *97*
    Roast, with Lemony Sauce Soubise, 232–34, *233*
    Soup, Brighter, 274, 275–76
Chickpeas
    Falafel, 184–85, *185*
    Roasted Cauliflower, & Sweet Potatoes, Tofu Curry with, *132*, 133–34
Chiles
    Hot Honey Labneh, 180, *181*
    Scallion Chimichurri, *94*, 95
    Spicy Cauliflower & Celery Pickles, 172, *173*

Chimichurri, Scallion, *94*, 95
Chives
    Au Poivre Dip, 58, *59*
    Blue Cheese Ranch, *246*, 247
Chocolate
    Cake, The Perfect, with Ganache Frosting & Raspberry Filling, 257–58, *259*
    Charoset Truffles, *288*, 289
    -Covered Halva-Stuffed Dates, *136*, 137
    Peanut Butter Hot Fudge Sundaes, 80–81, *81*
    Pecan Pie Brownies, 313–14, *314*
Chopped Liver, Mock, 270, *271*
Cilantro
    Amba-ish Mango Relish, 176, *177*
    Falafel, 184–85, *185*
    Harissa Carrot Salad, 126, *127*
Cobbler, Matzo & Almond Strawberry, 286–87, *287*
Cocktail Sauce, Bloody Mary, 248–49, *249*
Coffee
    Tiramisu Cake, 219–20, *221*
Cognac
    Au Poivre Dip, 58, *59*
    Filet Mignon au Poivre, *254*, 255–56
Corn, Grilled, & Green Bean Salad with Honey-Lime Vinaigrette, 92–93, *93*
Corn Muffins, Blueberry, *36*, 37
Cottage Cheese Frittata, Herby, *40*, 41
Cranberry Sauce, Sumac-Ginger, *295*, 295
Cream cheese
    Goat Cheese Schmear, 88–89, *89*
    Whipped Schmear, *28*, 29
Cucumber(s)
    -Avocado Cups, *156*, 157
    Bagel Toppings Salad, 30, *31*
    -Basil Shrub, *50*, 51
    Chopped Salad with Pepperoncini Dressing, *212*, 213
    Salad, Sumac-Smashed, *124*, 125
Curry, Tofu, with Roasted Cauliflower, Sweet Potatoes & Chickpeas, *132*, 133–34

D

Date(s)
    Caramelized Onion, & Brie Hand Pies, *108*, 109–10
    Charoset Truffles, *288*, 289
    Chocolate-Covered Halva-Stuffed, *136*, 137
Desserts. *See also* Bars; Cakes
    Apple Pie Calzone, *100*, 101–2
    Banana Cream Pie with Biscoff Crust, 117–19, *118*
    Charoset Truffles, *288*, 289

Chocolate-Covered Halva-Stuffed Dates, *136*, 137
Matzo & Almond Strawberry Cobbler, 286–87, *287*
Peanut Butter Hot Fudge Sundaes, 80–81, *81*
Saffron Panna Cotta, 150–51, *151*
Tarte Tatin, 235–36, *237*
Dill
    Bagel Toppings Salad, 30, *31*
    Blue Cheese Ranch, *246*, 247
    Brighter Chicken Soup, 274, 275–76
    Caraway-Roasted Beets, 196–97, *197*
    & Cornichons, Honey Mustard Potato Salad with, *90*, 91
    Herby Cottage Cheese Frittata, *40*, 41
    Rainbow Gefilte Fish, 272–73, *273*
    Spanakorizo (Greek Spinach and Feta Rice), *146*, 147
    Unstuffed Cabbage, 198–99, *199*
Dips
    Au Poivre, 58, *59*
    Blue Cheese Ranch, *246*, 247
    Brown Butter Tehina, *170*, 171
    Dipping Sauce for Kielbasa, 194, *195*
    Hot Honey Labneh, 180, *181*
    Minty Pea & White Bean, *60*, 61
    Mock Chopped Liver, 270, *271*
    Sun-Dried Tomato & Yogurt, 74, *75*
Dirty Martini–Cured Salmon, *24*, 25

E

Eggplant
    Honey-Balsamic Grilled Chicken & Summer Veg, 96, *97*
    & Tomato Salad, Za'atar Roasted, *178*, 179
Eggs
    Herby Cottage Cheese Frittata, *40*, 41
    Jammy, with Horseradish Mayo, *268*, 269
Equipment, 10

F

Falafel, 184–85, *185*
Farro & Cabbage Salad with Roasted Broccoli & Tahini Dressing, 158–59, *159*
Fennel
    Caramelized, & Green Olive Salad, Steamed Whitefish with, *148*, 149
    Crunch Salad Supreme, *278*, 279
    Fresh Cavatelli & Fennel-y Meatballs, *216*, 217–18
    Mock Chopped Liver, 270, *271*
Feta and Spinach Rice (Spanakorizo), *146*, 147
Focaccia with Whipped Ricotta & Peppadew Honey, 209–10, *211*

322   Index

French Toast Sticks, Challah, 38–39, *39*
Frittata, Herby Cottage Cheese, 40, 41
Fruit. *See also specific fruits*
    Salad, Honey-Lime, *164*, 165

G

Garlic
    Garlicky Matzo Balls, *276*, 277
    Matzo, *264*, 265
    -Parmesan Brussels Sprouts Gratin, 252–53, *253*
    Scallion Chimichurri, *94*, 95
Gefilte Fish, Rainbow, 272–73, *273*
Gin
    Dirty Martini–Cured Salmon, *24*, 25
Ginger
    -Honey Syrup, *50*, 52
    -Sumac Cranberry Sauce, *295*, 295
Goat Cheese
    Raspberry Bars, 68, *69*
    Schmear, 88–89, *89*
Gobble, Gobble
    German Green Bean Casserole, 299–300, *301*
    grocery list, 292
    Honey-Roasted Squash with Sunflower Seed Brittle, 304–5, *305*
    menu, 292
    Pecan Pie Brownies, 313–14, *314*
    prep list, 293–94
    Pumpkin Pie Blondies, *310*, 311–12, *314*
    Sour Cream & Onion Mashed Potatoes, 302–3, *303*
    Sourdough & Challah Stuffing, *296*, 297–98
    Spatchcocked Pastrami-Spiced Turkey & Gravy, *306*, 307–9
    Sumac-Ginger Cranberry Sauce, 295, *295*
Green Bean
    Casserole, German, 299–300, *301*
    & Grilled Corn Salad with Honey-Lime Vinaigrette, 92–93, *93*
Green Machine
    Avocado-Cucumber Cups, *156*, 157
    Beans & Greens, *160*, 161
    Cabbage & Farro Salad with Roasted Broccoli & Tahini Dressing, 158–59, *159*
    grocery list, 154
    Honey-Lime Fruit Salad, *164*, 165
    menu, 154
    prep list, 155
    Yogurt-Roasted Salmon with Leeks, *162*, 163
Greens. *See also* Kale; Lettuce
    Beans &, *160*, 161
    Socca with Artichoke & Arugula Salad, *142*, 143

Spanakorizo (Greek Spinach and Feta Rice), *146*, 147
Grenadine, Rose, *50*, 53
Grills Gone Wild
    Apple Pie Calzone, *100*, 101–2
    Burgers Provençal, 98–99, *99*
    Green Bean & Grilled Corn Salad with Honey-Lime Vinaigrette, 92–93, *93*
    grocery list, 86
    Heirloom Tomato Toasts with Goat Cheese Schmear, 88–89, *89*
    Honey-Balsamic Grilled Chicken & Summer Veg, 96, *97*
    Honey Mustard Potato Salad with Cornichons & Dill, *90*, 91
    menu, 86
    prep list, 87
    Scallion Chimichurri, *94*, 95

H

Halloumi & Roasted Tomato Salad, 144–45, *145*
Halva-Stuffed Dates, Chocolate-Covered, *136*, 137
Harissa Carrot Salad, 126, *127*
Hash Browns, Saffron, *44*, 45
Herbs. *See also specific herbs*
    Green Goddess Wedge Salad with Radishes & Crispy Capers, 226–27, *227*
    Herby Cottage Cheese Frittata, 40, *41*
Honey
    -Balsamic Grilled Chicken & Summer Veg, 96, *97*
    Brown Butter, Whipped, 243–44, *245*
    Cake, Zaftig (Medovik-ish), *200*, 201–2
    -Ginger Syrup, *50*, 52
    Hot, Labneh, 180, *181*
    -Lime Fruit Salad, *164*, 165
    -Lime Vinaigrette, Green Bean & Grilled Corn Salad with, 92–93, *93*
    Mustard Potato Salad with Cornichons & Dill, *90*, 91
    Peppadew, & Whipped Ricotta, Focaccia with, 209–10, *211*
    -Roasted Squash with Sunflower Seed Brittle, 304–5, *305*
    Saffron Panna Cotta, 150–51, *151*
Horseradish
    Bloody Mary Cocktail Sauce, 248–49, *249*
    Celery-Heavy Brisket with Caramelized Lemon & Leeks, 282–83, *283*
    Dipping Sauce for Kielbasa, 194, *195*
    Mayo, Jammy Eggs with, *268*, 269
    -Scallion Smashed Potatoes, 228–29, *229*

I

Ice cream
    Peanut Butter Hot Fudge Sundaes, 80–81, *81*

K

Kale
    Chicken & Biscuits Pot Pie, *114*, 115–16
    & Pomegranate Salad, *128*, 129
Ketchup
    Bloody Mary Cocktail Sauce, 248–49, *249*
    Burger Sauce, 66–67, *67*
Kielbasa in a Blanket, 194–95, *195*
KS&P (kosher salt and pepper), 10

L

Labneh, Hot Honey, 180, *181*
Lamb
    Veg-Heavy Shepherd's Pie, 111–12, *113*
Leeks
    Caramelized, & Lemon, Celery-Heavy Brisket with, 282–83, *283*
    Sourdough & Challah Stuffing, *296*, 297–98
    Yogurt-Roasted Salmon with, *162*, 163
Lemon
    -Almond Blondies with Sumac Glaze (Platinum Blondies), 186–87, *187*
    Caramelized, & Leeks, Celery-Heavy Brisket with, 282–83, *283*
    Lemony Turmeric Rice, 130, *131*
    Roast Chicken with Lemony Sauce Soubise, 232–34, *233*
Let My People Nosh
    Apricot Chicken with Roasted Asparagus, *284*, 285
    Ashkenazi Charoset, 266, *267*
    Brighter Chicken Soup, *274*, 275–76
    Celery-Heavy Brisket with Caramelized Lemon & Leeks, 282–83, *283*
    Charoset Truffles, *288*, 289
    Crunch Salad Supreme, *278*, 279
    Garlic Matzo, *264*, 265
    grocery list, 262
    Garlicky Matzo Balls, *276*, 277
    Jammy Eggs with Horseradish Mayo, *268*, 269
    Matzo & Almond Strawberry Cobbler, 286–87, *287*
    menu, 262
    Mock Chopped Liver, 270, *271*
    Paprika Potatoes, 280, *281*
    prep list, 263
    Rainbow Gefilte Fish, 272–73, *273*
Lettuce
    Chopped Salad with Pepperoncini Dressing, *212*, 213
    Creamy Pistachio Salad, 76, *77*

Lettuce (continued)
  Crunch Salad Supreme, *278*, 279
  Green Goddess Wedge Salad with Radishes & Crispy Capers, 226–27, *227*
Life of the Cocktail Party
  Au Poivre Dip, *58*, 59
  Cacio e Pepe Cheese Twists, *64*, 65
  Cheeseburger Arayes Sliders, 66–67, *67*
  Cucumber-Basil Shrub, *50*, 51
  grocery list, 48
  Honey-Ginger Syrup, *50*, 52
  Maple-Candied Nuts, *62*, 63
  Marinated Party Mix, *56*, 57
  menu, 48
  Minty Pea & White Bean Dip, *60*, 61
  Party Animal Mix, *54*, 55
  prep list, 49
  Raspberry Goat Cheese Bars, *68*, 69
  Rose Grenadine, *50*, 53
Lime
  -Honey Fruit Salad, *164*, 165
  -Honey Vinaigrette, Green Bean & Grilled Corn Salad with, 92–93, *93*
  -Wasabi Tuna Salad, *26*, 27

M
Mango Relish, Amba-ish, 176, *177*
Maple
  -Candied Bacon, *42*, 43
  -Candied Nuts, *62*, 63
Matzo
  & Almond Strawberry Cobbler, 286–87, *287*
  Balls, Garlicky, *276*, 277
  Garlic, *264*, 265
Mayonnaise
  Burger Sauce, 66–67, *67*
  Deviled Potatoes, *250*, 251
  Jammy Eggs with Horseradish Mayo, *268*, 269
Meatballs, Fennel-y, & Fresh Cavatelli, *216*, 217–18
Meatballs to the Wall
  Caesar Cabbage, 214–15, *215*
  Chopped Salad with Pepperoncini Dressing, *212*, 213
  Focaccia with Whipped Ricotta & Peppadew Honey, 209–10, *211*
  Fresh Cavatelli & Fennel-y Meatballs, *216*, 217–18
  grocery list, 206
  menu, 206
  prep list, 207
  Tiramisu Cake, 219–20, *221*
Mediterranean Spa Food
  grocery list, 140
  menu, 140
  prep list, 141
  Roasted Tomato & Halloumi Salad, 144–45, *145*
  Saffron Panna Cotta, 150–51, *151*
  Socca with Artichoke & Arugula Salad, *142*, 143
  Spanakorizo (Greek Spinach and Feta Rice), *146*, 147
  Steamed Whitefish with Caramelized Fennel & Green Olive Salad, 148, *149*
Mint
  Harissa Carrot Salad, *126*, 127
  Honey-Lime Fruit Salad, *164*, 165
  Minty Pea & White Bean Dip, *60*, 61
  Sumac-Smashed Cucumber Salad, *124*, 125
Mock Chopped Liver, 270, *271*
Muffins, Blueberry Corn, *36*, 37
Mushrooms
  German Green Bean Casserole, 299–300, *301*
  Mock Chopped Liver, 270, *271*
  Veg-Heavy Shepherd's Pie, 111–12, *113*
Mustard
  Deviled Potatoes, *250*, 251
  Dipping Sauce for Kielbasa, 194, *195*
  German Green Bean Casserole, 299–300, *301*
  Honey Potato Salad with Cornichons & Dill, *90*, 91

N
Nuts. *See also specific nuts*
  Maple-Candied, *62*, 63

O
Olive(s)
  Crunch Salad Supreme, *278*, 279
  Dirty Martini–Cured Salmon, *24*, 25
  Green, & Caramelized Fennel Salad, Steamed Whitefish with, 148, *149*
  Marinated Party Mix, *56*, 57
Onion(s)
  Bagel Toppings Salad, *30*, 31
  Caramelized, Date & Brie Hand Pies, *108*, 109–10
  Honey-Balsamic Grilled Chicken & Summer Veg, *96*, 97
  Mock Chopped Liver, 270, *271*
  Roast Chicken with Lemony Sauce Soubise, 232–34, *233*
  & Sour Cream Mashed Potatoes, 302–3, *303*
  Sumac-Smashed Cucumber Salad, *124*, 125

P
Panna Cotta, Saffron, 150–51, *151*
Paprika Potatoes, *280*, 281
Parker House Rolls, Brown Butter, 243–44, *245*
Parmesan
  Caesar Cabbage, 214–15, *215*
  Creamy Pistachio Salad, *76*, 77
  -Garlic Brussels Sprouts Gratin, 252–53, *253*
Parsley
  Blue Cheese Ranch, *246*, 247
  Brighter Chicken Soup, *274*, 275–76
  Falafel, 184–85, *185*
  Herby Cottage Cheese Frittata, *40*, 41
  Rainbow Gefilte Fish, 272–73, *273*
  Roasted Tomato & Halloumi Salad, 144–45, *145*
  Steamed Whitefish with Caramelized Fennel & Green Olive Salad, 148, *149*
Parties
  booze, 6–7
  conversation starters, 11–14
  food and hospitality, 5–6
  invitations, 8–9
  kitchen equipment, 9–10
  menus, 4–5
  music, 8
  table decor, 7–8
Party Animal Mix, *54*, 55
Party Mix, Marinated, *56*, 57
Pasta
  Fresh Cavatelli & Fennel-y Meatballs, *216*, 217–18
  Spicy Sausage Gnocchi Bake with Pesto Ricotta, *78*, 79
Peanut Brittle, *80*, 81
Peanut Butter Hot Fudge Sundaes, 80–81, *81*
Pea & White Bean Dip, Minty, *60*, 61
Pecan(s)
  Maple-Candied Nuts, *62*, 63
  Pie Brownies, 313–14, *314*
Pepperoncini Dressing, Chopped Salad with, *212*, 213
Peppers. *See also* Chiles
  Focaccia with Whipped Ricotta & Peppadew Honey, 209–10, *211*
  Honey-Balsamic Grilled Chicken & Summer Veg, *96*, 97
  Marinated Party Mix, *56*, 57
  Veg-Heavy Shepherd's Pie, 111–12, *113*
Pesto Ricotta, Spicy Sausage Gnocchi Bake with, *78*, 79
Pickles
  Burger Sauce, 66–67, *67*
  Honey Mustard Potato Salad with Cornichons & Dill, *90*, 91
  Spicy Cauliflower & Celery, *172*, 173
Pies
  Banana Cream, with Biscoff Crust, 117–19, *118*
  Caramelized Onion, Date & Brie Hand, *108*, 109–10
  Chicken & Biscuits Pot, *114*, 115–16

324   Index

Veg-Heavy Shepherd's, 111–12, *113*
Pistachio(s)
   Charoset Truffles, *288*, 289
   Salad, Creamy, 76, *77*
Pita Party
   Amba-ish Mango Relish, 176, *177*
   Brown Butter Tehina, *170*, 171
   Charred Cabbage Salad, *174*, 175
   Falafel, 184–85, *185*
   grocery list, 168
   Hot Honey Labneh, 180, *181*
   Lemon-Almond Blondies with Sumac Glaze (Platinum Blondies), 186–87, *187*
   menu, 168
   Pitas, 182–83, *183*
   prep list, 169
   Spicy Cauliflower & Celery Pickles, *172*, 173
   Za'atar Roasted Eggplant & Tomato Salad, *178*, 179
Pitas, 182–83, *183*
Pomegranate
   & Kale Salad, *128*, 129
   Rose Grenadine, *50*, 53
Poppy seeds
   Bagels, *20*, 21–23
   Kielbasa in a Blanket, 194–95, *195*
Potato chips
   Au Poivre Dip, 58, *59*
   Party Animal Mix, 54, *55*
Potato(es)
   Deviled, *250*, 251
   Paprika, 280, *281*
   Saffron Hash Browns, *44*, 45
   Salad, Honey Mustard, with Cornichons & Dill, *90*, 91
   Scallion-Horseradish Smashed, 228–29, *229*
   Sour Cream & Onion Mashed, 302–3, *303*
   Sweet, Roasted Cauliflower, & Chickpeas, Tofu Curry with, *132*, 133–34
   Veg-Heavy Shepherd's Pie, 111–12, *113*
Pot Pie, Chicken & Biscuits, *114*, 115–16
Puff pastry
   Cacio e Pepe Cheese Twists, *64*, 65
   Caramelized Onion, Date & Brie Hand Pies, *108*, 109–10
   Kielbasa in a Blanket, 194–95, *195*
Pumpkin Pie Blondies, *310*, 311–12

R
Radishes
   Avocado-Cucumber Cups, *156*, 157
   Creamy Pistachio Salad, 76, *77*
   & Crispy Capers, Green Goddess Wedge Salad with, 226–27, *227*
   Rainbow Gefilte Fish, 272–73, *273*

Raisins
   Ashkenazi Charoset, 266, *267*
Ranch, Blue Cheese, *246*, 247
Raspberry
   Filling & Ganache Frosting, The Perfect Chocolate Cake with, 257–58, *259*
   Goat Cheese Bars, 68, *69*
Relish, Amba-ish Mango, 176, *177*
Rice
   Lemony Turmeric, 130, *131*
   Spinach and Feta (Spanakorizo), *146*, 147
   Unstuffed Cabbage, 198–99, *199*
Ricotta
   Pesto, Spicy Sausage Gnocchi Bake with, *78*, 79
   Whipped, & Peppadew Honey, Focaccia with, 209–10, *211*
Ride or Pie
   Banana Cream Pie with Biscoff Crust, 117–19, *118*
   Caramelized Onion, Date & Brie Hand Pies, *108*, 109–10
   Chicken & Biscuits Pot Pie, *114*, 115–16
   grocery list, 106
   menu, 106
   prep list, 107
   Veg-Heavy Shepherd's Pie, 111–12, *113*
Rolls, Brown Butter Parker House, 243–44, *245*
Rose water
   Rose Grenadine, *50*, 53
   Saffron Panna Cotta, 150–51, *151*

S
Saffron
   Hash Browns, *44*, 45
   Panna Cotta, 150–51, *151*
Salad(s)
   Artichoke & Arugula, Socca with, *142*, 143
   Bagel Toppings, 30, *31*
   Cabbage & Farro, with Roasted Broccoli & Tahini Dressing, 158–59, *159*
   Caramelized Fennel & Green Olive, Steamed Whitefish with, *148*, 149
   Charred Cabbage, *174*, 175
   Chopped, with Pepperoncini Dressing, *212*, 213
   Creamy Pistachio, 76, *77*
   Green Bean & Grilled Corn, with Honey-Lime Vinaigrette, 92–93, *93*
   Green Goddess Wedge, with Radishes & Crispy Capers, 226–27, *227*
   Harissa Carrot, *126*, 127
   Honey-Lime Fruit, *164*, 165
   Honey Mustard Potato, with Cornichons & Dill, *90*, 91
   Kale & Pomegranate, *128*, 129

   Roasted Tomato & Halloumi, 144–45, *145*
   Sumac-Smashed Cucumber, *124*, 125
   Supreme, Crunch, *278*, 279
   Wasabi-Lime Tuna, 26, *27*
   Za'atar Roasted Eggplant & Tomato, *178*, 179
Salmon
   Dirty Martini–Cured, *24*, 25
   Yogurt-Roasted, with Leeks, 162, *163*
Sauces
   Bloody Mary Cocktail, 248–49, *249*
   Brown Butter Tehina, *170*, 171
   Burger, 66–67, *67*
   Dipping, for Kielbasa, 194, *195*
   Peanut Butter Hot Fudge, 80–81, *81*
   Sumac-Ginger Cranberry, *295*, 295
Sausage
   Kielbasa in a Blanket, 194–95, *195*
   Spicy, Gnocchi Bake with Pesto Ricotta, *78*, 79
Scallion(s)
   Brighter Chicken Soup, *274*, 275–76
   Chimichurri, *94*, 95
   Falafel, 184–85, *185*
   Herby Cottage Cheese Frittata, *40*, 41
   -Horseradish Smashed Potatoes, 228–29, *229*
Seafood
   Bloody Mary Shrimp Cocktail, 248–49, *249*
   Dirty Martini–Cured Salmon, *24*, 25
   Rainbow Gefilte Fish, 272–73, *273*
   Steamed Whitefish with Caramelized Fennel & Green Olive Salad, *148*, 149
   Wasabi-Lime Tuna Salad, 26, *27*
   Yogurt-Roasted Salmon with Leeks, 162, *163*
Sesame seeds
   Bagels, *20*, 21–23
   Maple-Candied Nuts, 62, *63*
Shallots
   Au Poivre Dip, 58, *59*
   German Green Bean Casserole, 299–300, *301*
Shepherd's Pie, Veg-Heavy, 111–12, *113*
Shrimp Cocktail, Bloody Mary, 248–49, *249*
Shrub, Cucumber-Basil, *50*, 51
Shtetl Chic
   Caraway-Roasted Beets, 196–97, *197*
   grocery list, 192
   Kielbasa in a Blanket, 194–95, *195*
   menu, 192
   prep list, 193
   Unstuffed Cabbage, 198–99, *199*
   Zaftig Honey Cake (Medovik-ish), *200*, 201–2
Sliders, Cheeseburger Arayes, 66–67, *67*

Socca with Artichoke & Arugula Salad, 142, 143
Soup, Brighter Chicken, 274, 275–76
Sour Cream
    Au Poivre Dip, 58, 59
    Blue Cheese Ranch, 246, 247
    Caraway-Roasted Beets, 196–97, 197
    Deviled Potatoes, 250, 251
    & Onion Mashed Potatoes, 302–3, 303
Sourdough & Challah Stuffing, 296, 297–98
Spanakorizo (Greek Spinach and Feta Rice), 146, 147
Spinach and Feta Rice (Spanakorizo), 146, 147
Spreads
    Goat Cheese Schmear, 88–89, 89
    Whipped Ricotta & Peppadew Honey, 209–10, 211
    Whipped Schmear, 28, 29
Squash
    Honey-Balsamic Grilled Chicken & Summer Veg, 96, 97
    Honey-Roasted, with Sunflower Seed Brittle, 304–5, 305
    Pumpkin Pie Blondies, 310, 311–12
Steak 'n' Cake
    Bloody Mary Shrimp Cocktail, 248–49, 249
    Blue Cheese Ranch, 246, 247
    Brown Butter Parker House Rolls, 243–44, 245
    Deviled Potatoes, 250, 251
    Filet Mignon au Poivre, 254, 255–56
    Garlic-Parmesan Brussels Sprouts Gratin, 252–53, 253
    grocery list, 240
    menu, 240
    The Perfect Chocolate Cake with Ganache Frosting & Raspberry Filling, 257–58, 259
    prep list, 241
Strawberry(ies)
    Cobbler, Matzo & Almond, 286–87, 287
    Saffron Panna Cotta, 150–51, 151
Stuffing, Sourdough & Challah, 296, 297–98
Sumac
    Amba-ish Mango Relish, 176, 177
    -Ginger Cranberry Sauce, 295, 295
    Glaze, Lemon-Almond Blondies with (Platinum Blondies), 186–87, 187
    -Smashed Cucumber Salad, 124, 125
Sundaes, Peanut Butter Hot Fudge, 80–81, 81
Sunflower Seed(s)
    Brittle, 304–5, 305
    Kale & Pomegranate Salad, 128, 129
Sweet Potatoes, Roasted Cauliflower, & Chickpeas, Tofu Curry with, 132, 133–34

Swiss chard
    Beans & Greens, 160, 161
Syrups
    Honey-Ginger, 50, 52
    Rose Grenadine, 50, 53

T

Tahini
    Brown Butter Tehina, 170, 171
    Dressing & Roasted Broccoli, Cabbage & Farro Salad with, 158–59, 159
Tarte Tatin, 235–36, 237
That Was Tonight?
    Creamy Pistachio Salad, 76, 77
    grocery list, 72
    menu, 72
    Peanut Butter Hot Fudge Sundaes, 80–81, 81
    prep list, 73
    Spicy Sausage Gnocchi Bake with Pesto Ricotta, 78, 79
    Sun-Dried Tomato & Yogurt Dip, 74, 75
Tiramisu Cake, 219–20, 221
Toasts, Heirloom Tomato, with Goat Cheese Schmear, 88–89, 89
Tofu Curry with Roasted Cauliflower, Sweet Potatoes & Chickpeas, 132, 133–34
Tomato(es)
    Bagel Toppings Salad, 30, 31
    Chopped Salad with Pepperoncini Dressing, 212, 213
    & Eggplant Salad, Za'atar Roasted, 178, 179
    Fresh Cavatelli & Fennel-y Meatballs, 216, 217–18
    Roasted, & Halloumi Salad, 144–45, 145
    Sun-Dried, & Yogurt Dip, 74, 75
    Tofu Curry with Roasted Cauliflower, Sweet Potatoes & Chickpeas, 132, 133–34
    Unstuffed Cabbage, 198–99, 199
    Veg-Heavy Shepherd's Pie, 111–12, 113
Treat Yourself Brunch
    Blueberry Corn Muffins, 36, 37
    Challah French Toast Sticks, 38–39, 39
    grocery list, 34
    Herby Cottage Cheese Frittata, 40, 41
    Maple-Candied Bacon, 42, 43
    menu, 34
    prep list, 35
    Saffron Hash Browns, 44, 45
Truffles, Charoset, 288, 289
Tuna Salad, Wasabi-Lime, 26, 27
Turkey & Gravy, Spatchcocked Pastrami-Spiced, 306, 307–9
Turmeric
    Rice, Lemony, 130, 131
    Spicy Cauliflower & Celery Pickles, 172, 173

V

Vegetables. See specific vegetables
Veg Out
    Chocolate-Covered Halva-Stuffed Dates, 136, 137
    grocery list, 122
    Harissa Carrot Salad, 126, 127
    Kale & Pomegranate Salad, 128, 129
    Lemony Turmeric Rice, 130, 131
    menu, 122
    prep list, 123
    Sumac-Smashed Cucumber Salad, 124, 125
    Tofu Curry with Roasted Cauliflower, Sweet Potatoes & Chickpeas, 132, 133–34
Vodka
    Bloody Mary Cocktail Sauce, 248–49, 249
    Dipping Sauce for Kielbasa, 194, 195

W

Walnuts
    Ashkenazi Charoset, 266, 267
    Maple-Candied Nuts, 62, 63
    Mock Chopped Liver, 270, 271
    Whipped Schmear, 28, 29
Wine
    Ashkenazi Charoset, 266, 267
Winner Winner, Chicken Dinner
    Green Goddess Wedge Salad with Radishes & Crispy Capers, 226–27, 227
    grocery list, 224
    menu, 224
    prep list, 225
    Roast Chicken with Lemony Sauce Soubise, 232–34, 233
    Roasted Broccoli with Buffalo Beurre Blanc, 230, 231
    Scallion-Horseradish Smashed Potatoes, 228–29, 229
    Tarte Tatin, 235–36, 237

Y

Yogurt
    Green Goddess Wedge Salad with Radishes & Crispy Capers, 226–27, 227
    Hot Honey Labneh, 180, 181
    -Roasted Salmon with Leeks, 162, 163
    Saffron Panna Cotta, 150–51, 151
    and Sun-Dried Tomato Dip, 74, 75

Z

Za'atar Roasted Eggplant & Tomato Salad, 178, 179
Zaftig Honey Cake (Medovik-ish), 200, 201–2
Zucchini
    Honey-Balsamic Grilled Chicken & Summer Veg, 96, 97

ABOUT THE AUTHOR

JAKE COHEN is the *New York Times* bestselling author of *Jewish* and *I Could Nosh*, the star of A&E's *Jake Makes It Easy*, and most importantly, a nice Jewish boy from New York. Jake and his recipes have been featured on *Rachael Ray*, *The Drew Barrymore Show*, *Live with Kelly and Mark*, *Good Morning America*, and Food Network, as well as in the *New York Times*, *Food & Wine*, the *Wall Street Journal*, *Bon Appétit*, and *Forbes*, among other publications. When he's not posting challah-braiding videos and recipes on his Instagram and TikTok accounts (@jakecohen), he's eating and gallivanting around New York City.

DINNER PARTY ANIMAL. Copyright © 2025 by Jake Cohen. All rights reserved. Printed in India. No part of this book may be used or reproduced in any manner whatsoever without written permission except in the case of brief quotations embodied in critical articles and reviews. For information, address HarperCollins Publishers, 195 Broadway, New York, NY 10007.

HarperCollins books may be purchased for educational, business, or sales promotional use. For information, please email the Special Markets Department at SPsales@harpercollins.com.

FIRST EDITION

Designed by Bonni Leon-Berman

Photography by Matt Taylor-Gross

Library of Congress Cataloging-in-Publication Data has been applied for.

ISBN 978-0-06-323972-2

25 26 27 28 29 MAI 10 9 8 7 6 5 4 3 2 1

"Jake's recipes bring me to my knees, and you can quote me on that! Wait, don't actually quote that . . ."
—Josh Groban

"Jake is the sweetest ingredient in the recipe for Moshiach energy."
—Modi Rosenfeld

"Jake is like a brother to me. A much less talented brother."
—Adam Met

"Jake is simultaneously the nicest and naughtiest Jewish boy I know."
—Jessie Ware

"Jake, despite being famously illiterate, writes beautiful cookbooks."
—Alex Edelman

"Jake is the gayest Jew on the planet!"
—Isaac Mizrahi

"Jake is the Jewiest gay on the planet! (Besides me and Isaac Mizrahi.)"
—Judy Gold

"Jake is the definition of a dinner party animal, whether he is wolfing down his delicious creations or fishing for compliments to put on this book."
—Benj Pasek